THE MOST
EVIL
WOMEN
IN HISTORY

THE MOST
EVIL
WOMEN
IN HISTORY

Shelley Klein

BARNES
&NOBLE
BOOKS
NEW YORK

First published in Great Britain in 2003 by
Michael O'Mara Books Limited
9 Lion Yard, Tremadoc Road
London SW4 7NQ

This edition published by Barnes & Noble, Inc.,
by arrangement with Michael O'Mara Books Limited

2003 Barnes & Noble Books

M 10 9 8 7 6 5 4 3 2 1

ISBN 0-7607-4556-0

Designed and typeset by Design 23

Printed and bound in Singapore by Tien Wah Press

CONTENTS

INTRODUCTION

The man who does not know sick women does not know women.

S. WEIR MITCHELL

Ever since Eve first plucked that infamous apple from the Tree of the Knowledge of Good and Evil in the Garden of Eden, womankind has enjoyed or suffered (depending on your point of view) from a borderline, split personality. As the bearers of children and the gender to whom nurturing is supposed to come as second nature, womankind has been called variously the gentler sex, the fairer sex and the weaker sex, but if a woman deviates from this path to commit the type of crime for which men are normally held responsible, then she is not only vilified for the act itself but also for the fact of her being female. How could she have done such a terrible thing? people cry, but the subtext is always, How could a *woman* have done such a terrible thing? Surely it's unnatural? Surely she must be some kind of monster?

This book gathers together fifteen women whose crimes have all, at one time or another, stained the pages of history. From Roman empresses to jealous daughters and bored housewives, they have all been found guilty of terrible acts. Whether you label the perpetrators more monstrous than their male counterparts because they were female is a matter for debate, but what isn't in question is that the crimes themselves were grotesque.

Even allowing for that, however, the histories of these women do fall, albeit broadly and imperfectly, into narrower categories, although it can be argued that several of them cross the borders into categories other than those in which they have been grouped. None the less, it can be said that Lizzie Borden and Audrey Marie Hilley arguably belong among women who have committed crimes because they were 'in it for the money'. Messalina, Agrippina the Younger and the Chinese Empress Dowager, Tz'u-hsi, may be categorized as 'scheming leaders', although they share much in common with 'enemies of the people' like Catherine II, 'the Great', of Russia, Queen Ranavalona I of Madagascar, and Elena Ceausescu. Mary Ann Cotton, Marie Noe and Rose West were all manifestly shown to have been 'bad mothers' – the worst, a reader might be forgiven for thinking – while other women have perhaps been no more than 'victims of the media' and of public prejudice, something to which both Grace Marks and Aileen Carol Wuornos have a powerful claim – or would have, were not both of them dead. Last, there are women, like Myra Hindley and Karla Homolka, so in thrall to their sexual partners that they will suffer any degradation, and commit or take part in any crime, however horrific, in order to remain close to a lover. That, in these two cases, both lovers were men, is not something that can be altogether ignored. I have followed these categories in ordering this book, rather than adopting a straightforward chronological approach which, in the end, adds little to an explanation of the nature of these women and their crimes.

Brutal and vicious, the crimes detailed here have sometimes involved rape and torture and at other times chemicals such as arsenic; there is nothing pretty or gentle about the acts described in this book. But having said that, how does one compare the criminal activities of a xenophobic Madagascan queen with those of a suburban housewife, and vice versa? How does Catherine II's treatment of the serfs compare with Marie Noe's treatment of her children, or Tz'u-hsi's murder of hundreds of foreigners compare with the Rosemary West killings? Although Catherine II and her ilk were responsible for the deaths of hundreds, if not thousands, of people, they were operating at a time when such atrocities were standard practice. The same can also be said for both Roman empresses, Valeria Messalina and Agrippina the Younger, for although murder was by no means sanctioned, neither was it regarded as such an unusual crime, given that it was the best way in which to rid oneself of political opponents. If you didn't murder your enemy, your enemy would undoubtedly murder you. That is not to say that any of these powerful women weren't despicable, but the moral framework in which such empresses and queens operated does set them apart from the Rosemary Wests and Karla Homolkas of this world.

But if Messalina or Catherine II can claim a certain immunity from prosecution then what of Elena Ceausescu? Born in 1919 and ruling her country alongside her husband during the 1970s and 1980s, she doesn't have the excuse of belonging to a different, less civilized era. In fact, if there is such a thing as evil then surely Elena Ceausescu is its personification. Even though she never directly bloodied her hands, through her actions thousands of children were sent to orphanages where they suffered not only degrading conditions but also an environment which caused many of them to endure long, painful deaths. Elena Ceausescu also ground an entire nation into poverty while she and her cronies lived the high life, importing luxurious foreign foods and clothing. At her trial her defence counsel advised her to plead mental instability but, arrogant until the end, she refused. Personally it was the worst mistake she could have made, but nationally it was a blessing. As Nicu Teodorescu (her defence lawyer) said in an interview with *The Times*, 'When I saw [the Ceausescus] dead, as a lawyer I didn't feel anything at all. But as a citizen, I, like everybody, rejoiced. It was the most beautiful Christmas in my whole life.'

Sadly though, if Elena Ceausescu wasn't certifiably insane, the same cannot be said of certain other individuals. For instance, two of the women included in this collection, namely Audrey Marie Hilley and Marie Noe, displayed such disturbing psychological symptoms that even if their mental condition wasn't entirely responsible for their crimes, certainly it didn't help either woman steer clear of trouble. Audrey Marie Hilley in particular could probably have benefited from psychiatric treatment rather than being incarcerated in a state penitentiary, for if we are to call ourselves a civilized society then surely we must treat our criminals (at the same time as punishing them) with a modicum of respect.

Which brings us to the extraordinary case of Myra Hindley who, up until the time of her death in 2002, was Britain's most reviled prisoner. As is common knowledge

Hindley, together with her accomplice Ian Brady, murdered four children and a seventeen-year-old boy, but what happened to her after she was incarcerated makes for a book in itself. Condemned as being that most perverted of beings – a woman who murders young children – Hindley quickly became an icon of everything unnatural. In this the public were aided by a mug shot of Hindley in which she stares straight into the camera's lens with an almost defiant air. Her hair is dyed suicide blonde, she is pouting and yet she looks harder than nails. 'Look at me,' the photograph screams. 'I am what I am.' Every time Hindley attempted to seek parole, petitions were drawn up, letters of protest were sent to Downing Street and interviews with the parents of Hindley's victims were broadcast on TV until the furore was such that no Home Secretary dared sign the papers that would signal her release. Yet in a civilized society where the prison system is based on rehabilitation, to deny one prisoner her rights smacks of injustice. Surely Hindley should have been dealt the same hand as other (male) prisoners who had committed similar crimes, only to be released on parole after they had admitted their guilt and served their sentences? What was it that separated Hindley from the rest of her group? The only answer that makes any sense was that she was a monster. Women do not murder children, therefore a woman who does so cannot be a woman. Nor, however, is this creature a man; she is worse than either, she is a hybrid, a monster who fits no socially acceptable role and therefore must never be allowed re-entry into society. In fact she is like the Victorian author Charlotte Brontë's creation, Bertha Mason, a madwoman who must at all costs be confined.

Which brings me neatly to the three Victorian murderesses included in this collection. How many times these days do we hear that 'society' is to blame for everything that is wrong in the world? It is a cry that has become so familiar it borders on the inane. But it could be argued that the crimes of Lizzie Borden, Grace Marks and Mary Ann Cotton could all be linked to their social status. Women in the Victorian era, unless very fortunate, had to rely on their fathers, brothers and husbands in nearly all aspects of life. Women couldn't vote, their work opportunities were mostly restricted to the mills or to domestic service and even after they were married they could not retain their own property. Strait-jacketed every which way they turned, life in the Victorian era was not especially kind to the female. Yet not every woman turned to murder. So what was it about Cotton, Marks and Borden that persuaded them otherwise?

On the face of it, Lizzie Borden's motive appears to have been inheritance money, but it could also be argued that, having suffered for years under the heavy patriarchal control of her miserly father, she murdered him in order to set herself 'free'. Grace Marks, on the other hand, had no rich daddy to keep a roof over her head; instead she had to go out to work as a servant. Only sixteen when she committed her crime, her low-standing position as a 'maid of all work', combined with her jealousy of another servant who had invidiously climbed up the social ladder, fired Marks into committing an atrocity which could be viewed as being as much an act against her impoverished background as against the victims themselves. Finally Mary Ann Cotton, who murdered so many husbands and children it was hard to keep count. What were her crimes in aid of? Again money seems to be at the root of the problem. Terrified of being left destitute, Cotton murdered her way through one family after another to ensure she would never have to face the ignominy of the Victorian workhouse.

Strangely enough, 'ignominy' was one of the main reasons cited by the most recent killer in this book, Karla Homolka, as to why she didn't step forward sooner when she realized her husband's true nature. Homolka (so she claimed) feared losing her parents' love as well as public disapproval if she revealed her crimes. In addition, she also said that she had been beaten so severely by her husband that she couldn't go to the police for fear that he might kill her. Battered-wife syndrome is of course a recognized condition (and one which claims the lives of many women throughout the world every year), but as a reason for participating in torture, rape and murder, it is hard to accept. Of course with this question, another is raised; had Karla Homolka not met Paul Bernardo would she have gone on to commit the vile crimes that she did? Indeed this is a question that could be asked of several of the women included in this collection. Had Rosemary West not met Fred West would she now be serving ten life sentences? What would have happened had Myra Hindley not met Ian Brady, or if Grace Marks had not met James McDermott? It is a question for which there is no answer, but it is none the less of interest because, more often than not, women who kill more than one person (apart from domestic murders) tend to do so as part of a team.

Aileen Carol Wuornos was an exception to this rule. When police in Florida first realized that a serial killer was on the loose, they initially decided a man was responsible. All seven victims had been stalked and shot and it was naturally assumed that a man was involved since guns and serial killing are more commonly associated with the male of the species. So unusual were the murders because a woman had committed them that Hollywood pounced on the story and several films were made as a consequence.

Statistically speaking, however, it must be pointed out that women are not the deadlier sex. In fact they represent less than 2 per cent of the world's serial killers,[1] so it must be concluded that the reason they make such a big splash in the newspapers has little to do with their crimes and, as was said earlier, much more to do with their gender. After all, at Lizzie Borden's trial the judge summed up by saying that for the jury to find her guilty of the crimes she was charged with they would need to believe she was a 'fiend': an unnatural being. He then told the jury (all of whom were men) to look at the accused and asked them if she resembled such a creature. Obviously she didn't, so obviously she was acquitted.

If a woman goes before a judge and is found innocent, then all well and good. However, if she is found guilty then, depending on what crime she has committed, she may as well be hanged for a devil.

SHELLEY KLEIN
April 2003

LIZZIE BORDEN

The Fall River Murders

Lizzie Borden took an axe
And gave her mother forty whacks.
And when she saw what she had done,
She gave her father forty-one.

VICTORIAN PLAYGROUND VERSE

At 11.15 on the morning of 4 August 1892, one of America's most notorious double murders was committed in the sleepy town of Fall River, Massachusetts. The annals of nineteenth-century crime would not be complete without its inclusion because it was, if not the most imaginative of murders, then certainly one of the bloodiest, and the key suspect was to become the subject of the most widely reported murder trial that America had ever seen.

Lizzie Borden was born in Fall River on 19 July 1860 to Andrew and Sarah Borden. Andrew Borden's first job was as an undertaker, but he was also an astute businessman who accumulated enough money to invest in property. By 1892 he was a rich man: a commercial landlord with a number of real-estate holdings and a director on the board of several banks. Photographs of him show a thin, greying man with a down-turned mouth, the epitome of a nineteenth-century patriarch: self-righteous, strict, thrifty with money and relentlessly dour. Of his wife, Sarah Borden, little is known other than she gave birth to two daughters, Emma and Lizzie, but died of complications after suffering a uterine congestion in 1863 when Lizzie was only three years old. Aged forty, Andrew Borden then took a second wife, Abby Durfree Gray. Contemporary accounts suggest that she was a very shy woman, heavy-set but not unattractive. Her husband, not one to display great amounts of emotion, was none the less said to have doted on her. Sadly the same cannot be said of his daughters, who resented their stepmother's presence from the outset, considering her to be an obstacle to their rightful inheritance. The resentment must also have been fuelled by the cramped conditions in which the four of them lived, because despite Andrew Borden's obvious wealth he chose to reside in a run-down, dowdy neighbourhood.

Fall River was not the prettiest of towns. Its main industry was cotton and there were several mills in the vicinity. Andrew Borden's house stood on 92 Second Street, a narrow building that was flanked by other narrow buildings, giving the impression that the whole street had been constructed without any thought to space or light. The inside of the house was no better. Starkly furnished, downstairs there was a kitchen, a living room and a dining room while upstairs there were four bedrooms, a dressing room and an attic. Further to compound the strained civility within the household, the upstairs apartments could be divided into two separate halves. This was achieved by bolting a communicating door between the master bedroom, the dressing room and the rest of the bedrooms. Once this was done, access to the master bedroom could only be gained by use of the back stairs, and that to the other rooms could only be gained by use of the front stairs. As evidence of just how unpleasant relationships had grown within the Borden house before the murders took place, the connecting door was kept permanently bolted on both sides. This was the set-up at 92 Second Street in 1892. There was only one other member of the household, an Irish maid-of-all-work called Bridget Sullivan. In 1892 Bridget was twenty-six years old and had been with the Bordens a little under three years. She knew both daughters quite well and, as far as the records show, the three women rubbed along nicely. Lizzie Borden was a not a particularly attractive woman; she had thick reddish-brown hair, light blue eyes and, like her stepmother, suffered from a rather plump waist. There, however, the similarity ends. Lizzie, unlike Abby Durfree Gray, was a reasonably gregarious woman. She taught Sunday school, was the Secretary to the Fruit and Flower Mission and enjoyed working with the Women's Christian Temperance Union. In 1890 Lizzie had also undertaken a grand tour of Europe. This was a popular pastime for young American ladies during the nineteenth century, as the novels of Henry James testify. Argumentative, Lizzie also had several run-ins with her father over money. She wanted to upgrade the house and live a more comfortable life, but Andrew Borden regarded her requests as unreasonable, if not downright profligate.

In contrast, Lizzie's older sister, Emma, was far quieter. She wasn't as involved with the church, certainly wasn't as extravagant with money and in general displayed an apathetic approach to life (which some rather unkind commentators have linked to her spinsterhood).

Late in July 1892 Emma Borden went to visit some friends of the family in Fairhaven. Few of their social class stayed on in town during June, July or August when the heat was at its most distressing, preferring instead to escape to the countryside. However, Lizzie Borden didn't accompany her sister; instead she visited friends in New Bedford, before returning a few days later.

On 3 August 1892, a day before the murders took place, Fall River was suffering from a heat wave.[1] The temperature, even before the sun reached its zenith, was in the region of eighty-nine degrees. Everyone was ill-tempered and lethargic, stifled by the heat, but in particular Andrew and Abby Borden were suffering because of an uncharacteristic bout of sickness. Abby had gone to visit Dr Bowen, the family physician, first thing that morning, complaining of a very bad stomach upset. On examining the patient, Dr Bowen thought that it was simply a case of mild food poisoning and sent Abby back home.

Later that same day, Mrs Borden's brother, John Vinnicum Morse, visited 92

Second Street only to find both husband and wife still feeling unwell. They told him they had been taken ill the previous evening and that Lizzie had also suffered a little during the night. On asking where Lizzie was, Vinnicum Morse was informed that despite her sickness she had managed to rouse herself and had gone out for the day. In fact Lizzie had gone on an errand to buy prussic acid from Smith's Drug Store. The acid was apparently to be used to clean an old sealskin cape. The chemist, Eli Bence, clearly remembers Lizzie Borden trying to make this purchase because, despite her protestations, he refused to sell her the liquid, saying that prussic acid was too strong for her needs. (He testified to this at the inquest, alongside two of his assistants, but Lizzie Borden insisted she had never been near the drug store.)

Lizzie then made a house call on a neighbour, a Miss Alice Russell, who said that she seemed agitated and out of sorts. She told Miss Russell that she thought someone was trying to kill the family. The previous year some of Andrew Borden's property, including 92 Second Street, had been burgled. Money had been stolen, as well as a watch and approximately thirty dollars' worth of gold. Being a frugal man who counted every penny, Andrew Borden was enraged. He called in the police and made a statement, but a few days later was heard telling City Marshal Rufus B Hilliard: 'I am afraid the police will not be able to find the real thief.' The word 'real' in this context struck the police marshal as odd, and it was generally believed among the rest of the force that Andrew Borden knew the thief (suspicion fell on Lizzie),

Lizzie Borden, photographed before the murders of her father and stepmother in August 1892. 'This church-going, forty-year-old spinster . . . looked more like a respectable matron than a bloodthirsty killer.' Nineteenth-century attitudes towards women of her class and background made it almost certain that she would, literally, get away with murder. (© BETTMANN/CORBIS)

Andrew J. Borden, wealthy and prominent citizen of Fall River, Massachusetts – 'self-righteous, strict, thrifty with money and relentlessly dour'. The eleven axe-strokes to his head and face left him virtually unrecognizable, while his wife's head had been all but separated from her body by a violent blow to her neck; in all, she was struck thirteen times.
(© BETTMANN/CORBIS)

but wasn't prepared to see them prosecuted.

Lizzie, meanwhile, in the presence of Miss Russell, said that she thought one of her father's enemies was out to get him. She was convinced that the sickness her father, stepmother and she had suffered overnight was as a result of someone deliberately poisoning their milk. Miss Russell tried to calm Lizzie down, but to little avail. Curiously, at her trial, Lizzie's defence counsel tried to blame the conversation on her 'monthly female condition'. Her parting words to Miss Russell were, 'I feel something hanging over me and I can't throw it off.'

4 August 1892 dawned just as hot as the previous day. Having stayed overnight with the Bordens, John Vinnicum Morse enjoyed a lavish breakfast with his hosts despite their still suffering from cramps to the stomach. In fact the breakfast was so gargantuan that Bridget, who later gorged herself on the leftovers, was sick in the back yard.

At 9.15a.m. Morse left the house in order to visit relatives and Andrew Borden set out to pursue some business matters in the centre of town. A short while later Lizzie came downstairs and, while Bridget busied herself with domestic duties, sat down to a light breakfast. Abby Borden then requested that Bridget clean the downstairs windows and so, fetching a bucket and cloth, Bridget made her way through a side door into the yard. Significantly the door was left unlocked. Scrubbing the windows, Bridget later testified that she saw no one in the ground-floor rooms other than the household's rightful occupants and about an hour later, having finished the job, she returned inside, locking the side door behind her.

Next, at approximately 10.40a.m., Mr Borden returned home. He had forgotten his key and, finding every door to the house firmly locked, had to knock in order to be let in. Bridget did the honours, but as Mr Borden entered the hallway she testified to hearing a strange laugh from the upstairs landing nearest the guest bedroom. Bridget insisted that the laugh belonged to Lizzie, but in court Lizzie swore she was in the kitchen when her father returned home. What is not in dispute is that on entering the house Mr Borden was informed by his daughter that Abby Borden had received a note concerning someone who was sick and had gone out. (This note was never found by the police and its absence would later be used by the prosecution as evidence of yet one more of Lizzie's numerous lies).

Ignoring his wife's apparent absence Mr Borden went upstairs to the master bedroom, only to return a short time later so that he could settle himself in the sitting room. He lay down to rest from the heat on a couch. Lizzie busied herself with some ironing and Bridget returned to washing the inside windows. At 10.55a.m. Bridget then retired upstairs to her room for a short rest before lunch and Lizzie went out into the yard or to the barn (during questioning at the inquest she was very vague as to where precisely she'd been or what precisely she'd been doing). What is not in dispute is that on her return she discovered what her principal defence lawyer, Mr George D. Robinson, would later describe as 'one of the most dastardly and diabolical crimes that was ever committed in Massachusetts'. He went on to say: 'inspection of the victims disclosed that Mrs Borden had been slain by the use of some sharp and terrible instrument, inflicting upon her head eighteen blows, thirteen of them crushing through the skull; and below stairs, lying upon the sofa, was Mr Borden's dead and mutilated body, with eleven strokes upon the head, four of them crushing the skull.'[2]

According to her testimony it was Andrew Borden's body that Lizzie first 'discovered'. He was still lying on the couch, his right cheek resting on a cushion, but due to his injuries he was virtually unrecognizable. Blood ran down his face, one eye was split almost in two and protruded from its socket, his nose was severed and there were in the region of eleven wounds to his face. His skull was mashed as if it were no stronger than the shell of an egg.

Confusion ruled. Lizzie started shouting for Bridget to come downstairs, after which she sent the servant rushing out to fetch the family doctor. There was blood on the walls of the sitting room and spots of it could be clearly seen on the carpet and on the sofa.

According to police records Doctor Bowen arrived at 11.30a.m. and by 11.45 seven police officers, together with the Medical Examiner, William Dolan, were all in attendance. Doctor Bowen left the house a short time later in order to send a telegram to Emma Borden, informing her of the crime. Sadly, by the time he returned there was even worse news, for Bridget and a neighbour, a Mrs Addie Churchill, had gone upstairs and discovered Abby Borden floating face-down in a pool of her own blood. Her head had nearly been separated from the rest of her body by a heavy blow to the neck while another blow had cut a huge flap of skin away from the back of her scalp. (Later it was conjectured that Abby Borden had died from the first blow she received, for although her wounds were extensive, there was very little blood spatter on either the walls or the furniture.)

The investigation now swung into action. First of all Lizzie Borden was asked by Officer Michael Mullaly if there were any hatchets in the house, to which she replied that there were several. Bridget showed the officer down into the cellar where Mullaly discovered four of the offending items, one covered in dried blood and hair (which later turned out to be from a cow) and one with a broken handle and covered in ash. This second hatchet was finally submitted in evidence to the court. In the meantime, Lizzie had been asked for an account of her whereabouts during the murders and, on telling the police that she had been in the barn searching for metal fishing sinkers (she had wanted to go fishing with her sister at Fairhaven), an officer, Sergeant Philip Harrington, and a colleague of his examined the room. The barn loft's floor was covered with a thin layer of dust but it was in pristine condition, with no evidence of either footprints, handprints or any other disturbance.

After photographing the bodies in situ, at 3.00p.m. both corpses were removed and lifted through to the dining room, upon whose table Dr Dolan now performed autopsies. Both Abby and Andrew's stomachs were removed, packaged up and sent by messenger to a Dr Edward S Wood, Professor of Chemistry at Harvard. The reason for this was to discern whether the two victims had been poisoned before being bludgeoned to death. No doubt Dr Bowen had mentioned how ill they had both been on 3 August and perhaps he now feared something more sinister had occurred. After all, it would be easier to beat someone to death who was already incapacitated by poison and, as this extract from the *Fall River Daily Herald* on 8 August 1892 suggests:

> **Josiah A Hunt, keeper of the house of correction, who has had an extensive experience as an officer of the law in this city, in speaking of the tragedy advanced a theory which has thus far escaped the notice of the police, or, if it has not, they are putting the public on the wrong scent.**
>
> **Said Mr Hunt: 'It is my opinion that both Mr Borden and his wife were dead before the murderers struck a blow, probably poisoned by the use of prussic acid, which would cause instant death. The use of the hatchet was simply to mislead those finding the bodies. I believe this to be the real state of the case, for if they had been alive when the first blow was struck, the action of the heart would have been sufficient to have caused the blood to spatter more freely than is shown from the accounts furnished by the papers. There was altogether too much of a butchery for so little spattering of blood.'**

Despite Josiah Hunt's suspicions, however, when the results of the autopsies were returned from Dr Wood's laboratory at Harvard they proved negative for prussic acid and other irritant poisons. The autopsy read as follows: 'I [Dr Wood] found that both stomachs were perfectly normal in appearance. They were in the condition of apparent good health. There was no evidence, no inflammation and no notice of the action of any irritant or anything of that kind.'

That said, there has since been much debate as to whether Lizzie might have used arsenic, the presence of which is hard to diagnose unless the victim has been administered it in small doses over a long period of time. In addition, samples taken from the stomach are not the best indicators when searching for the presence of this particular poison.

Meanwhile, as the bodies of Lizzie's father and mother were being examined downstairs, upstairs she was being placed under further scrutiny by Deputy Marshal John Fleet. On being asked whether she thought either her Uncle John or the maid Bridget could have committed the murders, she answered in the negative. As far as Lizzie was concerned, the murders had been perpetrated by someone who had broken into the house: someone unknown to its occupants. For as long as she lived, Lizzie never deviated from this story.

That evening Emma Borden returned from Fairhaven only to find that the body of her father and that of her stepmother were still awaiting collection by the undertakers. It must have been a highly fraught, emotional time and Dr Bowen, knowing this, prescribed sulphate of morphine to Lizzie in order to calm her nerves. Finally, at around 9.00p.m. that night, the bodies were taken away and the police left.

Saturday, 6 August 1892 was to be the day of the funerals. A service did take place, but burial of the bodies was postponed when Dr Wood informed the police that he wished to do further autopsies. Gruesomely this included the severing of both Andrew and Abby Borden's heads and plaster casts being taken of both. (Andrew Borden's head was never returned to its coffin).

Of course this type of request, i.e. the removal of body parts, wouldn't have seemed out of the ordinary, the Borden murders having become a high-profile case, picked up both by local and national newspapers. For instance, the *New York Times* headline for 5 August 1892 read: 'BUTCHERED IN THEIR HOME: Mr Borden and His Wife Killed in Broad Daylight.'[3] It soon became the first nationally prominent murder case to hit the newspapers throughout the United States. Meanwhile, the focus of the inquiry shifted to the burning of a dress by Lizzie Borden on Sunday, 7 August. At the inquest Lizzie testified that she was wearing a blue-and-white-striped cotton dress on the morning of the murders. However, when she was requested by the investigating officers to hand over this item, she gave them a dark blue silk dress, apparently nonchalant about its not matching her original description.

Finally, Miss Russell, who had slept over at the Borden house on the night after the murders in order to help comfort Emma and Lizzie, blew the latter's story out of the water. In evidence she insisted that she had witnessed Lizzie stuffing a light blue corduroy dress into the old kitchen stove. Emma Borden said that this was done on her instructions because the dress had been splattered with paint, but the police officers who had searched the house directly after the murders said they could not remember ever having seen such an item.

At the inquest, which was held over the following few days, this piece of evidence would be crucial in the decision to arrest Lizzie Borden. Even more damning was that, under questioning by District Attorney Hosea M Knowlton, Lizzie grew increasingly vague as to her whereabouts on 4 August. She became visibly agitated by Knowlton's examination, which was, as the following extract from the inquest transcript testifies, extremely persistent.

> QUESTION: **Where were you when your father came home?**
>
> ANSWER: **I was down in the kitchen. Reading an old magazine that had been left in the cupboard: an old *Harper's Magazine*.**
>
> QUESTION: **Are you certain of this?**
>
> ANSWER: **I am not sure whether I was there or in the dining room.**
>
> QUESTION: **Where were you when the bell rang?**
>
> ANSWER: **I think in my room upstairs.**
>
> QUESTION: **Then you were upstairs when your father came home?**
>
> ANSWER: **I was on the stairs when she [Bridget] let him in... I had only been upstairs long enough to take the clothes up and baste the little loop on the sleeve. I don't think I had been up there over five minutes.**
>
> **[A short time later the District Attorney returned to the subject.]**
>
> QUESTION: **You remember that you told me several times that you were downstairs and not upstairs when your father came home? You have forgotten, perhaps?**
>
> ANSWER: **I don't know what I have said. I have answered so many questions and I am so confused I don't know one thing from another. I am telling you just as nearly as I know.**[4]

At best this was vagueness, at worst a refusal to tell the truth. Together with Miss Russell's testimony, Judge Josiah Blaisdell of the Second District Court decided to charge Lizzie with both murders and on 12 August 1842 she was therefore arraigned to appear before a Grand Jury. Lizzie Borden pleaded not guilty.

By this time the press were having a field day. The crime was world famous and everyone was speculating as to whether Lizzie was indeed its perpetrator. Added to which, in a move that seems to foreshadow the Aileen Wuornos case, where feminists jumped to Aileen's defence, women's groups supported Lizzie's cause. These included the suffragettes, headed by a woman called Lucy Stone (a Massachusetts abolitionist and founder of the American Suffrage Association), together with the Women's Christian Temperance Union, led by a Mrs Susan Fessenden.

The trial, which was held in New Bedford in Bristol County, a little less than fifteen miles from Fall River, lasted just over two weeks, from 5 June 1893 to 20 June. There were three judges, as was the law at that time: Josiah Blaisdell

The house at 92 Second Street, Fall River, in which the murders took place. Despite his money, Andrew Borden insisted on living in this seedy property in an unfashionable part of town. Five weeks after her acquittal, Lizzie and her sister moved to a much larger house in a highly sought-after area of Fall River. (© BETTMANN/CORBIS)

presiding and, in attendance, Associate Justice Caleb Blodgett and Associate Justice Justin Dewey. The jury of twelve men was made up from a mixture of farmers and tradesmen. Also present were approximately thirty gentlemen of the press, who included representatives from the *Boston Globe* and the *New York Sun*.

When Lizzie Borden entered the courtroom she did so in style. Flanked by two of her most ardent supporters, the Reverends Buck and Jubb (who had conducted the service at the funeral of her father and stepmother), she was clothed fashionably in a black mohair dress with leg-of-mutton sleeves and a black hat made out of lace. Prosecuting the case for the State was Hosea Knowlton, assisted by William H Moody. Moody began by outlining three statements, all of which he said the prosecution would be able to prove beyond reasonable doubt.

First, he stated that Lizzie had planned the murders in order to gain substantial financial rewards; second, that she had carried through these plans to the letter; and third, that her consistent lying when questioned by the police was not the behaviour of an innocent woman.

Moody's case was very strong, with both a financial motive and a good deal of circumstantial evidence linking the accused to the crimes. However, he might have overdone the dramatics a bit when, throwing down a piece of clothing on to the desk in front of him (clothing which would later be shown in evidence), he disturbed some paperwork which was covering two very gruesome objects. These turned out to be the plaster-cast heads of Mr and Mrs Borden. Understandably, Lizzie fainted, but she was soon to recover and remained unnervingly composed throughout the rest of the trial, invoking her constitutional right to remain silent by saying only: 'I am innocent. I leave my counsel to speak for me.' Undeterred, the prosecution pressed ahead. In order to prove their first point, that of motive, Knowlton and Moody called John Vinnicum Morse to the stand, who claimed that Andrew Borden was in the process of changing his will. Morse testified that the new will would have left Emma and Lizzie with $25,000 apiece, while the remainder of the estate (estimated at half a million dollars) would go to Abby Borden.

Then Knowlton and Moody moved on to Lizzie's 'predisposition' to murder by attempting to enter into evidence her testimony during the inquest. Unfortunately for the prosecution, but very fortunately for Lizzie, her lawyers (in particular Andrew Jennings and Melvin Adams) objected strongly to this, saying that her statements had been made before she was formally charged. They also added that Lizzie's request for representation by counsel during the inquest had been refused. The trial judges agreed with Jennings and Andrews, thereby depriving the prosecution of some its most crucial evidence. This wasn't the worst of it, either, because the prosecution's troubles were then further compounded when one of the judges additionally ruled that Eli Bence's testimony, recording how he had refused to sell Lizzie the prussic acid, must also be disallowed as no evidence of poisoning had ever been discovered.

Moving on, the prosecution then attempted to establish that the hatchet in the cellar of the Borden's house was the one used in the murder. They stated that it showed signs of having been cleaned recently, not just with water and soap, but also with ashes. The length of the wounds found on both victims also matched the hatchet's blade for size. However, there was no one piece of conclusive evidence that could link the hatchet with the accused.

Finally the prosecution brought up Lizzie's inability to remember precisely where she'd been at the time of the murders. However, Dr Bowen testified that he had given Lizzie sulphate of morphine, not just on the evening after her father was killed but also during the inquest and while she was held in jail pending trial. Later Lizzie's defence would use this testimony, saying that the medication would have affected her mental abilities, perhaps even altering her recollections as to her whereabouts on 4 August.

After twelve days the prosecution rested its case. They had presented the facts clearly and logically but had been severely handicapped throughout the proceedings.

In contrast, the defence took only two days to present its side of the story, even though its case was much more far-fetched. Led by three lawyers – Andrew Jennings, George Robinson and Melvin Adams – the defence insisted that the scenario played out at 92 Second Street was nothing like that which the prosecution had described. Instead of Lizzie Borden being the perpetrator, they were convinced that someone had broken into the house and, unseen by any of its occupants, killed both Mr and Mrs Borden before slipping down into the cellar and escaping through the back yard. With this scenario in mind, the defence then called a number of witnesses to testify that there had been a mysterious stranger in the vicinity at the time of the killings. In addition, they also called Emma Borden.

Emma had stood by her sister from the moment Lizzie was charged with the murders. Now she was asked to take the stand and testify that there was no possible reason for her younger sibling to murder Andrew and Abby Borden. She acquitted herself well, taking centre stage and delivering her answers in a straightforward, believable manner.

On 19 June George Robinson delivered his closing argument which was, by anyone's standards, an extraordinary speech, the essence of which can be summed up in one short statement he made directly to the jury. 'To find [Lizzie Borden] guilty,' Robinson said, 'you must believe she is a fiend. Gentlemen, does she look it?'

Sitting sedately in the dock, this church-going, forty-year-old spinster, soberly dressed in black and flanked by two ministers, looked more like a respectable matron than a bloodthirsty killer. But as if that wasn't enough, Judge Dewey (who had been appointed to the Superior Court by George Robinson himself) then turned to the jury to sum up the case, only to regurgitate almost everything the defence had said as if it were gospel.

It took the jury a little over an hour to return with its verdict. On Monday 19 June, Lizzie Borden was found not guilty of murdering her father and stepmother. She left the court a free woman.

Today it seems impossible that such a flimsy defence could acquit a person so easily, but in 1893 it was practically unheard of for a respectable, middle-class lady to be accused of such a crime. Women were for the most part, in a phrase first coined by the poet Coventry Patmore, seen as 'angels in the house',[5] i.e. above reproach or anything as basic and venal as murder.

It is known that five weeks after the trial Lizzie and Emma bought a large, thirteen-room mansion at 306 French Street, which was in a highly sought-after and fashionable area of Fall River. Lizzie (who by then had changed her name to 'Lizabeth A Borden') led a comfortable life, often travelling to Boston, New York and Washington to attend the theatre, but in 1897 her name hit the headlines once again when she was arrested for the theft of two paintings from the Tilden-Thurber Company's store. Allegedly the paintings were traced to Lizzie Borden's house, but the case was settled out of court and nothing more was said about it. Echoes of the burglary at 92 Second Street did spring to mind.

Eventually Lizzie met an actress called Miss Nance O'Neil, a woman for whom she developed a huge crush. Over the following two years they became inseparable. Lizzie threw a huge party for her friend, inviting the whole theatre company to attend – an event which no doubt shocked the staid residents of Fall River. It certainly wasn't to Emma Borden's tastes, for it was during this time that Emma moved out of 306 French Street. Ever since the trial she had grown increasingly devout and no doubt found her sister's relationship with Nance highly unpalatable. Initially Emma lived with the Reverend Buck and his family, but eventually moved away from Fall River, moving to Newmarket in New Hampshire. Little is heard of her after that, but in 1923 a dispute broke out between herself and Lizzie over the sale of some property from their joint estate.

Lizzie Borden died on 1 June 1927, following complications after surgery on her gall bladder. Nine days later Emma Borden died. Both sisters left sizeable estates, Lizzie's amounting to approximately $266,000, which she divided amongst family and friends, as well as the Animal Rescue League. Both sisters were buried in the family plot, alongside their mother and the mutilated (and, in Andrew Borden's case, headless) remains of their father and stepmother.

AUDREY MARIE HILLEY

Secrets and Lies

Inorganic Arsenic compounds...are carried by the blood to different parts of the body, where they attack the tissues vigorously, producing their most pronounced effects on the capillaries. The intensity of the toxemia depends on the amount of the drug administered and the rapidity with which it is absorbed.

GONZALES, VANCE, HELPERN, AND UMBERGER,
LEGAL MEDICINE, PATHOLOGY AND TOXICOLOGY, 2ND ED.

Audrey Marie Hilley's story is one reminiscent of smalltown, 1950s America. On the surface everything appeared all white-picket fences, clean, bright and cheery, but underneath lurked secrets of a much darker nature. By the time Audrey Marie Hilley was arrested on 12 January 1983, her life had grown so murky, with mysterious stories of twins, unexplained fires, fabricated obituaries and tragic diseases of the blood, that one might be forgiven for thinking the whole sorry tale was something cooked up by the unconventional American film director David Lynch.

Audrey Marie Hilley was born on 4 June 1933 in the small mill town of Blue Mountain, North Alabama, during America's Great Depression. Blue Mountain wasn't a picturesque place; it was an industrial base featuring huge cotton factories. It was in one of these that Audrey Marie's parents, Huey Frazier and Lucille Meads, worked. They led a tough life, scraping a living together as best they could and taking nothing for granted. When Audrey Marie was born, Lucille couldn't even afford to stay at home and look after the baby and so shortly afterwards she returned to her job, leaving Marie (as she became known) with relatives. That said, it was never in doubt that Marie was a much-loved child who was given everything that her parents could afford. In fact they went out of their way to make certain she was always well dressed and well fed, things that could not always be said of other local children. They were determined that their daughter should have a better, more successful life than either of them had ever enjoyed. With this in mind, when Marie was twelve years old the Fraziers decided to move from Blue Mountain to the slightly larger, more cosmopolitan town of Anniston.

Whereas Blue Mountain was a fairly working-class area, Anniston housed most of the mill owners and industrialists. It also boasted a better-equipped school which

'Robbi Homan', who, after her 'death', returned as her twin sister, 'Teri Martin', even convincing 'Robbi's' bereaved husband, a photograph taken when she was living in New Hampshire while on the run from police in Alabama. In fact, her real name was Audrey Marie Hilley, and she was an extremely plausible con artist, but also a murderer.
(PHOTO FROM POISONED BLOOD BY PHILIP E. GINSBURG, 1987)

was important to the Fraziers as back in Blue Mountain the education, particularly for girls, was poor. Instead Marie was enrolled at Quintard Junior High School where she soon made her mark. She was a bright, pretty child who worked hard at her studies. Marie also joined various high-school clubs, including the Future Teachers of America and the Commercial Club, which prided itself on bringing together 'business women of the future' and in particular those who wished to go into secretarial work. Marie was also popular among her peers and had plenty of male admirers, but one boy in particular had caught her eye.

Frank Hilley became Marie's childhood sweetheart. He was a popular boy and came from a good Anniston family (he also had two sisters, Freeda and Jewel), though Marie's mother tried to dissuade her daughter from the relationship.

After high school, Frank went directly into the navy. This was the period between the end of the Second World War and the start of the war in Korea and the new recruit was soon assigned to a posting in Guam. Always a jealous man, while he was away he worried that Marie would meet somebody else, and so in May 1951, when Marie was eighteen years old, the two youngsters married. Afterwards Frank was posted to California to serve out his time in the navy, while Marie stayed on in Anniston and graduated from high school, after which she joined her husband. In 1952 Frank was posted to Boston and once again Marie went with him. It wasn't long before she fell pregnant and then, with Frank's service in the navy drawing to a close, the couple decided to return to Anniston, where they set up home. They both found jobs quickly, Frank in the shipping department of a company called Standard Foundry and Marie as a secretary. It all seemed such an ideal life. The Hilleys were blessed with everything that a middle-class American family could have wished for and this happy picture was further enhanced when, on 11 November 1952, Frank and Marie's first child, Michael Hilley, was born.

If everything on the surface looked rosy, then underneath cracks had begun to show, in particular financial cracks, because Marie Hilley had a penchant for spending large amounts of money. It had all begun when Frank was in California and had sent his pay cheques home for Marie to put in to the bank. Instead she had spent them, always wanting more clothes, better furnishings, more up-to-date kitchen appliances. Frank would earn the money and Marie would go out and buy something new, but instead of putting his foot down or taking control of the purse strings, Frank found it easier to give Marie her way. She wanted the best, so she would have the best. Besides, he was doing well at work.

By 1960 Frank had been made foreman at Standard Foundry and was on a comfortable salary. He was also well respected within the community and had become a member of the Elks Club, as well as the Veterans of Foreign Wars club. Marie, too, had made her mark in Anniston and did a lot of voluntary work for the First Christian Church. Soon the Hilleys had the excitement of a new baby to look forward to. Carol Hilley was born in 1960, and though Marie took maternity leave, she soon went back to work. Marie enjoyed her secretarial jobs although, unknown to her husband, her work colleagues were a little less than impressed. Marie didn't make friends easily and she tended to rub people up the wrong way (especially those beneath her in the office pecking order). It was only a matter of time before she would leave each job, having grown so unpopular that it was impossible for her to do anything else. But she always received good references and never found it hard to find fresh employment.

With two incomes coming in, Marie and Frank should have had no problem paying bills, buying the children what they needed, indeed having a comfortable, if not very exciting, life. However, Marie's profligacy was still taking its toll. When Frank finally put his foot down, instead of taking heed, Marie Hilley began renting a post-office box and had her bills sent there so that her husband couldn't see how much she was spending. The bills mounted up, as did the amount of credit that certain shops were willing to extend to her due to the fact that she was Frank's wife and therefore to be trusted. By 1974 the amount Marie owed had grown out of all proportion to the amount of money she and Frank earned. The strain on the relationship was enormous and it can't have been helped by the fact that around this time Frank began to grow ill.

Frank Hilley, who had hardly taken a day off sick from work in his life, now frequently suffered bouts of nausea. He also felt constantly fatigued and could barely raise himself in the mornings. By May 1975 he was ready to consult a doctor, but though he was prescribed all manner of medicines nothing appeared to alleviate his symptoms, let alone get rid of the illness. Frank also became aware that his wife was having an affair with one of her bosses, a man by the name of Walter Clinton. 'I got sick one day at work,' Frank Hilley told his son Michael, 'and came home early. Your mother was in bed with Walter Clinton.'[1] Never one to make a fuss, Frank Hilley brushed the event under the carpet and little was said about it either then or later on. Besides, Frank was feeling so sick that he didn't have the energy to argue with Marie. It was around this time that she began administering her husband with injections. Frank Hilley, explaining this to his sister Freeda, said that the injections were part of his treatment, something the doctor had told Marie she must do. But despite everything Frank's health did not improve. Finally he was admitted to hospital where he was diagnosed with infectious hepatitis. In retrospect, it is plain to see that the doctors were completely baffled by Frank's symptoms. They didn't know what was wrong with him and as a result his condition deteriorated rapidly. Michael Hilley, who was married by this time and studying at Atlanta Christian College, could barely recognize his father. Physically and

Audrey Marie Hilley hides her face as she is taken back to Alabama to face charges of murder. By then – January 1983 – she had been on the run for three years and two months, living first as 'Robbi Homan' and then as her twin, 'Teri Martin'. Her arrest came about when friends and co-workers of 'Robbi' became convinced that she and the woman posing as her twin were one and the same. (EDDIE MOTES/ANNISTON STAR)

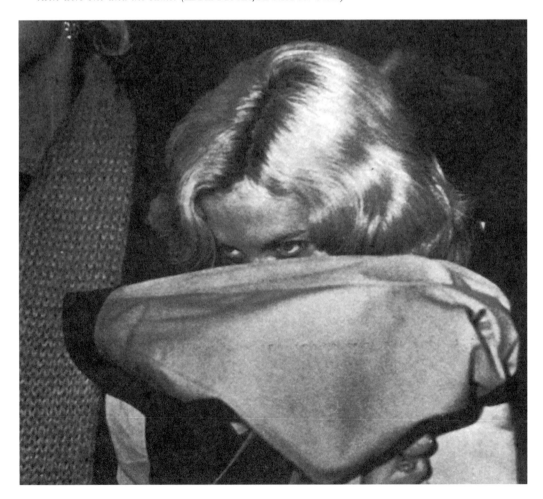

mentally Frank was a different man. He kept drifting in and out of consciousness, suffered severe headaches, bouts of nausea and on several occasions experienced bizarre hallucinations.

Frank Hilley died on 25 May 1975. The diagnosis of infectious hepatitis wasn't questioned by anyone, least of all by the family. Two days after his death Frank was buried at Forestlawn Gardens Cemetery.

Now a widow, Marie collected on her husband's life insurance. It wasn't a huge amount, being in the region of $30,000, but, if invested carefully, it might have been adequate. Never one to stint on spending, however, Marie went out and bought a new car, new clothes and more jewellery. She also spent a lot of money on presents for her children and when her son and his new wife, Teri, moved back into the area, she invited them both to live with her. At the time, Marie Hilley also had her mother, Lucille, who had been diagnosed with cancer shortly after Frank died, staying with her. Carol Hilley was also still living at home. It might have been a bonding experience for all concerned, a time to grieve, but also a time to come together. Sadly, however, nothing was further from the reality. Marie and Carol bickered constantly; they couldn't or wouldn't see eye-to-eye on anything, on top of which Marie was relying on Michael for complete emotional support. This didn't help his relationship with his wife who had, since moving in with her mother-in-law, begun to feel increasingly sick. Teri Hilley was admitted to hospital four times while she was staying with Marie and finally ended up suffering a miscarriage. Eventually she and Michael found their own apartment, but on the night before they were due to move into their new home there was a fire at Marie's house and, to their horror, Marie, Carol and Lucille all moved in with them instead.

Nor did the nightmare end there. In fact fire was to feature quite highly in Marie's life over the next couple of months. For instance, just when Marie's home was fit to move back into, the apartment next to Michael and Teri's burnt down and in turn damaged their home as well. Michael and Teri had to move back in with Marie. It was like a black comedy, only without the laughs. Then things grew even worse.

In January 1977 Lucille Frazier died and there then followed a succession of increasingly bizarre events which all centred on the Hilley's home. Directly after Frank Hilley had died, Marie had reported a number of petty thefts from the house. Now, with Lucille dead, the thefts started up again. In addition, Marie also began reporting gas leaks and on one particular occasion said that she'd discovered a fire in her hall closet. On top of this, Marie's neighbour, Doris Ford (to whose house Marie had a key) also began experiencing similar problems. She told the police of numerous gas leaks in her house, in addition to which the two women also began reporting strange phone calls that were being made to them at all times of the day and night. Precisely one month after Marie discovered the fire in her hall closet, Doris Ford found exactly the same thing had occurred in one of her hall cupboards as well. It was all too bizarre, all too much of a coincidence and yet, though the police traced some of Doris's nuisance calls back to the factory at which Marie worked, there wasn't enough evidence with which to charge her with anything substantial.

In 1978 Marie, with Carol at her side, decided to go to Florida and live with Michael and Teri. The arrangement was doomed and it wasn't long before Marie returned to Anniston where she and her daughter moved in with Frank's sister, Freeda.

Ever since Frank had died, Marie Hilley had seemingly become very conscious of just how many things could go wrong in one's life and therefore had begun taking out several different insurance policies. These included insurance for fire damage, for cancer and for burglary, as well as life cover. But most curious of all, Marie also took out life-insurance policies on both of her children.

Carol Hilley began feeling ill around April 1979. Although she didn't make any connection with the illness that her father had suffered, she too experienced bouts of nauseousness and was increasingly tired. She was also constantly vomiting. Instead of her symptoms improving with time, they grew steadily worse. Not wishing to admit defeat, Carol decided to move in to her own apartment. She was, after all, nineteen years old and it was very important for her to gain some independence and stand on her own two feet. But she hadn't reckoned on her mother who, on the pretext of caring for her daughter, came round to the apartment constantly. Marie would cook for Carol, help her with her medicines, talk to the doctors for her and in general make herself indispensable. Yet, despite several stays at Anniston's Regional Medical Center, Carol's health did not improve. It was at this point that Carol's doctor suggested to Marie that she take her daughter to see a psychiatrist called Dr John Elmore in Birmingham. On Dr Elmore's recommendation Carol was admitted to the psychiatric ward at Carraway Methodist Hospital. At the time it seemed a drastic step, but in retrospect it was a lucky escape; when Marie Hilley had moved back to Anniston, she had not only taken out several insurance policies but had also begun a series of complicated relationships and run up countless bills.

The relationships Marie had begun involved the owner of a local construction company, Harold Dillard, for whom she did some part-time work, and an old school friend of hers called Calvin Robertson. She told Robertson that she had been diagnosed with cancer but couldn't afford the very expensive treatment that was required if she was to stand a chance of survival. Robertson, who had always had a soft spot for Marie, duly sent money. Not long afterwards, Marie replied that miraculously she was cured.

Within three years of Frank Hilley's death Marie had spent all his insurance money and sold the family home. Even then she did not have enough money to live on. But instead of reining in her spending, when Carol moved into her new apartment Marie bought her daughter several expensive items of furniture. Unsurprisingly the cheques bounced and the bank filed charges. But if this wasn't enough to contend with, a friend of Marie's then began to suspect something was also amiss with Marie's treatment of Carol.

Eve Cole had met Marie Hilley through the First Christian Church where Eve taught Sunday school. The two had quickly become friends, so it wasn't unusual for Eve to call Carol at the hospital to find out how she was doing. Carol happened to mention that her mother had been giving her injections, something Eve Cole remembered Marie had done before when Carol first fell sick. Alarm bells started ringing and so Eve, to put her mind at rest, rang Carol's Aunt Freeda, who in turn rang Michael. Coincidentally, Michael had also begun to have his own suspicions with regards to his mother. In the light of his father's death, he wasn't happy about Carol's illness. In fact he was so unhappy that he'd rung the County Coroner's office to ask about an exhumation of his father's body. Now, with Aunt Freeda's information, he was genuinely concerned. Straightaway Michael rang Dr Elmore at the hospital who, though he didn't believe Carol was being poisoned, said he would put a stop to Marie visiting her daughter. But this was easier said than done. Marie Hilley was not a woman who could be crossed easily and, on hearing of Dr Elmore's plans, she immediately discharged her daughter from Carraway Methodist Hospital and took her instead to the University of Alabama Hospital where Carol was placed under the care of a Dr Brian Thompson.

Unfortunately for Marie, almost immediately after she had had Carol admitted to the new hospital the police arrested her as a result of all the bad cheques she had written.

Michael Hilley immediately seized upon his mother's absence to request that Carol be tested for poison. Although it sounded far-fetched, eventually Dr Thompson agreed. Firstly he examined Carol's fingernails and toenails for what are known as Aldridge-Mees lines, a clear sign of arsenic poisoning. The test was positive and on further investigation Carol Hilley's body was found to have a high content of arsenic.

This discovery prompted Michael to contact the County Coroner's office once again. He wrote Ralph Phillips a letter outlining all his suspicions, including that of Carol's poisoning by arsenic and his father and grandmother's untimely deaths. 'It is my belief that she probably injected my dad with arsenic as she has apparently done to my sister.'[2] Michael also wrote that he thought his mother was suffering from a mental illness and that he wanted to help her, but he needed to know the precise nature of her actions. Fortunately for him, Marie was still in custody at this point and he could therefore investigate without interference.

On 26 September 1979 Marie Hilley was interviewed concerning the death of her husband and mother, and the poisoning of her daughter. She tried to dodge the issue, but after two hours of questioning she did admit that she had administered injections to Carol both at home and at the hospital. At the same time, Freeda had gone round to Carol's apartment and found a small bottle which contained an unknown liquid. On analysis the liquid turned out to be arsenic. If that wasn't damning enough, on 3 October 1979, Frank Hilley's body was exhumed and when the toxicology report was returned it showed a huge amount of arsenic in his body tissue. Subsequently Lucille Frazier's body was also exhumed and, once again, the police were to find deposits of arsenic in her body too, although it was stressed that it was her cancer that had finally killed her.

Audrey Marie Hilley was charged with the murder of her husband and the attempted murder of her daughter in October 1979. Curiously, her son asked several family friends to help out with the bail money which, considering that Marie was on trial for murder, was extremely low – coming in at a mere $10,000. She was released on 11 November and her attorney, a man named Wilford Lane, suggested they stay in a motel somewhere in Birmingham so that they could avoid the press. Over the next few days Marie told Lane that she was terrified Frank's sisters would come after her. They wanted her blood, she said, and pleaded with Lane to change motels. Lane acquiesced, but on 18 November he and his wife decided to pay Marie an impromptu visit. Lane was stunned by what he discovered. The room was in mayhem, with clothes and other bits and pieces strewn everywhere. Marie, along with her credit cards and cheque books, was missing and the only clue to her whereabouts was a handwritten note which read, 'Lane, you led me straight to her. You will hear from me.' Naturally the inference was that one of Frank's sisters had caught up with Marie, but no one believed this version, preferring instead to surmise that Marie had simply made off to begin a new life somewhere else. Coincidentally, on the very same day that Marie disappeared, Carrie Hilley (Frank Hilley's mother) died of cancer, but tests which had been run on strands of her hair during the previous weeks showed arsenic in her system.

The FBI now swung into action. They put out numerous descriptions of the fugitive. 'Mrs Hilley,' they said, 'is 5 feet, 1 inch tall and weighs 110 pounds. Her eyes are green, her hair brown. Her only identifying mark is a scar on a knuckle.' But the elusive Mrs Hilley never turned up. The only clue to her whereabouts was a burglary which occurred in Blue Mountain a few days after she had gone missing. A car belonging to Marie's aunt, Margaret Key, was stolen, along with some of her clothes. Later on the car turned up in Marietta, Georgia, and the FBI then traced Marie to a motel in Savannah, but when they got there she had already escaped. A little later, officers concluded that Marie had most likely started a new life working as a secretary. They described her as a perfectionist in everything she did and surmised that she would never take a job that was beneath her evident skills. They also conjectured that she would be living a comfortable life and that on past experience she would still be taking great care of her appearance, perhaps even visiting beauty parlours on a regular basis. In addition, the FBI also advanced the theory that Marie Hilley might be suffering from a personality disorder and on 16 October 1980 the following headline appeared in the *New York Times:* 'FUGITIVE IN POISONINGS MAY CHANGE PERSONALITIES'. The article went on to say that 'interviews with Mrs Hilley's friends and relatives had led [the FBI] to believe that she might be exhibiting separate personalities. The FBI also said that she had used many aliases, among them Mandy Hilley, Julie Hilley, MF Hilley and Margaret Key, the real name of her aunt.'

Whatever the truth, it was almost without doubt that Marie Hilley had begun a new life somewhere else. But where had she ended up? The answer lay in Fort Lauderdale, Florida where, in February 1980, Marie met John Homan.

Homan was a well-off businessman, some years Marie's junior. She told him that her name was Lindsay Robbi Hannon, that she was thirty-five years old and that she came from a wealthy family in Texas. In addition, she also informed John that she had been married, but that her husband had died following a tragic car accident that had killed both of their children. Finally she told John that she herself was suffering from extreme ill health.

One month after they met, Marie and John had set up home together and, just as the FBI had predicted, Marie had found herself a good job at a firm of accountants in West Palm Beach. Then in October the couple decided to move to New Hampshire. It would be a fresh start for them both and consequently John found them a house in a small town called Marlow. In May 1981 the couple were married and John began a well-paid job in a company that made small components needed in the manufacture of jewellery, while Marie found herself work as a customer-service adviser for a company called the Central Screw Corporation. She did well at the company and for the most part the other employees found her pleasant to work with, although they did notice that she seemed to be ill a lot of the time. On further questioning they learned that the woman they knew as Robbi Hannon was dying. She told them something about a rare disease of the blood and on several occasions she left town for treatments. Robbi Hannon also began telling her co-workers of a twin sister of hers called Teri. Teri Hannon still lived in Texas and had arranged for Robbi to have treatment back there. It was going to be a make-or-break time; Robbi was not getting any better and this was her last hope.

Robbi/Marie left her husband in New Hampshire in early September 1982 and went to Texas as planned, but in the event she only stayed in Dallas three days after which she decamped and travelled to her old haunt of Florida. Once in the sunshine state she then registered at an employment agency under the name Teri L Martin. She also dyed her hair bottle-blonde. To all intents and purposes she was a different person; new appearance, new name. Nor did it take the employment agency long to find Teri/Marie new work, securing her a job as a secretary at Solar Testing Service. But it was only a matter of time before Marie's lies started up again. This time she told her boss, Jack McKenzie, that she had a twin sister called Robbi who lived in New Hampshire. Unfortunately Robbi had not only had a recent stroke, but was also suffering from cancer. As twins, Teri explained, the two of them were very close and she felt duty-bound to look after Robbi, whatever the cost. A few weeks later Jack McKenzie received a telephone call from Teri saying that she couldn't come into work because she'd had to go back to New Hampshire. Sadly her sister had died and she'd decided to stay on in the area and therefore wouldn't be returning to Florida.

One might have thought that this is where Marie Hilley would have ended her lies. After all, the tale was complicated enough as it stood, but somehow enough was never enough for Marie.

On 10 November 1982, while pretending to be Teri, Marie phoned her husband, John Homan, to inform him that his wife Robbi had died. Marie then said that she'd like to meet her sister's husband and therefore would be flying out to New Hampshire the following morning; perhaps the two of them could comfort each other?

It seems extraordinary to think that John Homan was duped into believing that the woman who turned up claiming to be his dead wife's twin sister was who she said she was. But this is the story he stuck to, saying that he only realized his mistake when Teri/Robbi/Marie was finally arrested in 1983. Besides, Teri and Robbi were supposed to be twins, and Teri did look slightly different from his wife in that she had bottle-blonde hair, was thinner than Robbi and walked with a slight stoop.

On arriving at her brother-in-law's Teri suggested that she and John place an obituary in the local newspaper, the *Keene Sentinel*.[3] Under the circumstances it wasn't an untoward suggestion, but this seemingly innocuous article stating that Robbi Homan had died 'after a long illness' was, in the long run, to prove Marie Hilley's final undoing.

Teri/Marie now moved in with John Homan under the pretext of offering him comfort. She also found herself a job at Book Press, a printing company located just over the state line in Vermont. Everything seemed settled and normal. That is, until Robbi Homan's former work colleagues saw the *Keene Sentinel* obituary and began asking questions.

Teri had visited the Central Screw Corporation to thank all Robbi's co-workers for their support during her sister's terrible illness. But immediately she entered the building several people decided that Teri and Robbi were one and the same. Now, with the appearance of Robbi's obituary, they started investigating the facts. Initially they tried calling the hospital to which Robbi's body was supposed to have been left for medical research, only to discover that the hospital didn't exist. Then they discovered that the church to which Robbi was supposed to have belonged in Texas was also a complete fabrication. If this wasn't strange enough, Robbi's co-workers also failed to turn up any record at the coroner's office in Dallas that Robbi's death had been registered. It was as if they were in the middle of an Alfred Hitchcock film. The more they researched, the murkier everything grew and eventually, not knowing where to turn next, they went to the head of the Central Screw Corporation, Ron Oja.

Oja started his own investigation but this only laid bare the same unsavoury facts: that the woman known to them as Robbi Homan/Teri Martin, was somehow trying to commit a fraud. Ron Oja called in the police, who interviewed most of the people who had worked alongside Robbi Homan. In addition the police also researched the obituary, coming back with much the same conclusion as everyone else.

On 12 January 1983, Teri Martin was apprehended at Book Press. The police asked for her name and, according to their records, she replied in a puzzled tone that she was called Audrey Marie Hilley. She also added that she was a fugitive from the law, wanted back in the state of Alabama on a charge of fraud. Of course, when this information was checked out, the police discovered the real reason why Marie Hilley was on the run from the law and she was returned to Anniston to stand trial.

This time, not wanting to take any chances, bail was set at $320,000 and, unsurprisingly, no one was willing to pay it. However, what did strike everyone as unusual was that Carol Hilley wanted to see her mother. After her initial visit to the jail, Marie's daughter then returned on many occasions to lend her mother moral support.

In May of the same year Marie Hilley went on trial for the murder of her husband and the attempted murder of her daughter. The key witness for the prosecution was, of course, Carol Hilley, and as such Marie's defence team decided the best angle of attack was to try to prove that Carol was a mentally unstable, drug-abusing girl who had administered the arsenic to herself in a bid to commit suicide. Thomas Harman, Marie's defence lawyer, said: 'We expect the evidence to show that Carol Hilley has used drugs extensively... that Carol Hilley is in fact either a homosexual or has engaged in homosexuality. In addition, we expect the evidence to show that Carol Hilley has, on at least three occasions, attempted suicide.'

Thankfully the defence's strategy failed, Carol Hilley not only withstood their attack but rose above it to deliver her evidence coolly and calmly. There were also further statements from Frank Hilley's sister, Freeda, who testified that her brother had said Marie had given him injections while he was ill. But the biggest blow to the defence came from Marie Hilley herself. Somehow she had forgotten that in 1979 she had given a long taped interview to police admitting to the administration of injections to her daughter. During that interview she also admitted that she might be mentally unstable and probably needed medical assistance. When the prosecution brought the tape forward as evidence, Marie Hilley's trial was effectively over.

On 8 June 1983 Audrey Marie Hilley was found guilty of the murder of Frank Hilley and the attempted murder of Carol Hilley and on the following day she received the requisite life sentence plus twenty years. She was moved to Tutwiler State Women's Prison in Wetumpka, Alabama, where, having been classed a medium-security prisoner in 1983, she was by 1986 reclassified minimum security. As such she qualified for a day-release programme, and on 19 February 1987 she secured an even better privilege: a three-day pass which she used to visit her estranged husband, John Homan.

Having spent two days with him in a hotel, she told Homan she was going to visit her parents' graves and would catch up with him later at a restaurant. Marie Hilley never showed up. Instead, on returning to their room, Homan found a note in Marie Hilley's handwriting that said: 'Dear John, I hope you will be able to forgive me. I'm getting ready to leave. It will be best for everybody. We'll be together again. Please give me an hour to get out of town. Destroy this note.'

Four days later, on 27 February, the *Los Angeles Times* reported the following:

> **BLACK WIDOW CAUGHT IN HER OWN WEB – Audrey Marie Hilley, who had received a three-day pass from prison to visit her second husband at a hotel, was muddy and incoherent when she was found Thursday on a porch in a rural area. Doctors pronounced Hilley dead three-and-a-half hours later, listing exposure and hypothermia as preliminary causes.**

It was an anti-climactic, dismal way for anyone to die, let alone for Audrey Marie Hilley, the great escape artist and con woman. But perhaps her death says more about her life than anything else ever could, for in its own way it spells out just how mentally unstable Marie must have been throughout most of her confused and confusing life.

VALERIA MESSALINA

A Roman Lolita

When a not very clever, not very attractive man of fifty falls in love with a very attractive and very clever girl of fifteen it is usually a poor look-out for him.

FROM *I, CLAUDIUS*, BY ROBERT GRAVES

The Roman Empire produced some of the most politically astute, cruelly ambitious women ever to grace the pages of history. Among their number are characters such as Livia Augusta, who was the vixen wife of the great Caesar Augustus; Poppaea, who was the treacherous second wife to the Emperor Nero; and the she-wolf herself, Agrippina the Younger (see pp. 45-55). But it is the name Valeria Messalina that over the centuries has become synonymous with all the vices and faults of womankind. When one considers that she was only fifteen years old when she met and married the Emperor Claudius and only twenty-two when she died, it is even more breathtaking that she achieved such a phenomenally evil reputation.

Valeria Messalina was the third wife of Tiberius Claudius Caesar, who became emperor after his nephew Caligula was assassinated in AD 41. Before Claudius ascended the throne he had never been valued as a man of importance, due primarily to the physical disabilities that he had suffered from since birth. Some modern commentators have attributed his condition to cerebral palsy, but at the time he was simply considered a dull-witted, misshapen cripple, attributes that probably saved his life when, after Caligula's death, soldiers purged the palace of all Caligula's known associates and relatives. However, Claudius, being of noble birth, did enjoy the support of some factions of the Praetorian Guard and so by the skin of his teeth survived the cull alongside his young wife, Messalina.

Messalina was of noble birth herself, with impressive familial connections. Her mother was Domitia Lepida (the granddaughter of Mark Antony) and her father was the famous Roman consul, Valerius Messalla Barbatus. Due to this parentage Messalina had enjoyed many privileges, but most specifically that of being a member of Caligula's household. It is therefore quite easy to understand how she would have grown up fully aware of the intrigues of court as well as being conscious of the precariousness of human life, particularly among the ruling classes and especially given Caligula's despotic, tyrannical leadership. During his reign Caligula enjoyed nothing better than attending the huge bloodletting ceremonies that were held in Rome's amphitheatres. There was also plenty of bloodletting to be witnessed at the palace, as well as sundry other cruelties and vile behaviour. During all this, Messalina's husband-to-be, Tiberius Claudius, was nothing more than an indolent shadow flitting around in the background, someone who enjoyed the pleasures of eating and gaming over political intrigue. No one supposed he would ever attain greatness, let alone the throne, so when Messalina married him it is most likely she did so in order to align herself with a powerful family, rather than in the hope that Claudius would ever be crowned emperor.

Claudius had been married before. He was twice betrothed while still a young boy, first to Aemilia Lepida, who was the great-granddaughter of the Emperor Augustus, and then to Livia Medullina. However, the first engagement was broken off when Aemilia Lepida's family insulted the Emperor, and although the second engagement reached the wedding day, the bride died of a mysterious illness. Finally Claudius married Plautia Urgulanilla, but he soon divorced her for 'scandalous misbehaviour and the suspicion of murder'.[1] Shortly thereafter he married again, this time to a woman called Aelia Paetina, but she fared no better than her predecessor and the couple were divorced, also on the grounds of her aberrant behaviour. Valeria Messalina

Valeria Messalina, third wife of the Roman Emperor Claudius Caesar – despite a difference of thirty-five years in their ages. Avaricious, licentious, cruel and occasionally murderous, her name became a byword down the centuries for all the supposed vices of women, a remarkable achievement given that she was Empress for only seven years, a reign that ended in AD 48 when her long-suffering husband ordered her execution.
(© MARY EVANS PICTURE LIBRARY)

was therefore Claudius's third wife, the two having first met when he was fifty years old and she was fifteen. From Messalina's point of view it can hardly have been an ideal union, but Robert Graves, in the first volume of his fictionalized autobiography of Claudius, describes the young girl from the older man's perspective as follows: 'Messalina was an extremely beautiful girl, slim and quick moving, with eyes as black as jet and masses of curly black hair. She hardly spoke a word and had a mysterious smile which drove me nearly crazy with love for her.'[2]

No doubt Graves based his description on those he found in contemporary sources, but even were that not so, it is easy to see how, to a fifty-year-old man, a vivacious child of fifteen would appear exquisitely beautiful. That nothing is mentioned in any of the history books as to how a girl of fifteen might view an ageing and crippled man might go some way to explaining why Messalina's reputation is as it is. For no matter how precocious she was as a child, Messalina must have felt a certain degree of trepidation, if not fear, at marrying and sharing Claudius's bed. Despite this the union went ahead and the two were married in a small ceremony *circa* AD 38. Shortly afterwards Messalina gave birth to a daughter, Octavia, in AD 39. After Caligula's assassination in AD 41, Claudius was crowned emperor and Messalina fell into the role of consort. This she took with great aplomb, revelling in her new-found position, which was further secured when, in AD 41, she bore Claudius a male child by the name of Britannicus. As mother of the heir apparent she now enjoyed even more influence over both her husband and his court. Certainly Messalina must have been bewitching, for it is said that even in the early stages of her marriage she enjoyed the attentions of several lovers. Her power over her husband was such that for years he turned a blind eye to her debaucheries and avarice. Even when Claudius did become suspicious of the life she was leading, he was too timid a man to take action, preferring instead to pander to her every whim.

Ironically, the first sign of her truly snake-like nature was only brought to light when she experienced a fit of unprecedented jealousy. On assuming the throne, the gentle, even-minded Claudius had made it known that he wanted his two nieces, Agrippina the Younger and Julia Livilla, recalled from exile in Pontia, where they had been sent by the Emperor Tiberius after their brother, Caligula, had abused and raped them. Agrippina and Julia were the children of Claudius's brother Germanicus and as such Claudius had promised that he would always keep an eye out for their safety. Messalina felt threatened by their return. She knew that her husband had always favoured these two women and when he gave them back their estates and had their former riches and titles restored to them, Messalina's jealousy seemed more than a little justified. She took a particular dislike to Julia, who appeared to be vying for Claudius's attention (see also the chapter on Agrippina the Younger). Julia was a handsome woman, well-practised in the art of seduction, and no doubt Messalina could see her hold over her husband slipping away. She swiftly pointed out to Claudius that what he was involving himself in was incest and Claudius, left with no other option, was forced to send Julia back into exile under the *Lex de Adulteriis* ruling, after which the unfortunate girl was secretly executed, probably on the orders of Messalina herself.

As a consequence of this sorry episode, Messalina took succour from the fact that her plotting had been so successful. Afterwards, anyone who dared stand in her way is said to have become an immediate victim of her cruelty. On her orders several courtiers were put to death and she engineered countless trumped-up charges of treason, adultery and embezzlement. Messalina's word became law and soon there was no one left in the land who would dare defy her.

But from what source did all this hatred and cruelty emanate? As a child at the court of Caligula, Messalina would have witnessed a great deal of precisely this kind of behind-the-scenes plotting. In addition, she would also have been aware of huge amounts of courtly corruption, not to mention all the pomp and circumstance which marked Caligula's reign out as one far removed from the Augustan virtues of morality and family values. Whereas the Emperor Augustus's wife, Livia Drusilla Augusta – the *Mater Patriae* of the Roman Empire to her husband's *Pater Patriae* – had tried to live a life based on Roman conservatism, Messalina adopted quite the opposite path.

Appius Silanus was one of the first to experience this at firsthand. He had married Messalina's mother, Domitia Lepida, while at the same time enjoying the friendship of the Emperor Claudius. In fact Silanus was a well-liked man tipped for high office, but disaster struck when the young Messalina made it known that she found him attractive. Spurning her advances, Silanus attempted to explain that he was her stepfather as well as being a close friend of her husband's. Humiliated, Messalina swore she would have her revenge. She inveigled the help of a servant called Narcissus who told the Emperor of a dream he had had in which Silanus had stabbed Claudius through the heart with a dagger. Adding fuel to the fire, Messalina then told Claudius of a similar dream in which Silanus had attempted to kill the Emperor and thus succeed to the throne himself. Never one to turn his back on signs and portents, Claudius felt he had no option but to have Silanus killed.

It was an event that was to stain Messalina's reputation as empress and one that several members of the Senate responded to by plotting to have Claudius and his scheming wife removed from office. One of their plans was to have the pair assassinated and to replace them on the throne with the Emperor of Dalmatia. However, the plans never came to fruition because, according to contemporary accounts, Messalina caught wind of what was afoot and, claiming to be acting on behalf of the state, had those men responsible hunted down. Estates were confiscated and anyone even remotely connected to the plot was executed. Intoxicated by the killings and by her unassailable position, Messalina then made certain everyone knew that even the slightest deviance from her commands would be severely punished. In addition, greedy for the riches of high office, she also began milking her position as the Emperor's wife, selling her influence to anyone who could afford it in return for imperial favours. These included selling citizenships for her own profit, giving out building contracts to the men who offered the highest bribes and awarding high office to those who likewise filled her purse with gold.

Herein lies one of the many reasons why Valeria Messalina enjoys the reputation that she does today, because after Caligula's demise the general populace was eager to acquire a ruler who respected tradition and valued true moral conservatism. In Claudius they had found the right man, but the good people of Rome also required a virtuous woman to be at his side. They needed a figurehead who was, if not beyond reproach, then at least judged to be beyond reproach: a woman in the mould of Livia Drusilla Augusta, who had assisted her husband in the laying down of traditional values. In every sense Livia had attempted to personify the feminine virtues by both dressing and behaving modestly. Even if neither came naturally (some commentators, including

If Messalina's name became synonymous with murder and adultery, she was also held to have been exceptionally beautiful, as this rather over-romanticized nineteenth-century painting shows. High-born and adept at court intrigue, she could, despite her youth, be extremely vengeful towards those who spurned or thwarted her. (© BETTMANN/CORBIS)

Suetonius, Tacitus and Plutarch, doubted it), the result was the same, for in the eyes of the people she and her husband managed to create a tempered, restrained autocracy.

Sadly, Messalina scorned tradition and was never going to live up to her predecessor's standards. Quite the opposite. The list of vices attributed to her was long and inglorious and, in addition to her debaucheries, her greed was second to none. For instance, for years she had coveted the Gardens of Lucullus, which were located on the Collis Hortorum (Rome's garden hill). It was an exquisitely crafted plot of land, renowned for its outstanding beauty, belonging to one of Rome's leading senators, Valerius Asiaticus. Knowing that she could acquire the gardens in no other way than by being underhand, Messalina accused Asiaticus of instigating the plot to assassinate Caligula. The evidence was flimsy, if not non-existent, but Messalina had Claudius believing every word that she spoke and accordingly Asiaticus was sentenced to death. The only concession that Claudius made to the poor man was that he could take his own life, and accordingly Asiaticus chose the Gardens of Lucullus in which to commit suicide. He had surgeons open a vein in his leg and then bled to death in a warm bath.

It was a tawdry affair, but one of many that stained Messalina's career. She was an insult to everything Roman, to everything that was considered fine and upstanding. Although certain accusations can be dismissed as being nothing more than idle gossip, certain other stories do have the ring of truth about them.

The affair with the famous Roman dancer, Mnester, is just such a case. Messalina was still only a young woman when she first set eyes on this man and immediately fell under his spell.

Mnester came from lowly peasant stock, having been a goatherd in his early days, but from humble beginnings this young man trained long and hard. When he finally entered Rome his reputation as a dancer preceded him. His name had become a byword for artistic merit much as the actor Roscius had enjoyed. Messalina was entranced. She had statues erected to Mnester both in the city and in the imperial palace and employed poets to write odes about his physical beauty. However, frightened of the implications of having an affair with the Empress behind her husband's back, Mnester is said to have spurned Messalina's advances. Undiscouraged, Messalina continued her pursuit until finally the young man said he would do what she demanded so long as Claudius consented to her wishes. Immediately Messalina returned to her husband and is said to have told him that the dancer had, in some minor way, refused to follow her orders. She wanted Claudius to inform everyone that her directions were to be treated with more respect. Accordingly Claudius did his wife's bidding, called the dancer to him and ordered that he should do precisely what Messalina wished. In this way Mnester became Messalina's lover – and all under the Emperor's nose.

But none of the foregoing comes close to the affair that finally put an end to Messalina's plotting and counter-plotting. It concerned a young consul-designate called Caius Silius, who was known as the most handsome man in Rome. Silius was said to have caught Messalina's eye, after which she grew fatally enamoured of him. Tacitus in *The Annals* describes the infatuation thus:

> **She [Messalina] had grown so frantically enamoured of Caius Silius, the handsomest of the young nobility of Rome, that she drove from his bed Junia Silana, a high-born lady, and had her lover wholly to herself. Silius was not unconscious of his wickedness and his peril but a refusal would have insured destruction, and he had some hope of escaping exposure. The prize too was great, so he consoled himself by awaiting the future and enjoying the present. As for her, careless of concealment she went continually with a numerous retinue to his house. She haunted his steps, showered on him wealth and honours and, at last, as though the empire had passed to another, the slaves, the freedmen, the very furniture of the Emperor were to be seen in the possession of the paramour.[3]**

That Messalina chose not to hide her affair from prying eyes either shows how naïve she was to believe that she could escape punishment, or how secure she felt in Claudius's love. After all, Claudius had never shown anything towards his young spouse but indulgence so he might have sanctioned her extramarital affairs in order to keep her content. There is ample evidence to support this, for it was during this period that Claudius bestowed on Messalina her own wing in the palace where she could live and entertain friends without interference. Messalina took full advantage of the gift and proceeded to hold countless orgies to which she would invite all and sundry: actors, freedmen, slaves, ambassadors. Indeed, most reference material labels Messalina a nymphomaniac. Although these reports were written exclusively by male commentators who were less forgiving when it came to sexually aberrant behaviour in women, there is surely some kernel of truth behind their speculations.

Whatever the case, history has it that several of Messalina's relationships went too far and, in an attempt to hide all trace of her debauchery, these friends and lovers were murdered. Claudius, as her husband and as the Emperor, was implicated in these executions. No doubt he was told that a certain lover was plotting against him or that another was embezzling state money, but he always did as his wife requested and had the men quickly despatched.

The Emperor was now in danger of becoming a laughing stock. To the people of Rome, his position was considered a semi-sacred one, and although Claudius acquitted his political duties with great intelligence, Messalina's headstrong, incautious behaviour had begun dragging him down. People said that his weakness was responsible for his wife's appalling reputation. They needed something to be done and eventually, after seven years of ever-increasing depravities, Messalina gave him the perfect excuse when she decided to marry her lover, Caius Silius.

There are several interpretations as to what happened. Some sources suggest that Messalina duped her dolt of a husband into agreeing to it by having him grant her a temporary 'divorce' on the grounds that she had received a premonition foretelling her husband's death in painful and mysterious circumstances. Claudius was, so the story then goes, only too happy to grant her wishes and allow her to marry some other simpleton who would consequently die as predicted.

But the most convincing argument was that Messalina had decided that Claudius's political position was beginning to look increasingly shaky. Claudius's own brother, Germanicus, was beginning to assert a claim on the imperial throne, and Caius Silius's family were a powerful clan who supported Claudius's rival. Marrying her lover would therefore help maintain Messalina's political survival should Claudius ever be assassinated. After all, when Caligula was murdered, his wife Caesonia was tracked down and stabbed by soldiers, while their two-year-old daughter, Drusilla, had her head repeatedly smashed against a wall. Claudius was seen as weak and unable to cope with the pressures of office, so who better to turn to than a powerful family who enjoyed the respect of the Praetorian Guard, and in turn of the army?

Of course both explanations seem ludicrous because the act itself was ludicrous, a point not lost on Tacitus:

> **I am well aware that it will seem a fable that any persons in the world could have been so obtuse in a city which knows everything and hides nothing; much more, that these persons should have been a consul-elect and the Emperor's wife; that, on an appointed day, before witnesses duly summoned, they should have come together as if for the purpose of legitimate marriage; that she should have listened to the words of the bridegroom's friends, should have sacrificed to the gods, have taken her place among a company of guests, have lavished her kisses and caresses, and passed the night in the freedom which marriage permits. But this is no story to excite wonder; I do but relate what I have heard and what our fathers have recorded.[4]**

The ceremony was said to have taken place while Claudius was on an official visit to Ostia performing a sacrifice to the gods. Much wine was drunk, music was played and Messalina and her new 'husband' Silius, who was crowned with an expertly woven wreath of ivy, danced to their hearts' content. On his return Claudius was informed what had occurred, although even then he wasn't convinced of Messalina's guilt. He was loath to act against his wife and it was only because one of his loyal advisers persuaded him otherwise that Messalina was finally brought to book.

Pallus was Claudius's most favoured servant and in later years became his Minister of Finance at the Imperial Treasury. At the time of the Messalina débâcle, however, he was a very close ally of Agrippina the Younger, who had set her sights on marrying Claudius herself. Between them, Agrippina and Pallus spied on Messalina. When Claudius returned from Ostia, Pallus and another of Agrippina's allies, Narcissus, made it their duty to inform the Emperor of his wife's misguided actions.

Claudius summoned his most powerful friends to the palace where he interrogated them for several hours on the subject of his wife's alleged misdemeanours. First of all he questioned a man called Turranius, superintendent of the corn market, after which he interviewed Lusius Geta, the leader of the Praetorian Guard. Eventually both men confirmed that Pallus was correct; Messalina had indeed 'married' her lover. They then counselled Claudius that it was of the utmost importance for him to assure himself of the army's backing, thinking first and foremost of his own safety before taking revenge on his wife.

Messalina's days were drawing to a close. Despite Claudius's love for her, despite the fact that she was the mother of two of his children and despite her aptitude for talking Claudius around, this time she had gone one step too far.

Claudius returned to the imperial palace determined to purge himself of not only Caius Silius but also his wife and all the guests at her so-called wedding. To this end Silius was hastily brought before a tribunal at which he neither defended himself nor begged for mercy, but instead asked that his execution be swift. Similarly several other nobles who had attended the wedding also asked for a speedy end to their miserable lives. The only man among the accused to be given a second thought was the dancer, Mnester, who threw himself on Claudius's mercy, saying he had no option but to take part in the ceremony. Claudius was inclined to agree and is said to have been on the point of pardoning the dancer, when at the last minute his advisers prevailed upon their emperor not to indulge in forgiveness. Claudius had to be seen to be strong, they said, particularly when it came to matters of state where the throne was in jeopardy. The wedding guests were therefore put to death, after which attention returned to the main player in the whole nasty affair: Messalina.

On reaching his bedchamber it is said that, despite his authority being in question, Claudius's resolution failed him and he began to waver over his wife's fate. Added to this was the spectacle of his two beloved children, Octavia and Britannicus, whom Messalina had sent to their father to plead for her life. It was the most grisly, distasteful situation; one which the Emperor couldn't cope with alone. Consequently Claudius's courtiers, in particular Narcissus, took over the reins of office and ordered the centurions to execute Messalina. Accordingly they located Claudius's wife in the Gardens of Lucullus where she was said to be sitting alongside her mother, Domitia Lepida, writing letters of entreaty to her estranged husband.

On seeing the guards Messalina attempted a dignified exit by trying to commit suicide. To the Romans this was the preferred manner of death, especially when the motive behind it was to avoid the dishonour of execution and particularly when he or she was of noble birth. Seneca eloquently argues the case for suicide in his *De Ira* as being one of the best expressions of freedom:

> **In whatever direction you may turn your eyes, there lies the means to end your woes. Do you see that precipice? Down that is the way to liberty. Do you see that sea, that well? There sits liberty – at the bottom. Do you see that tree, stunted, blighted and barren? Yet from its branches hangs liberty. Do you see that throat of yours, your gullet, your heart? They are ways of escape from servitude. Are the ways of egress I show you too toilsome, do they require too much courage and strength? Do you ask what is the highway to liberty? Any vein in your body.[5]**

Messalina, hoping to take the dignified way out, picked up a dagger and attempted to cut her wrists. She made several slashes with the blade but failed dismally. Instead, one of the centurions finished off the job for her by stabbing her to death. It was a sad ending to a young woman's life, but given her behaviour, combined with the precariousness of life within the imperial court, hardly a surprising one.

Almost immediately all the statues of Messalina were removed from all over Rome. Despite the fact that her children must have mourned her passing, Claudius didn't for a moment regret her execution. Although he swore he would never marry again, it wasn't long before he turned his attention to Agrippina the Younger, Messalina's former rival who was also Claudius's niece. But as Tacitus is at pains to explain: 'When the House next met, he persuaded a group of senators to propose that a union between him and her should be compulsorily arranged, in the public interest; and that other uncles should likewise be free to marry their nieces, though this had hitherto counted as incest.'[6]

Messalina did not fade from memory either easily or quickly. In life she had dazzled and amazed ancient Rome with her infamous behaviour and in death her reputation continued to hold people in thrall. Her scheming and violence ensured that her name would be remembered long after her death.

AGRIPPINA THE YOUNGER

Empress of Poison

I am obnoxious to each carping tongue
Who says my hand a needle better fits,
A poet's pen all scorn I should thus wrong,
For such despite they cast on female wits:
If what I do prove well, it won't advance,
They'll say it's stol'n, or else it was by chance.
FROM 'THE PROLOGUE' BY ANNE BRADSTREET.

Born into the very heart of the Roman Empire, Agrippina the Younger enjoyed an impeccable birthright. Her mother, Agrippina the Elder, was the daughter of Agrippa and Julia who represented two of the most prominent families in ancient Rome, the Julians and the Claudians, while her father was the famous military commander Germanicus (nephew to the Emperor Tiberius). With such an illustrious family background it is not surprising that Agrippina the Younger's life should see her at the centre of imperial Rome, nor that her early years influenced her craving for power. Even the most sanguine child would have been affected by the scheming and plotting that went on around her. Her father was assassinated when Agrippina was only three years of age and, as one commenter put it, she grew up in 'an appalling atmosphere of

Agrippina the Younger, great-niece of the Emperor Tiberius, sister of the Emperor Caligula, niece and fourth wife of the Emperor Claudius, and mother of the Emperor Nero. Her overweening desire for political influence, especially for her son Nero, coupled with her lust for wealth and contempt for human life, scandalized even the jaded court of Imperial Rome. (© HULTON-DEUTSCH COLLECTION/CORBIS)

malevolence, suspicion and criminal violence.'[1] In addition to being the sister of the future Emperor Caligula, Agrippina was also the mother of the Emperor Nero and became the third wife of the Emperor Claudius.

Agrippina the Younger was born at Oppidum Ubiorum on the Rhine to Germanicus and Agrippina the Elder *circa* AD 16. During her childhood her father enjoyed huge popularity amongst the people of Rome. Suetonius describes him as 'having been of outstanding physical and moral excellence. He was handsome, courageous, a past-master of Greek and Latin oratory and letters, conspicuously kind-hearted, and gifted, with the ability of winning universal respect and affection.'[2] Having succeeded in various military operations in Germany, the Emperor Tiberius granted him a full triumph in AD 15, the last such display any military commander who was not a reigning emperor would be granted. However, Tiberius was as formidable a foe as he was a friend, and when it became apparent that Germanicus not only enjoyed the support of the people as rightful princeps of Rome, but also that of the imperial troops, Tiberius is said to have had him poisoned. Germanicus died in the eastern city of Antioch in AD 15. On his deathbed he is supposed to have turned to his wife and pleaded with her to relinquish her anger and ferocity against the Emperor, if not for her husband's sake then for the sake of their children, and urged that when she had returned to Rome she was not to encourage her supporters to rile the Emperor or indeed anyone who was more powerful than she was. It was a tall order and one which Agrippina the Elder did not heed. Convinced of Tiberius's involvement in her husband's assassination, she made it clear on her return to Rome that she was no ally of the Emperor's. Finally Tiberius, afraid that her ambitions might lead her to try and replace him on the throne with one of her own sons, had her sent to the island of Pandateria, off the western Italian coast. In AD 33 Agrippina the Elder died of starvation, probably on the orders of the Emperor, although the official line went that she had committed suicide. Two of her sons, Drusus and Nero, had already succumbed to the Emperor's wrath and had died some time before their mother, Nero 'committing suicide' by supposedly slitting his own throat, while Drusus starved to death in prison. Having killed her elder sons it is surprising to learn that Tiberius spared her youngest child, namely Gaius Caesar, who was better known by the nickname Caligula. The boy was first sent to his grandmother Antonia's household, but then, when Caligula was nineteen years old, he received an imperial summons to join Tiberius on the island of Capri. For the next six years of his life Caligula lived with Tiberius and Tiberius even named Caligula, alongside his grandson Gemullus, as one of the heirs to the imperial throne.

Even as a teenager, Caligula had shown signs of the disturbed, maniacal nature that he displayed when in power. According to Suetonius, 'Caligula could not control his natural brutality. He loved watching torturers and executions and, disguised in wig and robe, abandoned himself nightly to the pleasures of feasting and scandalous living.'[3] This debauchery also included the rape of all three of his sisters (Drusilla, Agrippina the Younger and Julia Livilla), although it has been recorded that when this behaviour was reported to Tiberius, the Emperor saw to it that all three women were swiftly married off to allay any charges of misconduct on the part of their brother.

Agrippina's betrothed was a man called Cnaeus Domitius Ahenobarbus. He was twenty-five years older than his wife and extremely wealthy, but best known for his brutal temper and controlling ways. It was hardly an ideal union for the headstrong Agrippina or, in retrospect, for the people of Rome, as the product of the relationship was a son who later became known as the Emperor Nero.

In AD 37 the Emperor Tiberius died. He was seventy-seven years old and had reigned a little over twenty-three years. To the Roman people Caligula was the natural successor, so Gemellus was swiftly cast aside (within a year he was dead, presumed murdered) in preference to Germanicus's son. After all, who better to take over the reigns of power than the child of so revered and honourable a military leader? Caligula was born to be emperor, but no one had reckoned on his dubious mental state. Unnatural in almost everything he did, Caligula installed his favourite sister, Drusilla, as his mistress while also continuing an incestuous affair with the younger Agrippina. Caligula also arranged for Drusilla to marry one of his closest friends and allies, Marcus Aemilius Lepidus (who was rumoured to be Caligula's male lover). Drusilla had in fact been married before, to Lucius Cassius Longinus, but on her brother's insistence had divorced him and married Lepidus. The union suited Caligula's dynastic plans because, having no children of his own, he named Lepidus as his successor so that, should he die, his favourite sister would automatically become empress. Fortuitously, perhaps, this never occurred, as Drusilla died prematurely, but Agrippina, never one to miss an opportunity, tried to take her sister's place in Caligula's affections. On being rebuffed, Agrippina then switched tack and moved her attention to Lepidus, telling him that if he assassinated her brother, she would marry him. As well as recruiting her remaining sister, Julia, she also involved several others in her machinations. Of course the plan was doomed to failure and on its discovery Caligula had Lepidus executed and both his sisters sent into exile.

At this point one might have thought Agrippina would have toned her ambitions down, but nothing could have been further from the truth. With time on her hands she began plotting her future, waiting for the tides of fortune to turn. She did not have to wait long, either, because barely eighteen months after she had been removed from Rome, Caligula was assassinated. The year was AD 41 and though there are several different accounts as to how he was despatched, it is generally agreed that he died by the sword and that the fatal blow was delivered by Cassius Chaerea – a man whom Caligula had repeatedly mocked for being effeminate.

Thereafter there was a heated debate among the Senate as to who might succeed him, but it was finally decided, more by accident than design, that the fifty-year-old Tiberius Claudius Drusus would become emperor. Always considered something of a dunce, as well as a weakling, Claudius was none the less a kind man and one of his first acts was to bring his two nieces back from exile.

Agrippina, on her return, retrieved her son Nero from the care of her sister-in-law, Domitia Lepida. There was no love lost between these two women and this dislike only intensified when Domitia persuaded Claudius to marry her fifteen-year-old daughter, Messalina. Shortly after this union Messalina gave birth first to a daughter (Octavia) and then to a son (Britannicus), thus increasing Agrippina's wrath as she saw her chances of power rapidly slipping away. None the less, she remained determined to see herself and her own son in a position of power and began a well thought-out campaign to bring about Messalina's downfall.

Crafty in nearly everything she did, Agrippina now remarried, Cnaeus Domitius Ahenobarbus having died. The new candidate was a man called Passienus Crispus and he was both wealthy and highly regarded, qualities that ensured Agrippina became one of the most prominent, respectable ladies in Roman society. In contrast Messalina looked more and more inappropriate; she was wild, rowdy and outrageous, not qualities best associated with the Emperor's wife. It was a plan that, given time, was sure to work. After all, Messalina was bound to do something injudicious, thus incurring the wrath of her husband, who would then turn to the more stable, more socially acceptable Agrippina.

Not one to leave anything to chance, Agrippina also sent her younger sister, Julia, to Claudius in an attempt to test just how loyal he was to Messalina. But the plan failed dismally and Agrippina's sister was sent into exile and afterwards, through Messalina's agency, discreetly killed. Thereafter, Messalina decided that she was in an unassailable position and that Claudius would tolerate even her most aberrant behaviour. She began holding orgies at the palace, flouting herself before all and sundry, holding court and enjoying countless affairs.

Agrippina was still plotting behind the scenes, forging new alliances between herself and some of Claudius's most trusted courtiers. This latter plan of action included befriending a man named Pallus, who was the Imperial Treasurer. Between them Pallus and Agrippina spied on Messalina and spread stories about her debaucheries. Finally Messalina went too far and married another man, Caius Silius. Even then Claudius was reluctant to take action, but on the advice of Pallus and another court official by the name of Narcissus, both of whom were no doubt being instructed by Agrippina, Claudius eventually gave orders for his wife to be killed.

The path was now clear for Agrippina to make a play for the Emperor and in this she was again aided by Pallus who, when Claudius said he was ready to remarry, argued Agrippina's cause. He said that not only was she beautiful and intelligent but she was also the mother of Germanicus's grandson, added to which she was still young enough to sire more children. The choice was therefore made in favour of Agrippina – although there were still several obstacles to overcome. The first was that she was already married, but conveniently Agrippina's husband died shortly afterwards. Many sources are convinced that Agrippina poisoned Passienus Crispus, but with no firm evidence it can only remain speculation. The second obstacle was that Agrippina was Claudius's niece and under Roman law the marriage of uncle and niece was deemed incestuous. This potential roadblock was soon remedied, however, by creating a new decree in the Senate authorizing the union. Finally Agrippina had achieved her ultimate goal. She had gained power, been created empress and, according to Tacitus in *The Annals*, she entered the city of Rome in a ceremonial carriage, the intention being to emphasize 'the reverence felt for a woman who to this day remains unique as the daughter of a great commander and the sister, wife and mother of emperors'.[4]

Not one to rest on her laurels, Agrippina also made certain that everyone, but in particular her rivals, knew how much influence she now wielded. Lollia Paulina was just such a case. The third wife of the Emperor Caligula, she was a noted beauty and had been a rival with Agrippina for Claudius's hand in marriage. Agrippina therefore loathed Lollia Paulina and consequently she plotted her downfall, eventually deciding that the best course of action was to accuse Paulina of having consulted with astrologers and magicians, as well as the 'Clarian Apolla', regarding the imperial marriage. On hearing the charges Claudius, rather than questioning the accused as to whether the story was true, instead went straight to the Senate and stated that Lollia Paulina had evil designs on the state. Agrippina's plan had worked beautifully. The Senate, horrified to hear Claudius's accusations, immediately confiscated all of Lollia Paulina's property and had her sent into exile, where she was forced to take her own life. Robert Graves in his fictional work *Claudius the God* also adds that Agrippina ordered that Lollia's head be brought to her at the palace. 'Agrippina took it by the hair and, holding it up to a window, opened the mouth. "Yes, that's Lollia's head, all right," she said complacently to me [Claudius] as I came into the room.'[5]

Another victim of Agrippina's plotting was a woman called Calpurnia, who had incurred the Empress's wrath because Claudius had once, in passing, praised the young woman's beauty. Calpurnia was slightly more fortunate than Lollia Paulina, but none the less suffered greatly, having all her property confiscated.

After this Agrippina had Messalina's mother, Domitia Lepidus, executed (something which must, considering their rivalry, have given Agrippina a great deal of pleasure), as well as having all of Messalina's most trusted servants and aides either killed or cleared from the court. Agrippina also, in a move guaranteed to consolidate her position as empress, set her sights on marrying her son Nero to Octavia, Claudius's daughter by Messalina. There was only one hitch to the plan; Octavia was already betrothed. Agrippina swiftly threw this obstacle aside and, with her usual aplomb, began spreading rumours that the young man was conducting an incestuous affair with his sister (ironical, considering her own relationship with Caligula), and in turn this brought about the young man's quick despatch from Italy into permanent exile. Nero and Octavia were now betrothed and again one might have thought this would have brought to an end Agrippina's quest for supremacy. Yet nothing seemed to deflect her from her course.

The Roman Empire in its heyday has long fascinated film-makers. In this photo taken on the set of an Italian comedy, shot in 1956, called My Son, Nero, *Agrippina is played by the Hollywood legend Gloria Swanson (centre) and Nero's wife, Poppaea, by the young Brigitte Bardot; at left, Vittorio de Sica plays Nero's teacher, Seneca. (© BETTMANN/CORBIS)*

Immediately after Nero became engaged to marry Octavia, Agrippina began working on Claudius to adopt Nero as his son. As before, she employed Pallus to back her up, in particular by having him mention to the Emperor that Tiberius had 'adopted' Caligula: would it not be a similarly generous gesture if Claudius were to do the same for Nero? The implications were obvious. Claudius already had a son by his marriage to Messalina. The boy was called Britannicus, and it was obvious to all who knew him that Claudius felt very close to this child. On Claudius's death Britannicus would almost certainly succeed his father, but Agrippina couldn't bear the thought of losing power so easily. She therefore worked on her husband night and day until at last he gave in to her wishes and adopted Nero as one of his own. At this point things grew increasingly complicated, for the adoption meant that Nero was now betrothed to his legal sister and so the issue of incest once again raised its ugly head. Of course Agrippina had an answer, and Octavia was legally adopted into another family.

Agrippina's powers had now reached almost unassailable heights. She was constantly seen in the Emperor's company, sitting beside him at tribunals as well as riding up the Capitoline Hill with him in his chariot. She further consolidated her position by amassing huge wealth and placing her own supporters in key government positions. It is therefore not by any means certain, as some early historians (in particular Suetonius, Tacitus and Dio Cassius) have suggested, that it was Agrippina who was responsible for assassinating her husband. After all, she already controlled the imperial household as well as much of imperial policy, added to which she had secured her son's position as heir to the throne. According to Suetonius:

> **Most people think that Claudius was poisoned; but when, and by whom, is disputed. Some say that the eunuch Halotus, his official taster, administered the drug while he was dining with the priests of Jupiter in the Citadel; others, that Agrippina did so herself at a family banquet, poisoning a dish of mushrooms, his favourite food. An equal discrepancy exists between the accounts of what happened next. According to many of my informants, he lost his power of speech, suffered frightful pain all night long, and died shortly before dawn. A variant version is that he fell into a coma but vomited up the entire contents of his stomach and was then poisoned a second time, either by a gruel – the excuse being that he needed food to revive him – or by means of an enema, the excuse being that his bowels must be emptied too.[6]**

Bearing Suetonius's account in mind, if it was Agrippina who poisoned Claudius then it is likely she had an accomplice, and all the evidence suggests a woman called Locusta. It has been recorded that there was a growing incidence of poisoning in Ancient Rome, which had grown out of all control during the reign of the Julio-Claudian emperors. Horace in his *Satires* writes of three professional poisoners: Canidia, Martina and, last but not least, Locusta herself. The favoured potion would probably have been a vegetable derivative, i.e. plants that included belladonna alkaloids such as hemlock, aconite and yew, although contemporary sources rarely, if ever, mention anything specific. Whatever the case, Claudius was killed. He was sixty-four years old and had been on the throne a little over fourteen years so it was a sad, somewhat tawdry end to what had been a relatively peaceful rule. But this wasn't the only indignity the old emperor suffered, for after he had died it is said that Agrippina kept his body warm by various 'applications' until 'all arrangements had been made to secure Nero's succession.'[7]

At last, on 12 October AD 54, Nero was declared emperor by the Praetorian Guard and celebrations were held throughout Rome in his honour. Some citizens did question his right to succeed, citing that Britannicus had a more legitimate claim to the imperial throne, but luckily for Nero nothing came of these rumblings and he took over the reins of power. However, still being only seventeen years old, he could not legally rule in his own name. Agrippina therefore took on the role of self-styled regent and even after Nero came of age, it can be assumed he was still under her influence. She was given the title of 'AVGVSTA' meaning 'empress' and her portrait appeared alongside that of her son on every coin in the land. This last privilege was unique for, up until that moment women of the imperial household had only ever appeared on coins after they had died. Agrippina also made certain during this period that all rival claimants to the throne (except for Britannicus) were either sent into exile or killed. Whether he was aware of his mother's murderous activities or not, Nero must surely have been in awe of her as the two of them ruled for several years with absolute impunity. None the less, the deference that Agrippina inspired in her son was not to last for ever, for Nero soon began to discover as much pleasure in absolute power as his mother had done.

Nero was a dissolute young man who, despite an early yearning to become an actor or singer, later in life indulged his darker side by committing numerous vicious and atrocious acts. He squandered money as if it were water, enjoyed orgies, seduced both girls and boys and in general led a highly debauched life. Worse than this, and certainly worse in the eyes of his mother, was that he began to show Agrippina little respect. He started an affair while still married to Octavia with a former slave-girl, but now a freedwoman, named Acte. Agrippina was incandescent with rage not only at her son's flouting of his marriage but most of all because she didn't want an ex-slave girl as a rival for his affections or, worse still, as a future daughter-in-law. Nero also banished Agrippina's confidant, Pallus (whom some have suggested had become her lover by this point). This last act was perhaps the final straw and in desperation Agrippina now began threatening

Long before the advent of film, ancient Rome had often been a subject for writers and artists. This seventeenth-century engraving shows a scene from the play Britannicus *by the great French playwright Jean Racine, in which Agrippina reproaches Nero. She had persuaded her husband, Claudius, to adopt Nero, her son by a previous marriage, in preference to his own son by Messalina, Britannicus. After his accession Nero had Britannicus murdered, but his mother's machinations did her little good, for in the end Nero also had her killed after several botched attempts. (© MARY EVANS PICTURE LIBRARY)*

her son, telling him that she would have him replaced as emperor by his older step-brother, Britannicus. In order to make the threat seem more real Agrippina did begin to show an uncommon interest in her stepchild. Already paranoid that his position as emperor would be undermined, Nero took his mother's warning very seriously and not long afterwards engaged the services of Locusta, who in turn poisoned his stepbrother.

With Britannicus safely out of the way, Nero then further displayed his filial wrath by turning on his mother's closest friends and confidants. With the help of two of his own most trusted advisers, Seneca and Burrus, he had Pallus killed, after which he removed Agrippina's armed guard and had her titles revoked.

Agrippina was then told to leave the palace. Stripped of her titles and denied access to her imperial residence, Agrippina's powers were now greatly reduced. Yet this woman was still not deterred from seeking high office and, instead of lying low, now sought to find another candidate to replace Britannicus and threaten Nero. It was a bad, ill thought-out plan; Nero had spies everywhere and consequently Agrippina's plot was soon discovered. A commission was sent to her new place of residence in order to determine her guilt. This time Agrippina managed, by delivering a long and elegant speech, to extricate herself from all the accusations made against her, but with her next move she was not so fortunate. Extraordinarily, Agrippina decided that the best way to win her son back was to start an incestuous relationship with him

According to Tacitus, she waited until her son was satiated with wine and good food, then offered herself up to him 'carefully arrayed and ready for incest'. Agrippina caressed her son and smothered him with lascivious kisses, making such a display of herself that she couldn't help but attract the attention of several courtiers and officials. At this point, on seeing the Emperor struggling to escape his mother's clutches, Seneca intervened by sending Acte to Nero's side. The young ex-slave acted quickly and whispered into her lover's ear that rumours were fast spreading round the city that the Emperor was indulging in incest and that Agrippina, far from being ashamed of what she was doing, was revelling in her new role as seductress. In addition, Acte also pointed out that the army would not tolerate an emperor tarnished by such tawdry crimes.

Bearing this in mind and beginning to believe that his mother was the cause of everything that went wrong in his life, Nero resolved to have Agrippina killed. But this was no easy task. Despite having been stripped of many of her powers, Agrippina was still a formidable opponent. According to Suetonius, Nero attempted to poison his mother three times, but failed on each occasion as Agrippina had already devised antidotes in advance. Finally Nero had a collapsible boat built which, when set on water, would fall apart and sink. Under the guise of a reconciliation he wrote to his mother asking her to join him at Baiae to celebrate the Feast of Minerva. Agrippina duly attended, joining her son by galley, but as she arrived Nero arranged for one of his captains to cause an accident, thus making Agrippina's boat an unworthy vessel in which to sail home. The feasting and revelries over, Nero then offered Agrippina his collapsible boat, an offer she accepted. Even this plan failed. Nero sat up for the remainder of the night waiting for news of her death only to be informed by one of her freedmen that indeed the boat had sunk, but that thankfully Agrippina had been able to swim to shore. She had suffered only a minor injury to her left shoulder.

Perhaps Agrippina had suspicions of foul play even before this 'accident', but if not, then one incident surely convinced her. While the boat was sinking she had noticed a woman shouting out that she was the Emperor's mother and therefore had to be saved, but then Agrippina saw the woman being bludgeoned to death by some of the crew. Her suspicions that her life was in danger were confirmed, though as Tacitus remarks, 'she understood that the only way to avoid falling into traps was to appear not to suspect them'. With this in mind she sent word to her son that the gods had looked upon her with benevolence and, though Nero would want to visit her, he should wait as she was still recovering from the ordeal of the boat's sinking.

Far from waiting however, Nero rid himself of all caution and despatched a group of armed officers to his mother's villa with orders that she should never awaken.

Again, there are several differing reports of how precisely Agrippina died. Suetonius says that the murder was staged to look like a suicide and that after she was dead 'Nero rushed off to examine Agrippina's corpse, handling her legs and arms critically and, between drinks, discussing their good and bad points,'[8] while other historians record that she was killed with several blows of the sword to the stomach and that afterwards, in order to hide any evidence of foul play, her corpse was burnt on a bonfire.

Greedy in her ambition to achieve not just political influence, but also vast wealth, and implicated in the murder of so many others, it seems only fitting that Agrippina the Younger was now the victim rather than the perpetrator. Contemporary historians seem to think along much the same lines, noting that it was not only unnatural for a woman to use her femininity as a means of gaining power, but also beneath contempt. In fact, the only person who appeared to suffer after her death was the man who had her assassinated. It is said that for the rest of his life Nero was plagued by a bad conscience, sometimes being haunted by Agrippina's ghost, while at other times being pursued by the Furies. Even after employing occultists to exorcize her memory she still plagued his conscience and manifested herself in his dreams. Sadly, for the people over whom he ruled, even these horrors did not cure Nero of his blood lust. Until his death in AD 68 he still continued, as his mother had done before him, to live a bloody and brutal existence.

TZ'U-HSI

The Dragon Empress

Never should the word 'Peace' fall from the mouths of our high officials, nor should they even allow it to rest for a moment within their breasts. With such a country as ours, with her vast area, stretching out several tens of thousands of *li*, her immense natural resources, and her hundreds of millions of inhabitants, if only each and all of you would prove his loyalty to his Emperor and love of country, what, indeed, is there to fear from any invader? Let no one think of making peace, but let each strive to preserve from destruction and spoliation his ancestral home and graves from the ruthless hand of the invader.

FROM A SECRET EDICT OF TZ'U-HSI TO HER VICEROYS, 21 NOVEMBER 1899 (TAKEN FROM *COURT LIFE IN CHINA: THE CAPITAL, ITS OFFICIALS AND PEOPLE* BY ISAAC TAYLOR HEADLAND, NEW YORK, F.H. REVELL, *c.*1909)

In many ways Peking's Imperial City, with its labyrinthine streets and walls within walls, is a mirror image of the convoluted history of imperial China and in particular of the reign of the Dragon Empress. In the mid-1830s, when the Dragon Empress was born, China was at the height of its powers, but by the time of her death in 1908, due to numerous political upheavals and in particular to contact with Western civilization, the Ch'ing dynasty was all but dead, imperial China all but demolished.

Tz'u-hsi (pronounced Tsoo Shee or Cixi) was born on 29 November 1835 during the Manchu dynasty. She had two brothers and a sister, but her parents were not rich. Her father, Hui-cheng, was a minor Manchu mandarin, a nobody in relation to the thousands of other minor officials who populated Peking at that time. The only glory attached to his name was the hereditary honour of belonging to one of eight military companies, the 'Bordered Blue Bannermen'. Other than that, Hui-cheng was neither influential nor wealthy and, given the latter, he wouldn't have earned enough money to educate his children to any great degree. None the less, Tz'u-hsi, always a resourceful child, somehow managed to teach herself the rudiments of reading and writing, which was no small feat, for in those days Chinese women were nearly always illiterate. Her destiny, however, according to the society in which she lived, was to become a concubine and, in 1851, when Tz'u-hsi was only sixteen years old, she was sent to

A contemporary full-length portrait of the Empress Dowager Tz'u-hsi, after a Chinese painting. From a position as a humble concubine in the Emperor's court in 1852, she rose to preside over the Chinese empire for more than fifty years, although her cruelty and loathing of foreigners did much to destroy it, for it survived for only three years after her death in 1908. (© BETTMANN/CORBIS)

the imperial court where the new Emperor's harem was being chosen. Hsien feng had taken over the throne after the death of his father, the Tao-kuang Emperor, and Tz'u-hsi, being the daughter of a Bordered Blue Bannerman, was chosen, alongside her sister, to attend the imperial palace. She was one of sixty girls who were eligible for this time-honoured role and as such her family ensured that when she entered the palace both she and her sister were dressed in the finest clothes they could afford. In the event twenty-eight girls were picked and Tz'u-hsi was one of this number, although her entry into the Emperor's harem did not automatically mean she was any closer to the seat of power, as concubines quite frequently never set eyes on the Emperor.

On 14 June 1852, after the official mourning period for the old emperor was over, Tz'u-hsi was officially made a Kuei Jen (Honourable Person), which meant that she was a concubine of the lowest rank. At the same time another of the chosen few, a girl called Niuhuru, was made Pin, a concubine one rank higher than Tz'u-hsi. Only a few weeks later, Niuhuru was then elevated to become Hsien feng's consort. She was crowned Empress and, knowing instinctively that Niuhuru was destined for greatness, Tz'u-hsi immediately made herself a close friend of the young girl. Tz'u-hsi also began watching the intrigues within the imperial palace and soon gained the knowledge that the most influential people within its labyrinthine walls were the eunuchs.

Originally the order of eunuchs had been created to protect the authenticity of the imperial children: being castrated there was no question of them conducting illicit relationships with either the Empress or with the concubines. Over the years their position wasn't elevated as such, but instead they became very powerful in their own right, dealing on a day-to-day basis with all members of the imperial household. Tz'u-hsi, recognizing their influence, soon struck up an alliance with several of their number. However, this still did not bring her any closer to the Emperor who, at the time of her being created a concubine, was desperately trying to escape the ever-insurmountable duties of state.

Hsien feng wasn't an emperor who was greatly interested in his country's politics and at the beginning of his reign, China suffered internal rebellions and problems with several foreign powers. Instead of facing these concerns head on, Hsien feng decided to escape to his summer palaces in an attempt to ignore the political intrigues occurring around him.

In his absence, Tz'u-hsi occupied herself by making full use of the imperial palace's extensive libraries. It was time well spent. She also further ingratiated herself with the eunuchs and, when permitted, continued her friendship with Hsien feng's empress, Niuhuru.

Ironically it was Niuhuru who was to bring Tz'u-hsi her dream of power, for three years after Niuhuru's wedding to the Emperor she had still not provided him with a male heir to the Dragon Throne. Hsien feng's mother, along with his ministers, therefore advised the young emperor that it was now his official duty to spend more time with his concubines. There are several different versions as to how Hsien feng eventually chose Tz'u-hsi for this privilege, but most people believe that having ingratiated herself with the eunuchs, she now persuaded them to put her name forward as the best candidate for the role.

Her campaign was a success; Tz'u-hsi was sent for to share the Emperor's bed. Etiquette demanded that she be taken to his chamber naked and deposited at the foot of his bed, from where she would have to crawl upwards to where he lay.

Whether it was on this first occasion, or the second or the third, the union yielded results. On 27 April 1856, a son was born to the twenty-year-old Tz'u-hsi. He was named Tsai-ch'un and he was to be the only male child of the Hsien feng Emperor. As a reward, Tz'u-hsi, who had already been made a Pin, now became a Yellow Banner. As she later recorded, 'I must say I was a clever woman, for I fought my own battles and won them too. When I arrived at court, the late Emperor became very much attached to me… I was lucky in giving birth to a son, as it made me the Emperor's undisputed favourite.'[1]

Sadly, however, the relationship between emperor and concubine was never a stable one and it was further complicated when, under pressure from China's continued political crises, Hsien feng buried his head in the sand and refused to acknowledge his country's increasing difficulties. In particular Taiping rebels in the north had launched terrible attacks on the throne and this, combined with an invasion of north China by the 'foreign devils' of Britain and France, terrified the young ruler. Instead of standing firm and fighting these forces, Hsien feng retreated further and further from confrontation (eventually ending up in a palace at Jehol in the mountains). In the process he infuriated Tz'u-hsi who, embarrassed by his lack of courage, turned her back on the Emperor. Finally a special decree stating that all foreign prisoners should be decapitated was issued, but the voice that instigated it was not that of the Emperor; it was the voice of Tz'u-hsi.

Heads rolled, although in Hsien feng's absence from the capital his brother, Prince Kung, decided that the bloodshed could not continue and so, despite imperial decrees to the contrary, he signed a peace treaty with Britain and France. With the political situation thus calmed the Emperor was persuaded that he must return to the capital, but he fell desperately ill before he could do so. Tz'u-hsi's position was suddenly put in jeopardy; in China, primogeniture was not Ch'ing law. The Emperor, if he saw fit, could decree any one of his family's male children as successor to the throne. Bearing this in mind Tz'u-hsi once again sought out the friendship of Hsien feng's wife, Niuhuru. It was a cynical but worthwhile move, because shortly afterwards the thirty-year-old Hsien feng was on his deathbed. The Emperor grew increasingly ill and Tz'u-hsi grew increasingly worried. Then without warning, as she herself described:

The Emperor being practically unconscious of what was taking place around him, I took my son to his bedside and asked him

> what was going to be done about his successor to the throne.
> He made no reply to this, but, as had always been the case in
> emergencies, I was equal to the occasion, and I said to him,
> 'Here is your son'; on hearing which he immediately opened
> his eyes and said, 'Of course he will succeed to the throne.' I
> naturally felt relieved when this was settled for once and for
> all. These words were practically the last he spoke.[2]

On 22 August 1861, Hsien feng died and Tz'u-hsi's son, Tsai-ch'un, was declared emperor. But even this was not a simple matter, for in the three months between Hsien feng's death and his burial, several members of the court set different schemes in motion, all in the name of gaining power. The root of the problem stemmed from the fact that the new emperor wasn't old enough to rule. Tz'u-hsi, alongside seven other 'regents' (including Niuhuru), was named to administer the empire. Of course this division of power was bound to end with regent set against regent, and in due course Prince I and Prince Cheng were found guilty of crimes against the state and were 'permitted to commit suicide'. A third regent, Su-shun, was then executed by beheading, after which his estates and vast wealth were transferred into the hands of Tz'u-hsi and Niuhuru. This was the first time Tz'u-hsi had had such riches bestowed upon her and almost overnight she became a very wealthy woman.

But if the situation at court was more settled, in the country at large this was, sadly, far from the case. Civil war raged through five provinces and within the first few years of Tz'u-hsi's reign more than twenty million people died either as a result of the fighting or from starvation. Huge tracts of countryside were laid waste and cities were reduced to rubble. It was an inglorious page in China's history.

None the less, during this time Tz'u-hsi, far from being put off affairs of state, insisted on having an audience with Prince Kung every day in order to discuss political matters. In this way she began to learn how government worked and how to be skilful in political matters. What Prince Kung learnt from Tz'u-hsi, however, is less apparent, for he undoubtedly underestimated her intelligence, seeing her as a woman whom he could manipulate at will. As Marina Warner puts it in her biography of Tz'u-hsi: 'At this stage no one saw anything more in the twenty-six-year-old mother of the T'ung-chih Emperor than a pleasant, quite pretty, quite bright ex-concubine. She had stumbled on the highest power as if on a pebble in her path.'[3]

Besides, over the following few years the new administration had to face far greater problems, such as the internal uprisings within China itself. In particular this included the Taiping rebellion, which was still raging in the north, as well as further encroachments on China's territory by foreign powers. Then, as later on, Tz'u-hsi remained firmly entrenched in her belief that China could not and would not live in harmony with 'outsiders', whom she considered inferior to herself in every way possible.

In 1864, Tz'u-hsi celebrated her thirtieth birthday. She was still a young woman but had, over a short period of time, gained a huge amount of political acumen. Now she began putting some of it to use, first testing the waters by staging an unprecedented outcry during one of her audiences with Prince Kung. According to several historical documents, Tz'u-hsi began shrieking and crying until the Prince was forcibly removed from the chamber. She claimed he had tried to attack her and further accused him of sundry underhand dealings. Whether there was any truth in the matter is uncertain, but what is apparent is that Tz'u-hsi was no longer willing to remain demurely in the background. She wanted absolute power and in order to demonstrate this she had Prince Kung demoted and, to add insult to injury, she then proceeded to upgrade his younger brother, Prince Ch'un, who was married to Tz'u-hsi's sister.

The position Prince Ch'un was given was an important one, for he was to oversee the education of the boy emperor. Tz'u-hsi also demanded that all important affairs of state now be addressed to herself directly and not to either Prince Kung or to her co-regent Niuhuru, who was still obliged to co-sign all official court documents.

As her political stranglehold grew steadily stronger, so her private life grew more and more flamboyant. Tz'u-hsi encouraged her officials to increase taxes on an already impoverished population, and in order to keep the Dragon Court in feudal magnificence she began selling positions of influence in return for large donations to her own private funds. Within the safety of the palace it was further alleged that she lived a wild, frivolous existence. If Tz'u-hsi had one fatal flaw then this was certainly it; she adored wealth. During her time as interim co-regent, spending in relation to the upkeep of the Forbidden City, and in particular the palace, spiralled out of all control.

Meanwhile, Tz'u-hsi's young son, Tsai-ch'un,[4] was growing up. By the time of her thirtieth birthday, he was nine years old, but despite receiving the best education that his mother could provide, the young boy never showed any great intellectual flair. This must have been a huge disappointment to Tz'u-hsi, but she adored her son and he adored her. The two of them shared a love of the theatre and as well as watching plays they also enjoyed dressing up and play-acting themselves. None of this, however, could dispel the loneliness that the child must have felt as the only male living within a palace populated by eunuchs and women. The young boy had no playmates; there were no siblings and no cousins to whom he could turn for company. Instead he was cosseted and indulged by everyone around him. By the time he reached his mid-teens, Tsai-ch'un had turned into a spoilt, dissolute young man. Nor was Tz'u-hsi any help in this matter, for rather than insisting that her son pay attention to affairs of state, she preferred that he leave all such matters to her.

In 1872, the young emperor turned sixteen. This was the age at which he was supposed to choose a wife and accordingly several daughters of various Manchu officials were brought forward. In the event the girl who was picked turned out to be an eighteen-year-old of very high breeding called Alute.

Tz'u-hsi took an immediate dislike to her new daughter-in-law and though some commentators say this stemmed from the fact that the younger girl was more beautiful than Tz'u-hsi, most historians agree that the real reason stemmed from Alute threatening to replace Tz'u-hsi in her son's affections, which in turn meant she would lose all her hard-fought political influence.

None the less, the couple were married on 15 October 1872 and, a few months later, on 23 February 1873, Tsai-ch'un (now known as T'ung-chih) was officially crowned Emperor. Predictably, his reign was neither glorious nor happy. On gaining the throne he proved immediately that he wasn't interested in government, preferring instead to continue the wild days of his youth. The young emperor drank heavily and enjoyed many and varied sexual encounters. Tz'u-hsi couldn't have wished for more. With her son so uninterested in affairs of state she could continue her role as ruler without his interference. It was also during this period that she began the reconstruction of the Yuan Ming Yuan: one of the empire's most luxurious summer palaces. Always one to enjoy the trappings of royalty, Tz'u-hsi's sybaritic nature couldn't resist the opportunity of restoring this exquisite residence to its former glory. Besides, with her son on the throne she would have to live elsewhere and nothing would persuade her to move into a palace that didn't befit her royal status.

The Yuan Ming Yuan, once the jewel in China's crown, had succumbed to fire during the Taiping rebellion. The work that was required to repair it was extensive and from the beginning Tz'u-hsi encountered stiff opposition. Reports were made stating that it was obscene to spend this amount of money on one building when so much of the country was still on its knees after the Taiping rebellion. But a year after the work had begun it was discovered that the majority of builders were cheating over expenses and suddenly, on the orders of the Emperor, repairs to the palace were halted. Incandescent with rage, Tz'u-hsi had to put her dreams of a luxurious life on hold, though she didn't have to wait long to have them restored.

In 1874, T'ung-chih, having continued living the high life, fell ill with the smallpox. From his sickbed the young emperor stated that, 'in looking after the affairs of state for a time, the Empresses will crown their great goodness towards me and I will show them everlasting gratitude.'[5] Although privately she had never handed over the reigns of the empire to her son in full, Tz'u-hsi was now officially back in power. Despite a brief period of recovery in December of that year, the young emperor died on 12 January 1875. He was only nineteen years old and had been on the throne a little less than two years. Rumours abounded that Tz'u-hsi had precipitated her son's early demise by not only pushing him towards a life of debauchery, but in addition flying into a rage with Alute who had, while attending her husband's deathbed, tried to encourage his recovery by telling him of all the wonderful things they would do when they were in power again. The rumours further suggested that Tz'u-hsi had Alute dragged out of the bedchamber and beaten for her presumption. Tz'u-hsi did indeed have a foul temper, which she had displayed on many occasions. One witness describes it thus, '[Her eyes] poured out straight rays; her cheekbones were sharp and the veins on her forehead projected; she showed her teeth as if she was suffering from lockjaw.'[6]

On the day of her son's death, a meeting of the Grand Council was arranged in order to discuss who would succeed to the throne. Significantly Alute was not present. Instead, Tz'u-hsi sat on the Dragon Throne with the ever-compliant Niuhuru at her side. As Empress Dowager she had full authority to speak on behalf of her dead son and accordingly she suggested three possible candidates, two of whom she summarily dismissed as being unsuitable, preferring instead a third candidate, Kuang-hsu, son of Prince Ch'un and, not surprisingly, her very own nephew. It was also hardly an unexpected revelation that her preferred choice was only three years of age, thus giving her the perfect excuse to carry on as ruler until the young boy came of age. The child was not the first choice of the more conservative members of Confucian society because his birthright meant that he violated the deep-seated laws of 'ancestor-worship'. This latter meant that only a male heir (i.e. a son) could make sacrifices at the graveside of his forebears, while brothers or cousins could not. Kuang-hsu was the dead emperor's cousin and so by nominating him Tz'u-hsi was, in fact, defying ancient laws and throwing tradition out of the window. None the less, she braved the storm and when the candidates were put to the vote, fifteen out of twenty-five councillors agreed that Kuang-hsu[7] would be the best choice.

That same night, Kuang-hsu was brought to the Forbidden City where he was adopted by his aunt and, on 25 February 1875, he formally took his position on the Dragon Throne and was proclaimed Emperor.

Tz'u-hsi had now cleared the way for at least another decade in power, but she had also sparked off further rumours of foul play at the palace, for among other things it was said that Kuang-hsu might be her own bastard son, conceived during an illicit affair with a 'false' eunuch. The bad press continued when, on 27 March 1875, Alute, the former emperor's wife, committed suicide by taking an overdose of opium. It was implied that Tz'u-hsi had had a hand in this as well, possibly forcing her daughter-in-law to take her own life by repeating stories of how other, more loyal spouses had killed themselves after their husband's deaths, or perhaps Tz'u-hsi ordered someone else kill to her and make it look like a suicide.

Tragically for China, Tz'u-hsi's second reign as Dragon Empress, which lasted from 1875 to 1889, was a haphazard affair. It soon became clear that neither she nor her councillors had any idea which direction China should take and therefore policies were made up as they went along. This resulted in a rapid downturn in China's fortunes that also affected the economic status of China's neighbours (countries such as Korea, Burma and what is now Vietnam) who, so that they might survive, turned to other, more stable powers.

During this period China also locked horns with the French in Indo-China, with the Japanese in Korea and with Great Britain in India, all of whom wanted to do more trade in the East. In order to achieve their goal they began striking deals with China's neighbours. In 1874, for example, the French forced the King of Vietnam (then called Annam) to accept a treaty stating that France would now enjoy the privileges of sovereignty, which had formerly belonged to China. Infuriated by this show of defiance Tz'u-hsi wanted to declare war on her Vietnamese neighbours, but finding that she was not backed up by her officials she sacked the entire Grand Council instead. This ferocious dismissal included that of Prince Kung, a man who had always been a thorn in Tz'u-hsi's side. She stated: 'Prince Kung was wont to render us most zealous assistance but his attitude became modified as time went by, to one of self-confident and callous contentment with the sweets of office, and of late he has become unduly inflated with pride of place, displaying nepotism and slothful inefficiency.'[8]

In Prince Kung's place, Tz'u-hsi appointed a series of 'yes men' and proceeded with her plans for all-out war. The following events were bloody in the extreme, both sides inflicting and suffering huge defeats, but eventually the French won out and China conceded that Vietnam would from now on be under French rule. But that was by no means the end of China's difficulties abroad, for Japan now began to threaten another of her neighbours: Korea.

Ironically, what made Tz'u-hsi such a popular leader in China (i.e. her firm belief that not all nation states were equal) eventually brought the country to its political knees, because she refused to see that foreign powers could easily overthrow Chinese authority within China's own satellite states. However, war with the French in Vietnam and with the Japanese over Korea came at a price, and in order to raise funds it was necessary to raise taxes.

In 1876 a flood devastated huge tracts of southern China, bringing additional hardship to the Chinese. The floods were then followed by plagues of locusts, which all but devoured that year's crops. Suddenly the whole country was suffering a major famine, from which between seven and twenty million people died. In contrast, back in Peking, the imperial court continued to enjoy an extravagant lifestyle, something that was not lost on the people who gossiped about the palace's obscene profligacy in the face of disaster.

In 1881 Niuhuru died from a mysterious illness at the age of forty-four. Sadly, although the two empresses had been companions since both were brought to the Forbidden City as teenagers, they had never been close. Over the years a rift had grown between them, caused by the undeniable preference of the young emperor, Kuang-hsu, for Niuhuru, as opposed to his newly adoptive 'mother'.

Tz'u-hsi in later life, throned in splendour in the imperial court, and wearing all the trappings of her power. Deeply resistant to change, and utterly ruthless towards anyone whom she perceived as a threat, much less an enemy, she probably did more than any other person to bring China to defeat and economic ruin. (© HULTON-DEUTSCH COLLECTION/CORBIS)

But there were also deeper hatreds at play between the two women and, although the following story is no doubt apocryphal, it does throw some light on how Tz'u-hsi was seen by her subjects. After Niuhuru died it was said that during a discussion that the two women had had a few days previously, Niuhuru confessed to having in her possession a document from Hsien feng stating that should Tz'u-hsi become a nuisance to the imperial court then she was to be decapitated. After she had told Tz'u-hsi, Niuhuru then tore up the document saying she would never have referred to it anyway because Tz'u-hsi was her friend. A little later, Niuhuru received a gift from Tz'u-hsi of a plateful of cakes which she proceeded to eat, after which she fell down dead.

Whether this is a true story or not, the implication is clear: that Tz'u-hsi was a ruthless woman who would allow no one to stand in her way.

After Niuhuru died, Tz'u-hsi was free to rule by herself, something she did for the next six years; that is, until the young emperor was old enough to assume the throne himself. At this point Tz'u-hsi should have retired, but instead she enlisted the help of several key officials to the new emperor, who pleaded that she remain in government as an adviser. The young emperor accepted and so Tz'u-hsi secured another few years in power, during which time she obtained what she had always coveted, a summer palace to which, if the need ever arose (and some thought that it never would), she could retire.

Aiding and abetting the Empress Dowager was the new emperor's father, Prince Ch'un, who no doubt also wanted to see Tz'u-hsi safely tucked away so that his son could reign in peace. The fact was that the Emperor couldn't abide Tz'u-hsi, believing her policies were too inward-looking. In contrast Kuang-hsu thirsted for Western knowledge; instead of nurturing a repressive regime, he wanted to create something closer to a European democracy.

Meanwhile, Tz'u-hsi lavished money on her palace, clothes, jewellery and gardens. The latter was said to have overflowed with lilies, roses and jasmine, together with marble stairways, temples and lakes. Finally, when the young emperor reached the age of nineteen, the Dragon Empress, with her summer palace almost complete, retired from court. Now in her late fifties, Tz'u-hsi contented herself with frittering away even more of the country's funds and, as she grew older, this despotic women also grew increasingly cruel.

Her courtiers reported that she enjoyed punishing her household retinue with beatings and other sundry cruelties. On one occasion, having ordered a flogging, she went on to gloat, 'They have not been punished for several days and they are looking forward to it. I will not disappoint them, but give them all they wish to have.'[9]

In 1894 Tz'u-hsi outdid herself by planning the most extravagant of parties to celebrate her sixtieth birthday. Every courtier was obliged to donate twenty-five per cent of their salary to her funds and accordingly an obscene procession of luxury goods began to make its way through the poverty-stricken Chinese countryside towards her summer palace. At almost the same moment, however, an uprising broke out in Korea. The protagonists wanted both their Japanese and Chinese overlords thrown out and although the initial rebellion was quickly quelled, the Chinese and Japanese armies then began to fight among themselves over sovereignty. Realistically the Chinese stood little chance of success, for their army had been impoverished through the years of Tz'u-hsi's profligacy. In comparison, the Japanese were an elite fighting force that was fully equipped with up-to-date Western weaponry. It was a huge blow for China, being trounced by the Japanese whom they had always mocked as being 'dwarf barbarians', and for once in her life Tz'u-hsi's plans had to be put on hold; she was told to cancel her birthday celebrations.

While this wasn't a blow to the country, to the Dragon Empress the news was received with great bitterness. More was to follow. In the ensuing days and months China was to suffer huge losses, not in terms of life, but of land. On 17 April 1895, China signed the Treaty of Shimonoseki, which in essence gave Japan sovereignty over huge slices of China. Seeing this, other nations then pressed China for much of the same, seeking to gain an advantage from the country's apparent weakness.

Reform was the only way forward, but one person stood firmly and irrevocably against it: Tz'u-hsi.

Even in retirement this woman held great sway over the court. The Emperor's advisers therefore began advocating that she be placed under arrest until Kuang-hsu's reforms could be passed. However, on hearing of this, Tz'u-hsi, along with members of the army who were loyal only to her, stormed the Forbidden City and put Kuang-hsu under house arrest.

Once more Tz'u-hsi had regained power, only this time she wasn't going to be a puppet ruler. She was to be in total command.

Pressing on, she forced Kuang-hsu to recant all his previous reforms and, relying on the Chinese people's xenophobic tendencies, brutally closed China down to foreigners and dragged the country back to its more traditional roots.

Who then could have predicted that the next political uprising would stem from a group of youths who were equally eager to maintain China's traditions and who equally despised foreign interference?

The Boxer uprising first started in the Kuan district of Shantung, and derived its name from the shadow boxing which the youths performed to work themselves into a frenzy before attacking their foreign victims. However, although violent in the extreme, the Boxers were fiercely loyal to the Ch'ing dynasty. They were, indeed, as xenophobic as Tz'u-hsi herself, their aim being to 'exterminate the Barbarian'.[10] Tz'u-hsi chose to regard the Boxers as the 'people's army' and gave them her unstinting support.

Shortly after the Boxers had formed the killings began. Missionaries, Chinese converts, foreign merchants: all came under attack. Buildings were burnt and

An illustration from a French magazine of 1904, in which the Empress Dowager is seen showing to the Emperor, Kuang-hsu, the severed heads of mandarins suspected of sympathizing with the Russians during the Boxer Rising of 1899-1901. Tz'u-hsi supported the Boxers in their violent rebellion against foreign, and especially Western, domination of China.
(© MARY EVANS PICTURE LIBRARY)

prisoners beheaded. Dismayed by what was happening, foreign governments swiftly made plans to invade China and rescue those of their countrymen who were still alive. Most of the latter were holed up in the British Legation in Peking and therefore it was towards this city that the invading forces began to make their way. First they captured Tientsin, then they moved on towards the capital. Over 20,000 foreign troops now began marching towards Peking and it was only a matter of time before they overwhelmed the city completely. It wasn't difficult; the Chinese army was demoralized and the Boxers had never been paid for their trouble. Tz'u-hsi's fanatics hardly put up a fight.

Tz'u-hsi herself, along with the Emperor, his wife and the heir apparent quickly planned their escape from the imperial palace dressed as peasants. Seconds before they left, however, the Pearl Concubine (the Emperor's favourite from among his harem) begged Tz'u-hsi not to abandon the city and endanger the empire by turning her back on Peking. Instead of yielding to the Pearl Concubine's wishes, however, Tz'u-hsi ordered her to be thrown down a well in one of the Forbidden City's courtyards.

Traipsing through the countryside with a small retinue of loyal servants, Tz'u-hsi, for the first time in her life, saw the poverty and famine that gripped her country. Eventually she settled in Hsien and during this exile from Peking was forced to accept that several of the Boxer revolutionaries whom she had supported would, on the combined orders of the foreign powers, be executed. The foreigners also demanded that proper reparations be paid them for the deaths of 247 missionaries, 66 foreign citizens and 30,000 Chinese converts who had all been slaughtered during the siege of Peking. The sum mentioned was 450 million taels, equivalent these days to approximately £67 million. This settled, on 20 October 1901, Tz'u-hsi felt safe enough to return to the imperial city. Her re-entry was triumphant, but although she attempted to implement some of the reforms that had so infuriated her when Kuang-hsu was in power, China was now practically bankrupt.

In 1907, at the age of seventy-four, the Dragon Empress suffered a stroke. Almost simultaneously, it seems, Kuang-hsu also fell ill and on 14 November 1908, died. A day later, on 15 November, having dictated a valediction to the empire over which she had reigned for fifty years, Tz'u-hsi also died. Afterwards it was rumoured that the Empress, fearful that the Kuang-hsu Emperor might survive her, had had him poisoned, though the validity of the story can, of course, never be verified.

Tz'u-hsi, the Dragon Empress, was interred in a vault alongside the Hsien feng Emperor and his wife Niuhuru on 9 December. Her funeral was rumoured to cost the empire over one and a half million taels, no mean affair given the state of the government coffers. The Ch'ing dynasty lasted a mere three years longer, after which China turned to republicanism.

Humiliatingly, the last footnote concerning the Dragon Empress is the fact that in 1928 her mausoleum was ransacked and all the jewellery and other sumptuous treasures were stripped from the coffins. Tz'u-hsi's body was then further defiled by being stripped of its clothing and flung into the mud.

CATHERINE THE GREAT

Empress of All the Russias

She is ardent and passionate. She has a bright glassy hypnotic look like that of a wild animal. She has a big forehead and unless I am mistaken, a long and terrifying future marked upon it. She is thoughtful and friendly and yet when she approaches me I automatically back away. She frightens me.'
CHEVALIER D'ÉON, *CIRCA* 1756

The history of Catherine II is the history of highly complex, conflicting facts and figures. Her main aim as Empress was to make Russia great, yet she treated the serfs who populated her country so inhumanely that they might as well have been animals. Although never charged with murder, the mysterious deaths of both her husband Peter III and also Tsar Ivan VI undoubtedly left a question mark over her degree of involvement. Until the age of twenty-three she was a virgin and yet after she met her first lover she became notorious for the number of men she took to her bed. But the strangest dichotomy of all was that Catherine the Great, Empress of All the Russias, was in fact German.

Born in April 1729 in the Baltic seaport town of Stettin, Pomerania (now in Poland), Catherine was christened Sophia Augusta Frederica of Anhalt-Zerbst. Her parents, both minor royals, were Prince Christian Augustus, a Commandant at Stettin, and Princess Johanna, who was related to the ducal house of Holstein. Despite neither parent possessing a great deal of money and an apparent lack of interest shown by Johanna in her daughter, Sophia did enjoy a stable childhood. All that was to change, however, when, aged fifteen, she was chosen as a possible bride for the Grand Duke Peter of Russia, grandson of Peter the Great.

Sophia was amongst several contenders for this highly prestigious role and had probably been chosen because, being only a minor royal, everyone concluded she would be eternally grateful for the honour and thereby easily manipulated. Princess Johanna was certainly overjoyed at the news for, having always felt trapped within a very provincial life, this was her chance to break out, to prove to herself and to others that she was born to greater things.

On 10 January 1744 mother and daughter eagerly set off for the Russian Imperial Court and were initially received by the Empress Elizabeth (aunt to the Grand Duke Peter) on 9 February. According to contemporary sources the

Empress cut an imposing figure and the young Sophia is said to have nearly fainted when she first set eyes on her, for the older woman was wearing a silver, watered-silk dress strung with diamonds and pearls.

But Princess Sophia, despite several childhood illnesses that had taken their toll on her looks, was no ugly duckling herself. She had long, dark hair, pale skin and extremely blue eyes. Her mouth was shapely and her eyelashes long and black. In short, she was an attractive young woman and over the following few days she must have impressed herself upon the Empress, for she was finally chosen as the Grand Duke's future bride.

Here, sadly, the fairy tale ends. Sophia had never set eyes on her intended husband-to-be and when she did at last do so, the result was not pleasing. As a young boy the Grand Duke had suffered a severe bout of smallpox, which had resulted in his skin being badly pockmarked and his losing a lot of hair. According to contemporary sources, he had very thick lips that dominated his face. Worst of all, Peter was not the most mature of young adults, often preferring to play with toy soldiers rather than entertain his young guest. None the less, the union would establish Sophia at the head of a dynasty and so she dutifully complied with everything that was proposed.

The former Princess Sophia Augusta Frederica of Anhalt-Zerbst is crowned Empress of Russia as Catherine II, in St Petersburg (then the Russian capital) in 1762. Her accession had been made possible by a coup in July of that year which removed her husband, Tsar Peter III, from the throne; three weeks later, he was murdered. It is likely that, at the least, Catherine was secretly involved in both events. (© Mary Evans Picture Library)

On 28 June 1744 she took the new name of Catherine Aleksyeevna and renounced Lutheranism in favour of the Orthodox faith. The following day she became engaged and on 21 August 1745, with Catherine now aged sixteen, the couple were married at the Cathedral of Kazan in a huge ceremony the likes of which the girl could only ever have dreamed of. The wedding night, unsurpisingly, was a disaster, Peter preferring to play with his toys rather than consummate his marriage. Later, in her memoirs, Catherine wrote, 'I should have loved my new husband if only he had been willing or able to be in the least lovable. But in the early days of my marriage, I made some cruel reflections about him. I said to myself: "If you love this man, you will be the most wretched creature on Earth. Watch your step. So far as affection for this gentleman is concerned, think of yourself, Madame."'[1] Peter's behaviour became more and more unstable, and it is not surprising that night after night the royal marriage remained unconsummated. On one particular evening it is said that Catherine entered the bedchamber only to see a dead rat hanging by a rope from the ceiling. On questioning her husband he replied that the rat had committed treason. Other bizarre acts followed, including a period when Peter decided he wished to become a dog trainer and filled the bedroom with animals whose stench was so overpowering that it made Catherine ill. Catherine's marriage remained unconsummated for over seven years, but it was during this time, in contrast to her husband's increasingly erratic behaviour, that she dutifully applied herself to learning the Russian language and to conquering the intricacies of the Russian Orthodox faith. She was an extremely clever young woman who read voraciously and who enjoyed intellectual pursuits.

None the less, it was also expected of her to produce an heir to the throne. In the certain knowledge that this would not be achieved with her husband, Catherine (some say with the approval of the Empress Elizabeth) took her first lover, a chamberlain named Serge Saltykov. Saltykov was an extremely handsome man and, although married, was more than willing to begin a relationship with the Grand Duke's wife. Besides, the Grand Duke had entertained himself over the years with a bevy of mistresses, one of whom was the less than ravishing Countess Elizabeth Vorontsova.

In 1754 Catherine fell pregnant by Saltykov. Although it was common knowledge that the child was not her husband's, when she eventually gave birth the boy was given the title of the Grand Duke Paul. Saltykov was advised to travel abroad and the baby was handed over to the Empress Elizabeth, who stated that he would be brought up under her care. Bereft of her child, mourning the loss of her lover, Catherine's heart hardened to the vagaries of life at the imperial court. The Baron de Breteuil, a French diplomat who had been posted to Moscow, wrote of her during this time:

> **This Princess seems to combine every kind of ambition in her person. Everything that may add lustre to her reign will have**

some attraction for her. Science and the arts will be encouraged to flourish in the empire, projects useful for the domestic economy will be undertaken. She will endeavour to reform the administration of justice and to invigorate the laws. But her policies will be based on Machiavellianism; and I should not be surprised if in this field she rivals the King of Prussia. Cunning and falsity appear to be vices in her character; woe to him who puts too much trust in her. Love affairs may become a stumbling block to her ambition and prove fatal for her peace of mind. This passionate princess, still held in check by the fear and consciousness of internal troubles, will know no restraint once she believes herself firmly established.[2]

True to this description, Catherine's next move was to secure herself another lover, this time a Pole called Count Stanislas Poniatowsky. Although not as handsome as Saltykov, he was none the less a well-educated, kindly man who enjoyed Catherine's company. It was her next lover, however, who was to prove one of the most important in her life.

Gregory Orlov, like his four brothers, was an officer in the Imperial Guard who was noted for his good looks and physical prowess. As a youth he had been educated in the Corps of Military Cadets in St Petersburg and before he met Catherine he had already served and been wounded in the Seven Years' War. He wasn't a highly intelligent man, nor was he a statesman, but he did have a strong appreciation of current affairs and soon became a useful confidant. In any event, Orlov was an astute political choice for Catherine because the whole of Orlov's family, together with their friends and acquaintances, were proud that their future empress had chosen one of their number to be her companion. In turn this guaranteed Catherine the support of the Russian Imperial Army.

On 25 December 1761, the Empress Elizabeth Petrovna died and within a matter of days Peter was crowned Tsar of All the Russias. Throughout his time as Grand Duke he had always been an erratic individual, given to bizarre displays of temperament, and he now carried on in similar vein. He mocked his aunt's coffin and refused to wear the appropriate mourning attire. In direct contrast, Catherine donned black clothing from head to foot and, though she had despised Elizabeth, made a great show of being grief-stricken. It was also at this time that Catherine became pregnant with her second child, this time by Orlov. Having suffered so much at being separated from her first child, she was now hardened to the idea of motherhood and, when the baby was born, she had it sent directly to foster parents.

From the beginning of his reign, Peter III displayed the very same foolhardy behaviour as he had done while still a young man. He mocked the Orthodox faith, and began hero-worshipping Frederick the Great of Prussia, who had beaten Russia to her knees. But worse than either of these, within two months of his coming to the throne Peter had reversed his country's foreign policies to such an extent that he began talks with Russia's current arch-enemy, the King of Prussia. At the time, Russia had been at war with Prussia for over five years and had indeed almost vanquished her. Now, due to Peter's fresh foreign policy, a peace treaty was signed between the two sovereign states and Russia returned all the territories that she had won at such enormous cost. This was a very unpopular move in a country where so many families were still grieving, but one which Peter only added to by making several threats to Austria to comply with all Prussia's demands or face battle with her new ally, Russia. Peter picked a fight with Denmark and both countries teetered on the brink of all-out war. Then Peter III was suddenly ousted from power.

The *coup d'état* of 9 July 1762 was a swift, bloodless operation and, most important of all, a highly successful one. The Orlov brothers were its main perpetrators, but Catherine must have been involved, particularly because she would be its main beneficiary. Peter was forced to sign an act of abdication and on the following day, 30 June 1762, Catherine entered St Petersburg to artillery salvoes and the sound of bells ringing.

In contrast, Peter was unceremoniously removed from the city and dumped in the castle of Rophsha at Schlusselburg, which was located on a small island in the middle of the River Neva. Rophsha had a long association with both torture and murder and consequently Peter's imprisonment must have been terrifying. None the less he asked his wife if he could keep, among other things, his mistress, his dog, his negro and his violin. 'Fearing scandal,' Catherine wrote, 'I only granted him the last three.'[3]

It took some weeks to decide on Peter's fate. Initially there seemed to be only two choices: either to keep him incarcerated for the rest of his natural life or to have him repatriated to Holstein in Germany, but the latter was considered too risky and in the event a third option was followed.

On 18 July 1762, three weeks after he was deposed from the throne, Peter was murdered. Catherine maintained that her husband had died from apoplexy,[4] but all the available evidence (of which there is not a huge amount) points to the fact that the Orlov brothers, together with certain other agents and with the blessing of Catherine herself, did the deed and killed the Tsar. After all, Gregory Orlov could not marry the Empress if Peter were still alive, and Catherine could never be certain that Peter's supporters wouldn't attempt a military coup, so it was commonly believed that having tried to kill him with a glass of poisoned wine, Alexis Orlov strangled Peter by wrapping a table napkin tight around his neck.

On 7 July 1762 Catherine issued a statement to the effect that the deposed Tsar had died and on her instructions Peter was later interred at the Alexander Nevsky monastery, although Catherine did not attend the ceremony herself.

With her husband now safely out of the way, one might have thought that Catherine would have felt safe in her new position as Empress. Yet one last threat remained: a man better known to the authorities as 'Prisoner Number 1', but who in reality was Tsar Ivan VI.

Ivan VI had become Tsar of Russia on 5 October 1740 when he was only two months of age. As he was too young to reign a man called Count Ernst Johann Biron had been appointed regent in his name, but he was soon deposed and replaced by Ivan's young mother, Anna Leopoldovna. Sadly this reign too was short-lived for, on 25 November 1741, Elizabeth Petrovna, supported by the Imperial Guard, overthrew Anna Leopoldovna and took the throne for herself. The baby, along with his mother and the rest of his siblings, were sent into exile, first to Riga, then to Rannenborg Castle and finally to Kholmogory, where Anna Leopoldovna died. It was at this point that the rightful heir to the throne was incarcerated in the fortress at Schlusselburg. Deprived of every human dignity, including that of proper food and daylight, Ivan slowly lost his mind.

Despite being a gibbering wreck, however, Prisoner Number 1 still posed a serious threat to Catherine's position. After all, no sovereign enjoyed the support of all of the people all of the time; perhaps some future coup might be arranged with Ivan as its figurehead? With this in mind, she ordered an armed guard to be put in place specifically to execute Ivan should any attempt be made to free him.

They did not have to wait long. On the night of 5 July 1764, a lieutenant called Vasily Yakovlevich Mirovitch tried storming the fortress in an attempt to liberate the old Tsar. Immediately the soldiers guarding Ivan did as they were bid and stabbed him to death. Mirovitch was also put to the sword, but not before the rumours spread suggesting that Catherine was behind the executions. Whether or not it was true, the killings certainly worked in her favour.

Within the courts of Europe no one thought the new empress would last very long. She was born a German, not a Russian, and though no one dared mention it, hadn't she been involved in the murder of Peter the Great's grandson? It didn't bode well, but no one had reckoned on Catherine's determination to do her best for her adoptive country.

On 22 September 1764, in the Assumption Cathedral in Moscow, Catherine II was crowned Empress, after which she immediately returned to St Petersburg and turned her attention to affairs of state.

Initially her main aim was to raise Russia's profile in relation to Europe and to expand Russia's territories. To aid the former she began to make radical changes in government. A well-educated woman who numbered among her favourite authors philosophers such as Diderot, Voltaire, Locke and Montesquieu, she tried to accomodate their ideas within her own. To this end, in 1767 she had a new code of law drawn up.

'What is the true End of Monarchy?' she had her officials write. 'Not to deprive People of their natural Liberty but to

> correct their Actions, in order to attain the supreme Good.
> The Form of Government, therefore, which best attains this
> End, and at the same Time sets less Bounds than others to
> natural Liberty, is that which coincides with the Views and
> Purposes of rational Creatures and answers the End upon
> which we ought to fix a steadfast Eye in the Regulations of
> civil Policy.[5]

It all sounded very enlightened, and although Catherine has, down the centuries, become best known as a despot (hence her inclusion in this collection), she did make some very beneficial changes to the way in which Russia was run, namely in the fields of education, health, agriculture and industry.

However, despite progress on many of the above fronts and despite the fact that on paper her new reforms looked 'modern', some might even say liberal, there was one huge stumbling block to her plans: Russia's serfs. Serfdom was a hangover from the time of medieval feudalism when agricultural workers were owned by their landlords and enjoyed only a few more rights than the African slaves of North America. It was a deeply entrenched way of life: a mindset that had not changed since its very beginnings. Although the new empress had at first hoped to change the status quo and improve the living and working conditions of the serfs, she swiftly came to realize that the landlords on whom she depended for political support would not tolerate any such reforms. Instead she abandoned her plans and swiftly reverted to type, growing as autocratic as any previous ruler. In addition she drew up a new decree which was to strengthen the system she had previously condemned:

> The Governing Senate...has deemed it necessary to make
> known that the landlord's serfs and peasants...owe their
> landlords proper submission and absolute obedience in all
> matters, according to the laws that have been enacted from
> time immemorial by the autocratic forefathers of Her
> Imperial Majesty and which have not been repealed, and
> which provide that all persons who dare to incite serfs and
> peasants to disobey their landlords shall be arrested and taken
> to the nearest government office, there to be punished
> forewith as disturbers of public tranquillity, according to the
> laws and without leniency.[6]

To Catherine the serfs now deserved no human rights whatsoever. This was further compounded by the fact that under her rule it cost more to buy a dog than it did a peasant girl. She also imposed serfdom on the Ukrainians, who up until that time had enjoyed freedom. By the end of her reign there was barely a free peasant to be found in the whole of the land.

Nor was her rule of iron simply confined to the lower classes, for in an attempt to amass as much wealth as possible Catherine also began exercising her powers against the Russian Orthodox faith. This chipping away at the Church had in fact begun under the rule of Peter the Great, but Catherine, realizing the financial rewards she could garner, continued to strip the Church of its riches while at the same time turning its prelates and priests into government employees.

To add insult to injury, some of the wealth that Catherine stole then went into gifts bestowed on the Orlov brothers. Over a ten-year period they received between them in excess of seven million roubles, on top of which they were also given several palaces. But although Gregory Orlov remained her lover for quite some time after her husband's death, he did not achieve his ultimate goal, for when he suggested they be married, Catherine refused. Haughtily, Orlov is said to have stormed off, and on seeing this outrageous display of bad temper it is also said that Catherine decided the best course of action would be to have Orlov sent into exile. This was duly done, but not before she had conferred on him the title of Prince. His travels in Europe were a great success. Orlov dazzled high society and made a good ambassador for Russia, so much so that on his return Catherine further favoured him with a marble palace built on the River Neva between her own winter and summer palaces. Hoping perhaps to win her back and unaware that Catherine had taken a new lover to her bed, Orlov then presented the Empress with a huge blue Persian diamond. It was called the 'Nadir-Shah', but Catherine renamed it the 'Orlov Diamond' and had it mounted on top of the imperial sceptre, where it remains to this day.

Despite all this, Catherine's reign was not all palaces and fine jewellery, for in 1771 a horrendous plague broke out in Moscow. At the time the Empress was waging war against Turkey, an event many people thought responsible for the plague due to the soldiers returning from the front line riddled with disease. The Russian people, who were already beleaguered by the toll of the fighting, grew increasingly dissatisfied. In 1773, a former officer in the Cossacks, Yemelyan Pugachov, incited the greatest uprising Russia had ever experienced.

The revolt began in the Urals but spread rapidly to the south. By June 1774 Pugachov and his supporters were preparing to march on Moscow. Unfortunately, however, by the time he had Moscow within his sights the war with Turkey was over and Catherine swiftly sent in all her troops to crush the rebellion.

Pugachov was captured and beheaded in 1775, but the whole affair led to severe repercussions. Catherine resolved not only to tighten further her grip over her own people but also to tighten her stance when it came to foreign policy. With this in mind she decided to continue annexing territories on each of Russia's several borders as well as securing a 'window' on the Black Sea. Together with her close ally Austria, Russia declared a second war on Turkey.

By 1792 Catherine had got her own way, Turkey finally giving in to her demands and signing the Treaty of Jassy, which gave Russia a firm foothold on the northern shore of the Black Sea, a coastline that extended from the Caucasus Mountains to the River Bug in south-west Russia.

Meanwhile, during all these tempestuous political upheavals Catherine had managed to conduct two new love affairs. The first was with a man called Vasilchikov, but he was soon replaced by the most important of all Catherine's male companions: Prince Gregory Potemkin.

Potemkin had first come to the Empress's attention during the palace coup by which she had replaced her husband on the throne. Several years later, during Russia's first war with Turkey, Potemkin had served in the cavalry and distinguished himself so much that he swiftly rose through the ranks to become a major-general. But it was only on his return to Russia that he began his affair with the Empress. The two were besotted with one another, Catherine addressing him variously as 'Sweetheart', 'My darling soul', 'My heart', 'Kitten', 'Dear little heart' and 'Little Parrot'.[7] She also wrote him numerous love letters, an extract from one of which reads:

> **Darling, I think you really thought I would not write today. I woke up at five and now it is seven, I will write... I have given strict orders to the whole of my body, down to the last hair, to stop showing you the smallest sign of love. I have locked up my love in my heart under ten locks. It is suffocating there and I think it might explode. Think about it – you are a reasonable man. Is it possible to talk more nonsense in a few lines?**[8]

In Potemkin, Catherine had found a combination of all she could ever desire. He was not only a handsome man, but also an extremely intelligent one who could help advise her on political matters. Even after their relationship ended, Catherine remained fond of her old lover.[9] When, for instance, he succeeded in expanding Russia's border on the Black Sea by annexing the Crimea, she made Potemkin governor of the new province, and in 1787 he organized a grand tour for the Empress, which was one of the most lavish and costly in all of Russia's long history.

The tour was planned to take place over a period of four years and was to cover a distance of almost 1,000 miles. Potemkin, eager to show off his organizational skills, is said to have redeveloped vast tracts of land, had trees chopped down by the hundreds and, most bizarre of all, was accused of creating fake villages (hence the term 'Potemkin village', meaning a façade to cover up something which is unseemly). Everywhere Catherine travelled she saw beautiful, whitewashed hamlets from which happy, well-fed peasants would emerge to wave and cheer her on her way. Her glorification was further enhanced when the Emperor of Austria, together with the King of Poland and other notable

An unattributed portrait of Catherine the Great as Empress of All the Russias. Despite the enlightened reforms she instituted, she had by this time become a despot to whom any idea of liberalism was abhorrent, while her private life had been marked by a seemingly endless series of often unsuitable love affairs. (© MARY EVANS PICTURE LIBRARY)

dignitaries, joined in the festivities and came to honour her.

But at a time in her life when perhaps she should have felt most secure in her role as absolute ruler, yet another ugly phantom raised its head.

In 1789 the beginnings of a revolution were stirring in France. Ironically, as Catherine herself had proposed, the intellectual currents of the time were all pointing towards an Enlightenment when governments would be run constitutionally rather than ruled by divine authority. In 1790 a writer by the name of AN Radishev wrote a work that highlighted not only the lowly, ignominious position of the serfs, but also criticized the tremendous abuses they suffered. Catherine, who had always prided herself on being liberal-minded (in fact her own Reform Act of 1767 sounded much like Radishev's own) swiftly had the author arrested and condemned to death. Luckily he escaped the latter and instead was sent in to exile, but Catherine, wary of the type of doctrine he had been preaching and aware of the civil unrest in France, set about ruling twice as ruthlessly. When Poland began crying out for a more liberal constitution, Catherine sent in the troops. By 1794 she had wiped Poland off the map by dividing its territories between her country, Prussia and Austria.

In 1791 Gregory Potemkin died. It came as a terrible blow to the Empress, who had for so long relied on his support and advice, and it is said that she never truly recovered from the loss. Yet Catherine was not finished with men altogether, for she soon began yet another liaison, this time with a handsome individual called Plato Zubov. Zubov was forty years Catherine's junior and though he was 'pretty' he was certainly not as loyal as she might have wished; it was Zubov who later struck the first blow in her son's murder.

Catherine the Great died suddenly on 7 November 1796, at the age of sixty-seven, from what most people think was either a stroke or a heart attack. Her reign had been a long and, to many people, a successful one. Under her leadership Russia had increased its territories by 200,000 square miles, had succeeded in the long-held dream of gaining access to the Bosphorus Strait by way of the Black Sea, and had seen the construction of many marvellous palaces, government buildings and entire new towns. Catherine had also created a triumphant court atmosphere which attracted some of the greatest minds in Europe, and she had presided over huge military successes both abroad and at home.

But all this came at a cost. From arriving at court an idealistic, naïve young woman, she turned into a despotic creature to whom any idea of liberalism was totally abhorrent. With the onset of the French Revolution she grew increasingly conservative and reversed many of her more liberal policies. Sadly, this led to the further destitution of the Russian peasantry, just as it had done during the reign of Peter the Great.

On her death, Paul I succeeded to the throne. Catherine had never held her son in high esteem, regarding him as a bit of an imbecile. In the event his reign only lasted five years. After his assassination in 1801 he was succeeded by Catherine's grandson, Alexander I, who is best remembered as being the Tsar during Napoleon Bonaparte's disastrous Russian campaign.

QUEEN RANAVALONA I

Bloody Mary of Madagascar

If this woman's rule lasts much longer, Madagascar will be depopulated... Blood – and always blood – is the maxim of Queen Ranavalona, and every day seems lost to this wicked woman on which she cannot sign at least half-a-dozen death-warrants.

FROM *LAST TRAVELS* BY IDA PFEIFFER

Situated to the south-east of Africa lies the ravishingly beautiful island of Madagascar. Originally it was named St Lawrence by Portuguese explorers who had set sail from Lisbon to explore the Indian Ocean for spice routes on 2 March 1500. The fleet of thirteen ships was commanded by a man called Pedro Alvarez Cabral, but on 10 August 1500 disaster struck as one of his ships, commanded by Diego Dias, was separated from the rest of the fleet due to a storm. Searching for somewhere to dock until the bad weather had passed, Dias came in sight of a previously unmapped piece of land.

In fact, the first two-legged beings to have set foot on Madagascan soil had arrived many thousands of years previously and were probably from such diverse countries as India, Java, Arabia and Africa. But, as is the way of explorers, the Portuguese decided they had discovered the island and promptly rushed back to Europe to spread the good news. Suddenly France, England and Holland were all laying claim to what everyone agreed was a prime piece of property. The island was described as a 'paradise on earth', teeming as it did with such diverse creatures as lemurs, fruit bats, chameleons, golden frogs and the giant coua. Madagascar was also blessed with vast swaths of rainforest and rich arable land. It was therefore hardly surprising that everyone wanted a piece of this heavenly place and although the local tribes attempted to repel invading European forces time and again, eventually Europe did succeed in gaining a foothold. In 1642, Cardinal Richelieu ordered that Madagascar be claimed for the French and to this end established a military outpost at Fort Dauphin in the south-east of the island. The military expedition was named the Compagnie de l'Orient and its main duty was to exploit the island in every way possible.

Several Catholic missions were also established at Fort Dauphin, but the missionaries were killed and the French made little progress with the natives.

The success of foreigners settling in the country was due for the most part to

King Andrianampoinimerina (Nampoina). By 1794 Madagascar and its indigenous population had had enough of fighting so, in a monumental effort of diplomacy, Andrianampoinimerina brought as many tribes together as he could and united them to form the single kingdom of Merina, which was situated on the central plateau of the island. In addition, he then honoured every one of his subjects with their own piece of land upon which they could farm, thus ensuring no one would ever go short of food. By 1817 Andrianampoinimerina's son, King Radama I, following in his father's footsteps, also managed to strike up friendly relations with several of the major European powers and by 1818 had even begun permitting British missionaries into the country. Unbeknown to him, these missionaries viewed his people as little more than savages living in absolute wretchedness, but Radama, being an able, free-thinking monarch, was none the less eager to modernize his country. As a result of this he relied heavily on the British to bring his armed forces up to scratch. He also wanted to extend his reforms socially and politically, and so, once again along Western lines, he organized a parliamentary cabinet and encouraged the Protestant Missionary Society to visit.

Initially the missionaries consisted of two Welshmen – the Rev David Jones and the Rev Thomas Bevan – who arrived from Britain via Mauritius, bringing with them their wives and children. They landed at Toamasina on the east coast of Madagascar during October, the hottest part of the year when tropical rainstorms swept the coastline. It was an inauspicious beginning and one by one the small group was struck down by what was then known as 'coastal fever', but which is now recognized as malaria. At that time there was no known cure for this illness and over a period of two months everyone died except for the Reverend Jones, who swiftly beat a retreat back to Mauritius without having preached a word of the Gospel.

But Jones was not the type of man to take defeat lightly; once he had regained his strength he wrote to the London Missionary Society to send him new recruits so that he could restart his programme. In April 1820 (a much cooler, more temperate time of year) the new group set out for the island and slowly but surely made their way inland towards the capital. After fifteen days of battling through the tropical rainforests they finally arrived and were immediately given an audience with King Radama I, who sanctioned their request to set up a school to teach not only the Gospel, but also reading and writing. It was a revolutionary idea because the Malagasy people had no written form of language, which meant that David Jones had to go to great lengths to develop one. But by 1825 the task was complete, at which point the missionaries began to translate the Gospels, starting with the Gospel of St Luke, into Malagasy. They were supported in this venture by their friends back in England who sent out a small printing press together with a large supply of ink and paper.

By the mid-1820s David Jones had managed to translate and print the whole of the New Testament, but although this was a huge achievement in itself, it was nothing in comparison to trying to teach the natives the philosophical concept of such words as 'sin' or 'salvation'. None the less, the missionaries worked hard at their task and achieved a certain success. In addition to this they continued to translate the rest of the Bible and finally they produced a complete edition which they proudly bound in leather and began handing out to every Malagasy man, woman or child who requested one.

But the equilibrium struck between native and foreigner was sadly not to last long. King Radama I was growing weak and in 1828, after a protracted illness, he died aged thirty-six. Radama and his wife Queen Ranavalona did not have any children and therefore his nephew, a boy by the name of Rakotobe, was next in line for the throne. Foreseeing a bitter struggle for ascendancy, several government ministers concealed the news of King Radama's death, hoping that this would enable Rakotobe to succeed to power before his political opponents were any the wiser. But how long can you keep the death of a husband from his own wife? Less then twenty-four hours after Radama had died, a young army officer named Andriamihaja reported the King's death to Ranavalona, who in turn swiftly started spreading the rumour that 'the idols' to which all the Malagasy people referred for guidance favoured her as Queen in opposition to Rakotobe. No sooner had this piece of misinformation been circulated than Rakotobe and all his supporters were brutally slaughtered – a move that prompted one nineteenth-century commentator to describe the new monarch as being 'quite willing to wade through slaughter to the throne'.[1]

Afterwards, when the killings were finished, Andriamihaja was rewarded for his services by being elevated to commander-in-chief of the army. In addition he also had the title of the Queen's official lover conferred upon him, although neither of these two roles were to last long, for shortly afterwards he was accused of treason and swiftly executed.

Ranavalona was born *circa* 1782/90 into the Menabe tribe, whose king ruled the west of the island; despite Andrianampoinimerina's and Radama I's best efforts to unite Madagascar's different factions, the island was still split into four different kingdoms. Firstly there was the Merina kingdom in the central highlands; secondly there was the Betsileo kingdom in the south highlands, thirdly the empire of Betsimisaraka; and finally the kingdom of Menabe. Having failed to unite this last kingdom with the Merina, Radama had decided that the best policy was to marry the eldest daughter of Andrian-Tsala-Manjaka and his wife Rabodo Andrian-Tampo. During the early years of their union nothing of note is heard of Ranavalona other than that her appearance was said to have been very imposing. Take for example this description of her by the novelist George MacDonald Fraser who, though writing fiction, is said to have based his novel on several contemporary accounts: 'She might have been anywhere between forty and fifty, rather round-faced, with a small straight nose, a fine brow, and a short, broad-lipped mouth; her skin was jet black and plump – and then you met her eyes, and in a sudden chill rush of fear realized that all you had heard was true, and the horrors you'd seen needed no further explanation. They were small and bright and evil as a snake's, unblinking, with a depth of cruelty and malice that was terrifying.'[2]

From the outset Ranavalona was loathed and feared by all who knew her. The *British Quarterly* described her as 'the Diocletian of our days', referring to the Roman emperor who persecuted the Christians. Even to this day Ranavalona I is spoken of as either the 'Modern Messalina', 'Bloody Mary of Madagascar' (in reference to Bloody Mary Tudor of England) or 'Wicked Queen Ranavalona'. She distrusted all foreign influence, be it British, Dutch or French. Neither was she alone in these views, for a decade earlier Samuel Copland had described the people of Madagascar as 'the children of Abraham' who had been corrupted and exploited by the Europeans. Indeed, Copland felt that the missionaries, and through them Great Britain itself, had 'abused, insulted and betrayed'[3] the Malagasy people. Ranavalona thought along much the same lines, and yet despite her intense hatreds it is said that she tolerated the missionaries due to the fact that she coveted various skills they possessed. In particular she was fascinated by the idea of soap, and told the missionaries that if they could teach her people to make it then they could stay on indefinitely. Her obsession with cleansing materials stemmed no doubt from a custom she had begun shortly after assuming the throne. Queen Ranavalona I used to take baths in full view of the public on a balcony overlooking the city. Naked except for a hat, she enjoyed nothing more than to sit in a tub being washed by her slaves before a fully appreciative audience who would stand below and clap and cheer. Nor was this the only one of her eccentricities. Despite her hatred of the French, Ranavalona enjoyed collecting Napoleonic paintings with which she would adorn the walls of her palace; her clothes were more often than not an eclectic mix of fashions and fabrics (taffeta and tartan being two of her favourites), and she also loved throwing parties.

Every year, on the anniversaries of her birth and her accession to the throne, the palace gardens would be decorated and everybody who was anybody in Malagasy society was invited to join in the revelries, at which huge amounts of alcohol were consumed and toasts drunk to the Queen.

But what of the soap and the missionaries? After Ranavalona had declared an interest in the former, the missionaries swiftly set about concocting a suitable recipe which bought them a few extra months on the island. However, once the secret recipe was revealed, Ranavalona's true loathing of the outsiders bubbled up to the surface. Apart from soap, she could see no benefit in anything the missionaries brought with them, and she found their religion particularly abhorrent. Christians had a very hostile attitude towards the islanders' ancient customs and beliefs and so, with the support of her prime minister, Rainiharo (who was rumoured to have gained his position in government by sleeping with the monarch), Ranavalona slowly began to implement edicts forbidding all baptisms, communions, Christian marriage rites and public worship. Finally in July 1836 she summoned her people to the capital, Antananarivo (which can mean either the 'City of a Thousand Towns' or the 'City of a Thousand Soldiers'), where she had decided to make an announcement. Suddenly all roads into Antananarivo were thronged with people. Men, women and children travelled for days in order to reach their destination in time to hear what their queen had to say. They were not to be disappointed. At the appointed time a procession of soldiers carrying long silver spears made its way out of the hillside palace, followed by a large group of slaves carrying a platform upon which sat Queen Ranavalona dressed from head to foot in bright scarlet. It was an impressive sight and one made all the more so by the number of people who prostrated themselves on the ground as the Queen passed. Eventually the procession reached the Royal Garden of Andahalo from where, on a high platform surrounded by armed guards, the Queen began her speech:

> **It has come to my notice that the Bible is wicked. It teaches about a new King, called God, and about his Prime Minister, Jesus Christ his son. They try to persuade my subjects to become part of his Kingdom of Heaven, and to pray to their King of God and ask favours of him. Now you all know there is only one Kingdom here – the Kingdom of our ancestors Randriamasinavalona, Randrianampoinimerina, Radama and myself! From henceforth, I intend that this kingdom shall not be divided. I will have none of this Kingdom of Heaven, none of this God ruling over us, none of this Jesus Christ! These are the white men's rulers from over the seas; I will not have my people misled by them.**
>
> **I know that some of my people have been led astray; I believe that they knew no better, but allowed themselves to be swayed by these wicked men. So I am willing to pardon them if they confess their wickedness and return to their belief in our ancient idols, charms and sacred mountains. From today, it is an offence punishable by death and by confiscation of property to pray, to possess Bibles or hymn books, to hold meetings of worship to God or Jesus Christ, or to teach others to read.[4]**

Deprived of their right to practise their beliefs, the missionaries decided that the best course of action would be to leave Antananarivo. Consequently they travelled to the east coast of the island, to Tamatave, although they left behind a small group of approximately fifty committed Christian activists to keep an eye on the school and the churches. As time passed, the group grew in size until it numbered well over two thousand. Under strict instructions to monitor their position on a day-to-day basis so that, should things deteriorate, they could make their escape, they sent countless letters to their Christian brothers and sisters in Tamatave. In these letters they spoke frequently of reading John Bunyan's allegorical treatise *The Pilgrim's Progress,* from which they gained immense strength. They also saw their own situation reflected in the trials endured by the book's main character, Christian. Christian, as all those who are familiar with this text will know, suffered immense persecution for his beliefs and had to struggle every step of the way on the road towards salvation. Variously he contended with characters such as Giant Despair, Sloth and Presumption, as well as having to travel through the Slough of Despond and the Valley of the Shadow of Death. No wonder the missionaries found this book so inspiring. Sadly, however, in contrast to Christian's success in reaching the Celestial City, a large number of missionaries were far less fortunate. In the early part of the 1840s a group of thirty-seven Christians were found guilty of having preached the word of God to the community at large and, alongside their wives and children, were condemned to a life of slavery. Later, forty-two Christians were accused of having a Bible in their possession, and although they escaped the death penalty they had all their worldly goods confiscated, and they too were sent into slavery. These were harsh times, but they were about to get even harsher

On 7 July 1857 Queen Ranavalona ordered the exile of all Europeans from the island, thus leaving Madagascar isolated from the rest of the world. Infuriated that the death penalty was not being implemented for crimes which she viewed more wicked even than murder, Ranavalona also insisted that from now on anyone caught preaching Christian doctrine or in possession of a Bible be put to death immediately. In this she displayed a fanaticism similar (if not worse) to that of the Emperors Caligula and Nero, who between them executed thousands of Christians during their respective reigns.

On Queen Ranavalona's command, soldiers began to spy on anyone they suspected of being a convert. Soon long lists of offenders were being drawn up and circulated among government officials. But there were still ways and means of reading the Bible and the ever-resourceful Malagasy soon found that if they split the Bible up into booklets they could easily hide these smaller texts in the thatched roofs of their houses, in rice-storage pits or various other cubbyholes around the house. A young woman named Mary Rasalama was one such who turned to subterfuge rather than relinquish her faith.

Situated outside her house was a large rice pit which was used for storage and which she now made twice as big by digging out the walls. Afterwards she then covered the top of the pit (its mouth) with a huge stone and on top of this she placed leaves, branches and rubbish as camouflage. At night, when the wind was up or the rain was falling, Rasalama and her friends then congregated in the pit

Ranavalona I, Queen of Madagascar, at the height of her power – a somewhat fanciful portrait, painted after her death in 1863, of a woman who employed murder, massacre, torture and imprisonment to subdue her subjects. Her persecution of Europeans, and especially of Christian missionaries, did untold harm to her country.

<small>(IMAGE TAKEN FROM A COLOURED POSTCARD OF THE PORTRAIT, WHICH MAY HAVE BEEN LOST WHEN THE QUEEN'S PALACE IN ANTANANARIVO WAS DESTROYED BY FIRE)</small>

where they would sit and quietly sing and pray to the Lord. It wasn't ideal, but at least people had somewhere to congregate. Unfortunately it wasn't long before neighbours, realizing what was afoot, reported Rasalama's activities to the relevant authorities. Rasalama was arrested and, although given the opportunity to recant and admit her error, she refused. In August 1838 she was led out of the city to a barren field where she was told to kneel down. Her guards permitted her to pray and she began 'Lord Jesus, into Thy hands I commit my spirit'. Before she could say any more several soldiers crept up behind her and stabbed her in the back with their spears. When she was finally dead, her body was thrown to the dogs. It was an inglorious event, but one which would be repeated in various guises for years to come.

Immediately after Ranavalona had vowed that every missionary or convert caught reading the Bible would be put to death, a large number of men were condemned to die either by being thrown from high rocks, burned at the stake, beheaded, boiled or, in some cases, forced to drink poisonous liquids. A particularly gruesome description of 'death by boiling' appears in *Flashman's Lady*, in which the author describes in meticulous detail exactly how the torture was implemented. At the bottom of a steep mountainside pits were dug out in which those condemned to die were made to stand with their hands tied behind their backs to long wooden stakes. At the far end of each pit stood blazing fires upon which were balanced huge cauldrons of water. When the water was at boiling point guardsmen then slowly tipped the cauldrons upwards and over so that the boiling liquid would run down specially constructed channels into the pits. The water caused steam to rise up but when this evaporated 'I saw to my horror that [the water] only filled the pit waist deep – the victims were boiling alive by inches'.[5] Meanwhile, all this was being watched by countless natives who stood at the top of the mountain baying and jeering at the victims below. Another method of execution, equally repulsive, was to yoke several victims together by the neck with a heavy iron wheel and then dump these unfortunates in the wilderness, where they would either starve to death or break each other's necks in an attempt to get free. No torture was too gruesome or too inhumane to use. Ranavalona was a sadist with a whole kingdom of people with whom she could play. However, it was always Christians who exercised the Queen's anger most. In March 1849, for instance, the following exchange was recorded between a group of Christians who had been arrested and the interrogatory officer in charge of their trial:

> **'Do you worship the sun, the moon or the earth?' the officer asked, to which one of the accused replied, 'I do not pray to them, because the hand of God made them.'**
>
> **'Do you worship the twelve sacred mountains?'**
>
> **'I do not worship them, because they are only mountains.'**
>
> **'Do you pray to the idols which preside over the consecration of kings?'**
>
> **'I do not pray to them, because the hand of man made them.'**
>
> **'Do you pray to the ancestors of the rulers?'**
>
> **'Kings and governors are given to us by God so that we obey them and pay them homage, but they are only men like us. When we pray, it is God alone whom we address.'**
>
> **'Do you distinguish other days and do you observe the Sabbath?'**
>
> **'It is the day of the great God, for in six days the Lord made all His works, then He rested on the seventh day and declared that day holy. That is why we rest and keep that day holy.'**

One by one the accused replied in the same manner until the whole group of approximately twenty-five men and women were pronounced guilty, and afterwards condemned either to be burned at the stake, thrown down from the summit of Amapamarinana until their necks had been broken, or flogged till their hearts gave out and they died. The prisoners were then each bound hand and foot and led away and incarcerated until the hour of their execution. They didn't have to wait long.

The following morning, before the sun rose, the condemned were led to Analakely, where they were joined by a group of soldiers and the judges who had previously sentenced them. Each of the prisoners' names was read out aloud, after which they were told which punishment they would receive. The prisoners were then divided into groups and it is recorded that those who were about to be burned to ashes began to chant out hymn number 137 in the Malagasy hymn book:

> **When I die, when I leave my friends**
> **When these friends lament over me**
> **When my life has departed from me**
> **Then I shall be truly happy.**

Understandably, perhaps, the singing did the Christians no favours, for it infuriated the soldiers and judges to such an extent that when the condemned pleaded that they be killed before their bodies were burnt, their pleas were ignored. Queen Ranavalona insisted the prisoners be burnt alive.

As for those whose bodies were going to be hurled down from on high, they were tied by their hands and feet to long poles which the soldiers then slung over their shoulders to carry them to their place of execution. Along the way the prisoners spoke to passers-by and, according to one account, 'those who laid eyes on the condemned said that their faces were like the faces of angels.'[7] Nothing could save them and, trussed up like chickens, they were taken to the summit of Amapamarinana and hurled over the edge to certain death below. Afterwards the bruised and battered corpses were then dragged to the far side of the capital and placed on the same pyres upon which those who were condemned to be burned at the stake were to die. It was a horrific sight and the stench of burning flesh, together with the screams of the dying, were enough to curdle even the strongest man's blood. None the less, as with those who were thrown down from the mountain, it is said that those burnt alive sang hymns throughout their ordeal and eventually died gently and in peace.

Over the years there were further massacres of the innocents, but for every convert who was executed or banished from the island, two sprang up in their place. Bibles, which were scarce, were surreptitiously passed from one family to another, secret prayer meetings were held every Sabbath, and children were baptized behind locked doors. No matter what threats Ranavalona made, nothing stemmed the Christian community from growing and, as noted in the following extract, from establishing stronger and stronger roots:

> **The pure and unselfish lives of those who met death joyfully**
> **for their attachment to the Christian faith has had its influence**
> **on the multitudes […] and whenever it is possible, there are**
> **those who even now meet together in secret places to**
> **commemorate that ordinance whereby the disciples of the**
> **Lord Jesus do show forth His death till He come.**[8]

Perhaps a more intelligent monarch, noting that her policies were not having the desired effect, might have revised her plans, but Ranavalona did nothing of the sort, leading most historians to speculate that either she loved torture for torture's sake or that she was certifiably insane. The latter theory is tempting – there is plenty of evidence to show her mind was unbalanced – and yet throughout her reign she managed to avoid being assassinated or removed from the throne, which in itself testifies to her having had a certain degree of intelligence.

None the less, no one lives indefinitely and, in 1863, after almost thirty-five years of misrule and persecution, Queen Ranavalona I fell ill and died. She was hated not only in Madagascar but also in Britain and France, having either exiled or executed citizens from both of these countries.

In her place her son, Radama II (also known as Rakota, who was born from one of her illicit relationships), succeeded to the throne. In general he was a progressive ruler who abolished slavery and implemented a 'freedom of religion' act, but unfortunately after three years on the throne he was assassinated.

Rasoherina, Rakota's widow, succeeded him, but again her reign was very short-lived.

Finally, in 1869 Queen Ranavalona II was crowned ruler. At her coronation she is said to have converted to Christianity, after which she began welcoming new missionary activity back to the island.

Notwithstanding this new turn of events, the martyrs of Madagascar were never forgotten and, as if to back this up, recent aerial photographs have revealed that:

> **at 10,000 meters of altitude, in the plane which from Europe takes you towards Madagascar, well before seeing its shores you are suddenly intrigued by an immense reddish spot which stands out sharply against the blue water of Mozambique without mingling in it... That red water, spurting out from everywhere like a fatal haemorrhage whose power forces the sea waves beyond the horizon, is *the blood of the earth*.**[9]

Perhaps this is the blood of the martyrs? It certainly seems to speak of their deaths.

ELENA CEAUSESCU

Mother of the Fatherland

Dreptatea e cum o fac domnii (**Justice is as the rulers make it**)
ROMANIAN PROVERB

O n Christmas day 1989, an elderly couple dressed in thick winter overcoats stood hand-in-hand at the back of a small courtyard in Tirgoviste, Romania. Seconds later both were dead, having been executed by a three-man firing squad. A close-up revealed that the right side of the man's head was stained with blood, as was that of his wife, as well as the bullet-ridden wall behind them. It was a gruesome scene, but over the following days this picture was splashed over every newspaper's front page in the world, for the couple were none other than Romania's President Nicolae Ceausescu and his wife, Elena. Accused of causing the deaths of over 60,000 people during their twenty-four-year reign of terror, in life they had been an unassailable force governing their country with a rod of iron. In death their strength, their pride and their arrogance all but disappeared. In their place lay the crumpled bodies of two lonely senior citizens.

Elena Petrescu (nicknamed 'Lenuta') was born on 6 January 1919. Her parents were of peasant stock and lived in Oltenia, a rural region of Romania that lies south-west of the capital, Bucharest. Her father farmed a small plot of rented land and ran a small shop which sold sundry items such as bread, candles and flour. With money hard to come by, Elena left school at fourteen before she had taken any exams, moving instead to Bucharest where she found unskilled work, first as a laboratory assistant and then as a seamstress in a textile factory.

Given her background, it is somewhat surprising that she expressed an interest in so dry and academic a subject as politics and yet, early on in her life, she began attending meetings of the Young Communist League. However, it wasn't until she met and married Nicolae Ceausescu in 1939 that her real interest in politics was ignited, first and foremost because her new husband was the leader of the Young Communist Party itself.

Ever since he was a boy, Nicolae Ceausescu had always expressed an interest in affairs of state. As a member of the communist youth movement he was twice imprisoned, first in 1933 for inciting a strike and distributing political pamphlets, and again in 1940 for distributing communist propaganda and 'political organizing'. It was while he was in jail at Tirgu Jiu that he met and became friends with Gheorghe Gheorghiu-Dej, who would later, in 1952, become Romania's leader. Ceausescu was Gheorghiu-Dej's protégé and when the Communists succeeded to power in 1947, Ceausescu was immediately made head of the country's Ministry of Agriculture, after which he was elected Deputy Minister of the Armed Forces.

At this stage Elena was working as a low-paid secretary in the Romanian civil service, although she was soon given the sack due to her incompetence. Elena's lack of education was to dog her throughout her life and was undoubtedly the driving force behind one of the more curious aspects of her career as the wife of Romania's leading politician. Having not even completed an elementary education it seems that Elena was desperate to convince people that she was a strong, intelligent woman. To this end she somehow managed to 'acquire' a PhD in chemistry. Although everyone knew the doctorate was a fake, no one questioned its authenticity. This madness continued when she was later elected chairman of the main chemistry research laboratory in Romania. Elena also sought recognition for her academic achievements abroad, accepting honorary degrees for her scientific work from almost every country she visited. Mircea Codreanu, a Romanian diplomat posted to Washington, states: 'Being an ignorant, uneducated, primitive kind of woman, she really thought that if she had some titles after her name, it would change her image.'[1] To add insult to injury she also forced many renowned Romanian scientists to relinquish their own research and have it published in various journals under her name. But Elena Ceausescu did not only seek academic recognition; she also craved political influence. It was this desire to move into government that sealed the fate of the Romanian people for almost twenty-five years.

With the death of Gheorghiu-Dej in 1965, Nicolae Ceausescu succeeded first to the leadership of the Communist Party, then to the general secretariatship and finally, in December 1967, he was elected President of the State Council and thereby became head of state. This latter was a role that Ceausescu had coveted all his life and Elena, who had always craved power, was equally elated.

Elena's rise through the ranks of the Communist Party was almost as impressive as that of her husband. In 1968, one year after Nicolae had become General Secretary of the Romanian Communist Party (PCR) and President of the State Council, Elena Ceausescu joined the PCR's Bucharest Municipal Committee. Thereafter her rise through the ranks was swift; by 1972 she had been elected a member of the Central Committee and by 1973 she had reached the Executive Committee. To say that she was eager to gain more and more political influence would be naïve; Elena was desperate for power and with her husband's aid grasped every opportunity that was put in her way.

Besides, when Ceausescu first succeeded to the leadership he was considered very popular, winning immediate support from the people for his independent political stance, which challenged the dominance of the Soviet Union over Romania. In the 1960s, Ceausescu ended Romania's participation in the Warsaw Pact military alliance and in 1968 he further broke ranks with the USSR, condemning the invasion of Czechoslovakia. But all was not sweetness and light under Ceausescu, for at the same time as maintaining an independent foreign-affairs policy, at home he baulked at the suggestion of introducing more liberal laws and instead followed the party's Stalinist legacy, which recommended a strict centralized administration. Ceausescu's secret police (the Securitate) swung into action, denying people their right to free speech as well as maintaining a rigid censorship over all forms of the media and the mail and, as the following extract from Julian Hale's book, *Ceausescu's Romania*, outlines, they left no stone unturned:

> **The State Security is far more powerful and dangerous, liaising with military intelligence and playing a watching role in all branches of State activity. In Article Twenty-eight of the Constitution of the Romanian Socialist Republic it is written: 'The freedom of speech, press, assembly, meetings and demonstrations is guaranteed to the citizens of the RSR.' In the following Article Twenty-nine the situation is clarified: 'The freedom of speech, press, assembly, meetings and**

Nicolae Ceausescu, President for Life of Romania, and his wife Elena during a cruise on the Black Sea, circa 1975. By 1979 Elena had been named 'Mother of the Fatherland', among other sonorous titles, and a year later became First Deputy Prime Minister, the most powerful person in Romania after her husband. (© HULTON-DEUTSCH COLLECTION/CORBIS)

**demonstrations must not be used for purposes which are contrary
to the socialist system and the interests of those who work.'**

Naturally, the Securitate's job was to implement Article Twenty-nine at the expense of Article Twenty-eight, and over the course of Ceausescu's reign it is estimated that they coerced over one million people into informing on their fellow countrymen. Past mistakes or indiscretions could at any time be raised and used against an individual. The Securitate knew everything about everyone; phones were tapped, rooms were bugged, private correspondence was opened and read, and more often than not hotel staff, shop assistants, bus drivers and petty officials of all ranks worked for the security forces. The strain on people's everyday lives to do and say the right thing was enormous.

But what of Elena Ceausescu's role in the day-to-day running of this police state? As the saying goes: behind every powerful man stands an even more powerful woman, and this 'truism' was never more appropriate than when applied to the Ceausescus.

In 1966 Nicolae Ceausescu, with the full backing of his domineering wife, began to pass a series of laws making abortion illegal. Further, he prohibited the use of contraception and decreed that each married woman under the age of forty have a minimum of four children (a number that was later increased to five). Ceausescu also made divorce almost impossible to obtain and increased taxes not only on childless couples but also on those who had three children or less. From beginning to end it was a disastrous policy. Families who could barely support one or two children suddenly had to fill even more mouths. And women in particular suffered huge hardships. Unable to escape unhappy marriages and forced into one pregnancy after another (or into backstreet abortions) they soon became no more than glorified birth machines.

But Elena Ceausescu, for all her 'scientific' education and for all her being a role model for women, lifted not a finger to help. As Julian Hale comments, 'Ceausescu is reputed to be something of a puritan, but here he may be affected by the influence of his wife, Elena, who is a keen reformer of national morals. Some say she was responsible for the decree curbing divorce and abortion.'

Elena encouraged her husband in every way that she could. This included his next disastrous step, which was to begin exporting huge amounts of the country's agricultural and industrial production.

In the early 1970s Nicolae Ceausescu borrowed vast amounts of foreign money from Western credit institutions to support his plans to turn the country from an agrarian state into an urban society. This included depopulating rural communities, bulldozing their villages and relocating their inhabitants to new urban settlements, where they could work in the factories and increase Romania's industrial production. However, through the 1970s and into the 1980s Ceausescu accumulated such large foreign debts (approximately $10 billion)

The Ceausescus are greeted by well-wishers on their arrival in New York from New Orleans during a state visit to America in 1978. Although personally extremely rich by now, back in Romania their disastrous economic strategies, coupled with a repressive state regime, were beginning to bring the country to the brink of disaster. On their return from such visits, citizens would be bussed in from surrounding areas to wave flags and applaud them. (© BETTMANN/CORBIS)

that in order to pay the money back he made the decision to export everything that he and his ministers could lay their hands on. At this point Romania, though not rich in natural resources, could boast that it had homegrown deposits of oil, gas and coal, in addition to which it also produced satisfying amounts of wheat, maize, fruit, vegetables, meat and salt. With all these resources shipped abroad, however, suddenly Romania began to suffer chronic food shortages, not to mention a lack of medical supplies, energy for lighting and heat, petrol and other basic necessities. A typical Romanian joke during this period would go something like this:

> **A Romanian official dies and goes to Hell. At the entrance to Satan's palace he sees two vast identical chambers, one marked 'East' and the other 'West'. The frightened official**

asks the attendant devil:

'What is the difference between the two? Which one should I choose?' The reply comes:

'Oh, the services we provide are the same. Monday, boiling in oil, Tuesday, roasting on a spit, Wednesday is fire and brimstone, Thursday, baking in an oven, Friday, frying in a pan...'

'But why is East so crowded and West so empty?'

'Well in East Hell they're always running out of oil, then the spits don't turn up and there is a permanent shortage of sulphur and brimstone.'

Sadly, however, the reality of the situation was far from amusing. Indeed, it was as if the country had been plunged into the Dark Ages. Shopping for food became a task that required huge amounts of patience and stamina and, more often than not, having queued for hours for a loaf of bread or a couple of eggs, people were turned away empty-handed.

Tragically the population boom and food shortages weren't the only catastrophes that the long-suffering Romanians had to face, for a further disaster began to loom on the horizon.

Orphanages began springing up throughout the country, for as the birth rates rose and the food decreased, families were no longer able to support their offspring. Another incentive compounded this horrendous situation: money.

Nicolae Ceausescu began offering financial rewards to all parents who off-loaded their children on to state-run institutions in the hope that when the youngsters reached adulthood

Elena Ceausescu stands to applaud at the closing of the Romanian Communist Party Congress. Among her titles was 'Leading Fighter of the Party for the Glorious Destiny of Romania', which would have been laughable had not the times, for most Romanians, been so terrifying. (© BERNARD BISSON/CORBIS SYGMA)

they could form a Romanian Workers' Army. Naturally the orphanages weren't luxurious; they weren't even basic. Designed like factories and staffed by the minimum number of nurses required to keep things operational, the children were treated worse than animals. No mental stimulation was given them, no love, no education, no medical care, no physical activity and, worst of all, there was little if any food to go round. As a result, those children who survived grew up severely impaired, either physically or mentally. Worse still, in later years it was also discovered that the majority of them were suffering from AIDS. Doctors, who had for years been prevented from keeping up with advances within the medical community, had misguidedly thought blood transfusions might help the children regain their health. Tragically, the opposite occurred. In addition to the doctors' ignorance, Ceausescu and his 'scientist' wife, believing AIDS to be nothing more than a disease of the 'decadent West', had forbidden the testing of blood.

Of course, as a woman, it might have been hoped that Elena Ceausescu would have been appalled by what was occurring right under her nose. Surely no one, let alone a member of the female sex, let alone a woman who was a mother herself, would wish this type of life on any infant or, worse still, sanction it as a political necessity? But while the country starved and the orphanages increased in size, in stark contrast the Ceausescus were enjoying a boorishly lavish lifestyle.

On 28 March 1974 Nicolae Ceausescu was made President for Life of the Republic by the Grand National Assembly. It was a position created especially for him and one that he began to abuse almost the moment it was bequeathed. Suddenly members of Ceausescu's family, including his own son and two of his brothers, were given key roles either in government or in the army.[2] But it was Elena who reaped the greatest reward, and on her sixtieth birthday in 1979 the daily newspaper *Scînteia* devoted two days' worth of eulogy to her, showering her with titles such as 'Leading Fighter of the Party for the Glorious Destiny of Romania', 'Mother of the Fatherland', the 'Party's Torch' and 'Great Example of Devotion and Revolutionary Passion'. If it hadn't been such a terrifying time then it would have been laughable, but by 1980 Elena had become first Deputy Prime Minister: the most powerful person in Romania after her husband.

There now began a concerted effort on the part of Mrs Ceausescu to control and promote her image as Romania's leading lady. Orders were issued that whenever the names of Nicolae and Elena were printed (i.e. in a newspaper) they were to appear on the same line together, so that Elena's name was imbued with the same importance as that of her husband. As if this wasn't manipulative enough, it was further ordered that no other names be quoted in the same articles so that the dictators' names would appear all the more impressive.

Photographs were to be treated with much the same delicacy. No photograph of Nicolae was to appear without Elena by his side and all photographs had to be given a red background, as red was the official Communist Party colour. If Elena and Nicolae travelled abroad on state visits (to China and North Korea, the USA and Great Britain) then on their return citizens were bussed in from the surrounding towns, villages and schools so that they could wave flags and sing the praises of their esteemed leaders. Nothing was left to chance; everything was organized in order to promote the two dictators. In particular, after the National Conference of Women, Elena was praised by a large group of children who sang out the following praise:

> **We gaze with esteem, with respect, at the harmony of this family life. We attach special significance to the fact that her life, as a former textile worker, communist youth militant, member of the Party since the days of illegality, today hero of Socialist labour, scientist, member of the Central Committee of the PCR, together with her husband – offers us an exemplary image of the destinies of two communists. The three children of the Presidential couple work, like any of us, following the example of their parents, to bring socialism to Romania. All this attests clearly to the truth that work and personal example are obligations in the Ceausescu family.**[3]

Despite this whitewashing of her career, however, behind the scenes Elena was neither well liked nor respected.

By 1980, after twenty-seven years of relative prosperity, bread rationing was reintroduced to the country. In addition, measures were also taken to limit the consumption of other basic foodstuffs, including rice, sugar, coffee and corn. It was a bitter blow to the Romanian people, a clear signal that the Ceausescus' economic strategies weren't working. But if the country was on its knees, the Ceausescus were not.

The disparity between the lives that the Romanian people led and those enjoyed by its leaders was obscene. The Ceausescus enjoyed the luxury of over forty palaces and in one of these – a building situated on Bucharest's Primaverii Boulevard – an entire room was set aside and filled with Elena's vast collection of dresses, not to mention jewellery and over fifty fur coats. Elena's extravagance makes Imelda Marcos's expenditure on shoes look miserly. But clothing wasn't the only luxury item that the Ceausescus favoured. Nicolae and Elena owned two yachts, the *Snagov I* and the *Snagov II*, as well as several speedboats which they moored on a lake north of Bucharest. And if the country was starving, those people fortunate enough to live in the palaces certainly weren't. Banquets were organized during which Elena was said to have eaten enough for two people. Nor was any expense spared in pursuit of the finest wines, the best meat, the sweetest cakes and the richest coffee. Yet if this was the scene inside the palace walls, then outside it could not have been more different. As Mircea Kivu, a Romanian research director for the Institute of Marketing and Polls in Bucharest, recalls:

'One winter day in 1988, I queued for potatoes for five hours and when there were only ten people in front of me, the potatoes ran out. I remember that I cried. Sometimes I think it wasn't real.'

The country was on the verge of a complete socio-economic collapse. Its citizens, starved of food, heating and medical aid, were totally demoralized and finally, on 16 December 1989, discontent boiled over into public protest when a riot broke out in Timisoara.

The riot had begun as a protest in support of a dissident Hungarian minister named the Reverend Laszlo Tokes, who was facing deportation for speaking out against the Ceausescu regime. But what began as a small gathering of his parishioners soon turned into a large anti-government campaign which the police had to bring under control. Suddenly Securitate troops joined forces with the police, and in turn the army came out. On the command of General Victor Stanculescu, the troops opened fire, killing hundreds of citizens. It was a disastrous event, not just for those killed and wounded, but also for the President

In March 1990, three months after the collapse of the Ceausescus' regime and their execution, an auction of the vast hoard of property they had corruptly amassed was held in Bucharest. Here an auction guide shows a prospective bidder a wall hanging featuring portraits of the late President and his wife. (© PA PHOTOS/EPA)

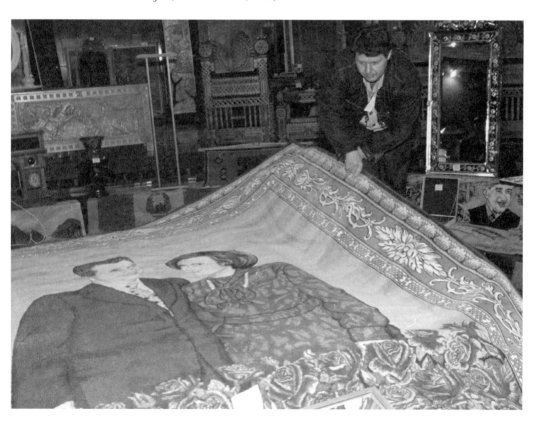

and his wife, whom many felt were responsible for giving General Stanculescu his orders to open fire.

On 20 December 50,000 people once again took to the streets of Timisoara. This time they were protesting against the government in general, and Nicolae Ceausescu in particular. But the President remained resolutely undisturbed by this turn of events and, egged on by Elena, decided on 21 December to hold a mass rally in Bucharest's central square, then called the Pieta Republica (Republican Square), but now known as the Pieta Revolutiei (Revolution Square).

Some 80,000 people turned out to hear their President speak and they weren't disappointed. Ceausescu soon appeared on the balcony of the Central Committee Building flanked by various officials, as well as his wife. However, while Nicolae began spouting out his rhetoric concerning 'scientific socialism', certain people in the crowd below began to heckle and scream slogans such as 'Down with the dictators!' and 'Timisoara! Timisoara!'

The rally was being broadcast on Romanian television and when one looks back on the tapes it is easy to see the shock written all over Ceausescu's face, not to mention Elena's obvious disgust and anger. Shortly afterwards the broadcast stopped, to be replaced by patriotic songs, but the damage had already been done. Thousands of people all over the country had witnessed their leader's humiliation. There was no coming back from a defeat such as that.

The Ceausescus retreated back into the Central Committee Building, but instead of making their escape from the city they made the first of several fatal mistakes and decided to wait until the following morning. In the meantime, encouraged by the hecklers at the rally, huge numbers of Romanians took to the streets and began demanding that Ceausescu be overthrown. Even the army was on the side of the people; although the troops had been ordered to stop the rioting, they joined in the demonstrations.

By morning the protestors had broken into the Central Committee Building, but they were to be disappointed because their prey, suddenly aware of the danger they were in, had arranged to be picked up by helicopter from the building's roof. However, it was a short-lived escape. Without any precise destination in mind, the helicopter landed and both Nicolae and Elena were swiftly arrested by the armed forces and taken to a military base at Tirgoviste (fifty kilometres north of Bucharest), where they were put on trial before a military tribunal. The panel comprised of three civilians, five judges and assessors, two prosecutors, two defence lawyers and a cameraman.

The charges, as outlined by the prosecutor, General Dan Voinea, were as follows:

> **Crimes against the people. They carried out acts that are incompatible with human dignity and social thinking; they acted in a despotic and criminal way; they destroyed the**

people whose leaders they claimed to be. Because of the crimes they committed against the people, I plead, on behalf of the victims of these two tyrants, for the death sentence for the two defendants. The bill of indictment contains the following points: Genocide, in accordance with Article 356 of the penal code. Two: Armed attack on the people and the state power, in accordance with Article 163 of the penal code. The destruction of buildings and state institutions, undermining of the national economy, in accordance with Articles 165 and 145 of the penal code.[4]

But, on being requested to give a response to the above charges, Nicolae Ceausescu, instead of pleading mercy, replied that he wouldn't answer anything the tribunal asked him. 'I will only answer questions before the Grand National Assembly,' he said. 'I do not recognize this court. The charges are incorrect, and I will not answer a single question here.'[5]

Elena Ceausescu was in no mood to beg for mercy either, and she interrupted the trial with inappropriately sarcastic comments on more than one occasion. When the prosecutor pointed out to Nicolae that thirty-four people had been killed during the rioting, Elena said: 'Look, and that they are calling genocide.'[6] Elena also whispered to her husband throughout the main part of the trial, prompting the prosecutor to accuse her of always being talkative even if she didn't know what she was saying. 'I have observed,' said the prosecutor, 'that she is not even able to read correctly, but she calls herself a university graduate.'

Elena then answered: 'The intellectuals of this country should hear you, you and your colleagues.'

After this spat the prosecutor went on to list all of Elena's fake academic titles.

Later, Ceausescu was accused of ruining the country by exporting all its main assets, of destroying Romanian villages and Romanian soil and of deliberately starving the people while he and his wife gorged themselves on sumptuous meals made from imported foreign goods. But no amount of goading persuaded Nicolae to rise to the bait. Elena obviously thought the trial beneath her contempt.

In certain respects she was right, for the trial was little more than an opportunity for the prosecution to air its disgust at the couple's years in power. The opening statement that the defence counsel, Nico Teodorescu, put forward was also heavily weighted against the accused. Teodorescu (who viewed the couple as a 'monster with two heads') said: 'Even though he, like her, committed insane acts, we want to defend them.'[7]

Teodorescu had earlier tried to persuade both Nicolae and Elena to plead mental instability, pointing out to them that this was their best chance of survival. But the couple ignored his advice. 'They felt deeply insulted,' he said, 'unable or unwilling to grasp their only lifeline. They rejected my help after that.'[8]

Teodorescu went on to recite a long list of charges, all of which the defence team agreed Nicolae and Elena were guilty of, and summed up that both defendants should therefore be punished. It was hardly the type of democratic hearing to which the phrase 'innocent until proven guilty' could be applied.

Finally, in summation, the prosecutor stated that, 'I have been one of those who, as a lawyer, would have liked to oppose the death sentence, because it is inhuman. But we are not talking about people. I would not call for the death sentence, but it would be incomprehensible for the Romanian people to have to go on suffering this great misery and not to have it ended by sentencing the two

The body of Elena Ceausescu photographed at an undisclosed location after her execution by firing squad on Christmas Day 1989. The anti-communist rising had started in Timisoara on 16 December. So great was Romanians' feeling against their leaders that, despite repressive measures by the army, the Ceausescus were on trial before a military tribunal within a few days. (© CAMERA PRESS DIGITAL)

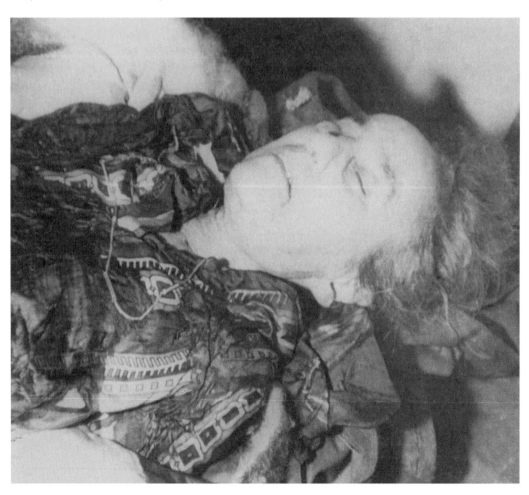

Ceausescus to death.'[9] Nicolae and Elena's fate was sealed.

Moments later they were led out into a small courtyard and shot. Voinea, who had stepped outside for a quick cigarette, witnessed the whole, gruesome event:

> **When they were taken out of the room where they'd been tried, there was this 10-metre-long corridor, and then they entered the yard of the military unit. From the exit to the wall where they had them shot, it was about fifteen metres. When they took them out into the yard [Ceausescu] stopped as he saw the soldiers. It was then that he realized he would be executed, I believe. First they took him and put him up against the wall. They took two steps back and the officer shot first. The other members of the firing squad were behind him. When they shot, he jumped, I think out of reflex... because they aimed at his feet. More than half a metre he jumped. And maybe you've seen on TV that he died on his back with his feet under him... And then they shot her.'**

It was an ignominious end to a political career that had spanned almost a quarter of a century. Seen in one light it could be viewed as a tragedy. After all, from very humble beginnings Elena Ceausescu had carved out a career of unparalleled success. She was a prominent scientist whose academic credentials had contributed to her country's scientific progress both at home and abroad. She was also a successful politician who had worked her way tirelessly through the Communist Party's ranks to attain a leading governmental position. From scarce appearances in public she had grown to become the female face of Romania, her image appearing not only on TV broadcasts, but in newspaper articles, on billboards and posters. Romanians adored her, children sang her praises and foreign dignitaries showered her with honourable titles. To all intents and purposes, her's was a success story.

Seen in a different light, Elena's life was far from savoury. Barely able to read or write, her scientific titles weren't worth the paper upon which they were printed, and her political successes were entirely due to her husband's position. Romanians had been forced into loving Elena, when in reality they despised her. The only people who loved this boorish, power-crazed woman were her husband and children. In the light of this, it could be seen as quite poignant that Nicolae and Elena's corpses, though taken to the same cemetery (the Ghencea in south-west Bucharest), were buried in separate plots. Today, very few people lay flowers on either of the Ceausescus' graves.

MARY ANN COTTON

The Black Widow

Mary Ann Cotton
She's dead and she's rotten
She lies in her bed
With her eyes wide open.
Sing, sing, oh, what can I sing?
Mary Ann Cotton is tied up wi' string.
Where, where? Up in the air
Sellin' black puddens a penny a pair.
FROM A CHILDREN'S RHYME *CIRCA* 1873

When Mary Ann Cotton died on 24 March 1873, she had been accused of killing four of her husbands and almost three times as many children. The fact of the murders and of her guilt has never been disputed (except by Mary Ann herself) but one enigma behind these gruesome killings remains; why would such a seemingly respectable woman wish to perpetrate so many foul crimes?

Mary Ann Cotton was born in the small English village of Low Moorsley in County Durham in October 1832. Her parents, Michael and Margaret Robson, were a young, working-class, Methodist couple, who struggled all of their lives to keep themselves and their family from poverty. Michael Robson was a miner, in those days a gruelling job. He was also fiercely religious, attending chapel every Sunday, and a strict disciplinarian. No doubt he ruled his household with a rod of iron and probably handed out various physical punishments to both Mary Ann and her brother, Robert. None the less, both children felt secure within this tight-knit family unit; they had a father and a mother and although money was scarce, there was food on the table. Tragically, however, when Mary Ann was eight years old, all this changed. The family moved to a mining town called Murton where, a year after they had settled, Mary Ann's father suffered a fatal accident, falling down a mineshaft to an untimely death. Without a breadwinner in the house, the family was exceedingly vulnerable. Life for a working-class family in nineteenth-century England, and in particular a family headed by a widow, was rough in the extreme. The shadow of the workhouse would have loomed over Mary Ann's head and few things could have been worse, both because of the ignominy and the grim conditions she would have had to endure once she was there. As Charles Dickens wrote in an article for the magazine *Household Words* around 1850:

> **In one place, the Newgate of the Workhouse, a company of boys and youths were locked up in a yard alone; their day-room being a kind of kennel where the casual poor used formerly to be littered down at night. Divers of them had been there some long time. 'Are they never going away?' was the natural inquiry. 'Most of them are crippled, in some form or other,' said the Wardsman, 'and not fit for anything.' They slunk about, like dispirited wolves or hyenas; and made a pounce at their food when it was served out, much as those animals do. The big-headed idiot shuffling his feet along the pavement, in the sunlight outside, was a more agreeable object everyway.**
>
> **Groves of babies in arms; groves of mothers and other sick women in bed; groves of lunatics; jungles of men in stone-paved down-stairs day-rooms, waiting for their dinners; longer and longer groves of old people, in up-stairs Infirmary wards, wearing out life, God knows how – this was the scenery through which the walk lay, for two hours.**

But, as luck would have it, it was at this crucial point in Mary Ann's life that fate intervened, for not long after Michael Robson's death, Mary Ann's mother remarried. Although there was no love lost between Mary Ann and her stepfather, he did serve a purpose. The new man in the household had a small salary and thus Mary Ann escaped the workhouse and almost certain destitution. What she didn't escape, however, was a lesson that would affect her for the rest of her life: that she had to have money, whatever the consequences.

At sixteen Mary Ann decided to leave home. One can only speculate that this was due to the uneasy relationship between her and her stepfather, but it would also have been appropriate for her to start earning some wages. With this in mind she found a job as a servant in the household of a family in South Hetton. The job was to last three years and there is no reason to believe that at this stage she was anything other than a hardworking, average young woman. Then, after three years, Mary Ann left this job in order to train as a seamstress.

By now she was almost twenty years old and many of those who later spoke about her to the newspapers recalled that she was a pretty young girl (although a photograph taken after her imprisonment, aged forty, reveals a rather heavy-set, plain woman). None the less, Mary Ann must have had something about her, as she was obviously attractive to many men during her lifetime. One such was her first husband, William Mowbray, whom she met shortly after she turned twenty. Mowbray, like her father, was a miner and the couple were wed at St

A contemporary photograph of the notorious arsenic poisoner Mary Ann Cotton, nicknamed 'the Lucrezia Borgia of the North'. It is possible that this is one of the prints that an enterprising Durham photographer had made, and which he sold after her execution in 1873. (REPRODUCED BY PERMISSION OF THE DURHAM RECORD OFFICE)

Andrew's Church in Newcastle-upon-Tyne in July 1852. After the marriage Mowbray decided he no longer wanted to work down the mines, instead taking various jobs that included a few on railroad-construction projects in Cornwall and Durham. This must have put a considerable strain on the marriage since, for a lot of the time, Mowbray worked away from home. He and Mary also had five children in quick succession. Four of these infants died only a few days after they were born and, although child mortality rates were extremely high in Victorian England, this does appear to be the first sign of Mary Ann's murderous inclinations. Gastric fever was claimed to be the cause of death in each case, a diagnosis that over the years was to become increasingly familiar.

Having worked as a miner, then on the railroads, William Mowbray subsequently landed himself a job on a steamer called the *Newburn*, which docked in Sunderland. The family moved there, eager to be together again, but Mowbray was to spend long periods away at sea and on a couple of occasions even sailed abroad. All this changed, however when, in January 1865, following an injury to his foot, Mowbray returned to Mary Ann in order to be nursed better. He was soon struck down by a mysterious intestinal disorder, however, and died in fits of agony a few days later.

Mary Ann, now a widow, withdrew her husband's insurance money and decided to make a new life for herself by moving to a place called Seaham Harbour. It was here that she met a man named Joseph Nattress.

Nattress, who lived with two of his brothers, was engaged to a local woman, and although Mary Ann was greatly attracted to him she couldn't manage to make him break off his engagement. Instead she moved locations again, returning to Sunderland where, ironically, she took a nursing job in the Sunderland Infirmary, House of Recovery for the Cure of Contagious Fever. As with her previous job as maidservant, all surviving records maintain that Mary

Ann was a diligent worker, a nurse who was always concerned for the welfare of her patients. One of those under her care was a man called George Ward. Nurse and patient soon fell in love and, on Ward's release from hospital, the two were promptly married. Not long after this, however, Ward fell ill and despite the attention of several physicians he died in October 1866, after suffering a protracted bout of paralysis and intestinal problems. Before he died, Ward had made out a will bequeathing everything he owned to his wife and immediately after his death Mary Ann is known to have taken a short holiday, only to return to Sunderland, where she now met her third husband, James Robinson.

Robinson was a foreman in the shipbuilding industry; a widower after his first wife, Hannah, had died. He was also the father of four young children and, in order to return to work, he needed a housekeeper. Consequently Mary Ann applied for the job and was hired, but shortly after she had begun in her new post, the youngest Robinson child, who was in fact still only a baby of ten months, died of gastric fever. Overcome with grief, James Robinson promptly turned to his new housekeeper for comfort. Soon enough the couple were engaged, but their wedding plans had to be put on hold for a short time when, in March 1867, Mary Ann's mother, Margaret, fell ill. Mary Ann returned home only to find Margaret's health had dramatically improved but, ever the dutiful daughter, she stayed on with her mother in order to help the older woman regain some of her strength, Within a few days of Mary Ann's arrival, her mother complained of severe stomach cramps, and died shortly afterwards.

Subsequent to her mother's death, Mary Ann returned to her fiancé and, in June 1867, she and James Robinson were wed at Bishopwearmouth Church. However, the honeymoon period was not to last long, because by the year's end tragedy struck not once, but three times, as each of the remaining Robinson children succumbed to gastric fever and died.

Nicknamed by later commentators the 'Lucrezia Borgia of the North',[1] during her trial in 1873 the general public speculated as to why no one had picked up on the unusually high death toll that surrounded Mary Ann. After all, she had left three dead husbands in her wake, not to mention numerous children. Shouldn't someone have noticed? However, during each illness Mary Ann would have had a different doctor in attendance, in addition to which, after each death she was careful to move house, often relocating to a different town, if not county. Mary Ann also gave all the signs of being a respectable, honest woman. She was of good appearance, well spoken and had worked as a nurse, which was a responsible job. Finally, but by no means least, the chemical she had chosen by which to despatch her victims, arsenic, was a common household item. Many people used it as a rat poison and some people would combine it with soap powder in order to scrub their floors clean. It is not surprising therefore that no eyebrows were raised when a woman went into her local chemist or hardware shop in order to purchase the product. Arsenic was also an easy method by which to dispose of someone, a) because it could be administered behind closed doors, and b) because it was almost colourless, and having no smell or taste of its own, could be slipped into food or drink without the victim being able to detect it. On top of this the symptoms of arsenic poisoning (stomach pain, nausea, vomiting, diarrhoea etc) parallel countless other more common illnesses, so that unless you are looking specifically for arsenic poisoning, someone's true condition could be (and more often than not was) completely misdiagnosed.

With all these factors in mind it is not surprising that Mary Ann escaped notice for so long, but after the death of the Robinson children her fortunes took a turn for the worse; James Robinson began to grow suspicious of his wife. All through their short marriage Mary Ann had constantly pestered her husband for larger and larger amounts of money. She also insisted he take out life insurance, and now his children, who had all enjoyed good health prior to his meeting Mary Ann, had died one after the other. Being the foreman at a shipyard Robinson had considerable financial acumen and was meticulous when it came to keeping household records. He was therefore unpleasantly surprised when he began receiving letters detailing various debts that Mary Ann had accrued. On top of this Robinson then discovered that his wife had pawned several of his most valuable belongings. Enraged, he threw Mary Ann out of his house, an act that undoubtedly saved him from a most gruesome death.

Homeless, Mary Ann trudged the streets, something she had feared since her days as a child when the threat of the workhouse had loomed ever closer. But her destitution was not to last long, because she soon seems to have secured herself a job as matron in the Sunderland Penitentiary. During this period Mary Ann met and fell in love with a young naval officer, but while he was abroad on one of his trips, she decided to steal everything she could lay her hands on in his house, after which she swiftly relocated and secured a job with a Dr Hefferman. Given her track record it would not be unreasonable to surmise that Mary Ann probably had an eye to marrying this, her latest employer, but fortuitously for Dr Hefferman, he discovered that she had stolen some money from a drawer in his bedroom and promptly dismissed her.

Mary Ann relocated once again, only this time she travelled north to Walbottle in Northumberland. It was here that a friend of hers, Margaret Cotton, introduced her to her brother Frederick. Like James Robinson before him, Frederick Cotton was a widower, in addition to which he had already suffered the loss of two out of his four children. His sons Frederick Jnr and Charles were, on the other hand, the picture of health.

Before Mary Ann showed up, Frederick Cotton's sister, Margaret, had kept her brother's house in order and his children well fed and washed, but shortly after the newcomer's arrival Margaret died. The diagnosis was a stomach ailment of unknown origin. Bereft and seeking consolation, Frederick Cotton turned to his sister's friend, Mary Ann, and subsequently the couple struck up a

The house at 20 Johnson Terrace in the mining town of West Auckland, Co. Durham, where Mary Ann Cotton lived for a time with one of her many husbands. In all, she is thought to have killed between fifteen and twenty-one people, including her mother, four of her husbands, and many of her children and stepchildren. Unfortunately for her, by the 1870s there had been great scientific advances in detecting arsenic poisoning.
(WITH THANKS TO MR DARREN FAIRCLOUGH, WWW.WESTAUCKLANDWEB.COM)

relationship, one that resulted in Mary Ann falling pregnant. Thereafter, it didn't take Frederick long before he asked Mary Ann to marry him. This (although unknown to him) would have been a bigamous act, as Mary Ann was still married to her third husband, James Robinson. However, to a woman who had committed several murders, bigamy must have seemed paltry in comparison and the couple duly wed in September 1870 at St Andrew's Church, Newcastle-upon-Tyne, the very building in which she had married her first husband, William Mowbray.

After the wedding Mary Ann persuaded her new husband to take out not only life insurance for himself, but also for his two remaining children. In early 1871 a son was born to Frederick and Mary Ann Cotton. The boy was christened Robert Robson Cotton, his middle name presumably referring to Mary Ann's maiden name – or perhaps it was meant as a reminder of a more innocent time in her life. Whatever the reason, the family, which now consisted of Frederick, Mary Ann and their three young children, moved to West Auckland in County Durham. This last relocation was due to the constant disputes between Mary Ann and her neighbours, whose livestock, in particular a significant number of pigs, kept dying. Accusatory fingers began pointing in Mary Ann's direction so the Cottons left. Another explanation for their departure, however, was Joseph Nattress.

Nattress was the man with whom Mary Ann had fallen in love so many years previously and as luck would have it she had lately discovered that he was no longer married but was living as a bachelor in West Auckland. So the family left Newcastle-upon-Tyne, only to meet with disaster; in December 1871, barely a year after his second marriage and only a few months after the birth of Robert, Frederick Cotton died.

Frederick had begun the day as normal, setting off for work in good health, but had soon succumbed to excruciating stomach pains and vomiting and on being brought home faded away swiftly. Once again the diagnosis was gastric fever. Mary Ann collected the life-insurance money and not long afterwards Joseph Nattress moved into her house as a lodger. The following sequence of events is hard to put in chronological order, especially since contemporary historians have written conflicting accounts, but it is known that after Frederick Cotton's death two of his children – Frederick Jnr and Robert Robson Cotton – died at some time in 1872, after which Mary Ann began a new job nursing a man called John Quick-Manning, a government excise officer who was recovering from a bad case of smallpox. Mary Ann, in a macabre echo of her early days with James Robinson, soon fell pregnant by Quick-Manning and intended to marry him. Apparently he was a far better prospect than Nattress, who soon fell ill with gastric fever only to die a few days later, but not until he had conveniently made out a new will leaving everything to his landlady. Mary Ann collected £30 in insurance money after Nattress's death, then proceeded to try and get rid of Frederick Cotton's last surviving child, Charles. Why she didn't kill him as she had all the others remains a mystery to this day, but instead of administering arsenic to the young boy, she attempted to get him a place in a workhouse. She was interviewed by the establishment's administrator, a minor government official called Thomas Riley, who informed Mary Ann that children were not taken in without being accompanied by their parents. In response, Mary Ann is supposed to have said, 'I could have married again but for the child. But there, he won't live long and will go the way of all the Cotton family.'[2]

Sadly, that is exactly what occurred. In early 1871, Charles Cotton was sent out to a nearby chemist with instructions to buy a small amount of arsenic. The shopkeeper refused the boy, telling him that he could only sell arsenic lawfully to persons over twenty-one years of age. It is then recorded that Mary Ann asked one of her neighbours to purchase the chemical. Perhaps she thought that she had purchased so much over her lifetime, it would be more sensible if someone else's name appeared on the poisons register. Whatever the case, Charles Cotton died a short time afterwards and the diagnosis was, unsurprisingly, gastric fever. Mary Ann was now free to marry Quick-Manning, and no doubt she would have done, but suspicions had been aroused. Charles Cotton's doctor, for example, was surprised to hear that the young boy had died; he had seen him several times during the week and couldn't detect anything to worry about. But it was Thomas Riley who went to the police and outlined his suspicions, recalling what Mary Ann had said to him at the workhouse. He now requested that Charles Cotton's doctor not sign a death certificate until the police had had time to investigate. The death certificate was an essential document that Mary Ann would need to collect on Charles's insurance. And it was the insurance that Mary Ann went for, even before looking into funeral arrangements for Charles: hardly the action of a caring woman. Mary Ann's plans were unravelling, because now a formal inquest into Charles's death was going to be held.

At the inquest there were initially no signs of foul play. The investigating physician said that nothing he had found indicated anything other than death by natural causes. Mary Ann must have been relieved, but this was by no means the end of the matter, because by this time a handful of local newspapers had got hold of the story. Calling her 'Lady Rotten' they inevitably reported on the inquest, but in addition they also mentioned that local gossip had branded Mary Ann a serial poisoner. Quick-Manning, horrified by these reports, broke off all relations with his intended bride, despite her being pregnant with his child, while she, ruffled by the newspapers' accusations, started making arrangements to move out of the area. It didn't seem to occur to her that, in so doing, she might make herself look guiltier than ever. Suspicions were already running exceedingly high and before she could relocate, her whole world collapsed; one of the investigating physicians during the inquest had saved samples of Charles Cotton's stomach and he now began testing them for signs of poisoning.

Unfortunately for Mary Ann, during the mid-nineteenth century tests to detect the presence of arsenic in the body had dramatically improved. In part this was due to a growing tendency for people to take out life insurance (arsenic was often nicknamed 'inheritance powder'), thus making those insured highly profitable targets for murder. In order to prosecute more people successfully it was therefore very important to improve forensic medicine, and in particular the science of toxicology. Significant milestones included the Marsh test in 1836 and the Riensch test in 1841, both well established by the time of Mary Ann's killing spree.

Normally the stomach is not the best place to determine the presence of arsenic, the hair, nails, blood and urine being far better indicators as to whether someone has unnaturally high levels of the poison in their system. However, the examining physician persevered and it wasn't too long before the results came back. They were positive. The doctor then asked the police to exhume the rest of the body, which in due course was also shown to have high levels of arsenic. Directly afterwards the police exhumed several other of Mary Ann's nearest and dearest (including the body of Joseph Nattress), only to make precisely the same discovery.

On 6 May 1873 Mary Ann Cotton was arraigned at Durham Assizes for the murder of eight-year-old Charles Edward Cotton. Her trial was then delayed until she had given birth to Quick-Manning's daughter (the infant was later adopted), after which event it continued apace.

The prosecution first of all made a request to the judge, a Mr Justice Archibald, that in order to prove her systematic approach to the murder of Charles Cotton, evidence should be heard in respect of the deaths of Joseph Nattress as well as several other victims. Much to Mary Ann's horror the judge agreed and the prosecution continued full speed ahead by bringing forth numerous witnesses to testify to Mary Ann's frequent purchase of arsenic. The prosecution also produced several doctors who confirmed the unusually high death rate from gastric fever in Mary Ann's households, and finally called Thomas Riley to the stand, who confirmed that Mary Ann had stated Charles Cotton was an obstacle to her marrying John Quick-Manning.

Defence counsel, a Mr Campbell Foster, put up a good fight. He maintained that Charles Cotton, as well as several other of the victims, had slept in a room covered in green floral wallpaper which was known to contain elements of arsenic. The pigment had in fact been developed *circa* 1775 by Carl Scheele, who named it Paris Green, so it wasn't beyond reasonable doubt, Mr Campbell Foster argued, that the child had died from inhaling airborne particles of arsenic.[3] In addition, because Mary Ann was scrupulously clean, she had also used soap and arsenic to scrub down her floors. When the water dried it would have left a residue of the poison, which could also have been inhaled by the unfortunate child. It was a clever defence, but the jury believed not a word of it and shortly after they retired they returned with a verdict of guilty. When Mr Justice Archibald read out her death sentence Mary Ann fainted, and had to be carried out of the courtroom by two prison warders.

Mary Ann Cotton continued to insist on her innocence right up until the time of her death. She wrote numerous letters not just to her supporters (who numbered amongst them some of her former employers) but also to her husband, for legally she was still married to James Robinson, pleading with him to bring her child to the prison as well as her two remaining stepchildren. James Robinson did not reply to the letter but, undeterred, Mary Ann again wrote to him begging that he visit her. Instead Robinson enlisted the help of his brother-in-law, sending him to the prison where Mary Ann asked that he put together a petition stating her innocence and demanding her release. Robinson's brother-in-law refused to do any such thing but, astonishingly, given the weight of evidence against her, Mary Ann was able to persuade several others to produce such a document and have it circulated, though unsurprisingly nothing came of it.

On 24 March 1873, at the age of forty-one, Mary Ann Cotton was led to the scaffold situated inside Durham Gaol. It is said that, always having been a meticulously tidy woman, she insisted on brushing and neatly tying her hair back before being led to the place where she would be hanged. The hangman, a man by the name of William Calcroft, was an expert in his field. Having begun his illustrious career while in his mid-twenties by flogging children for 10 shillings a week, he had since progressed to hanging for £10 a 'drop'. His career as public executioner had spanned almost fifty years by the time Mary Ann stepped up to the noose, so the chances are that she met with a swift if not a painless end.

Naturally, because Mary Ann didn't confess to any of the killings there are no accurate records of the number of people she actually murdered, but given the century she lived in, it would not be far-fetched to speculate that some of them did in fact die of natural causes. That said, most researchers believe that she killed between fifteen and twenty-one people, including her mother, her lover Joseph Nattress, her sister-in-law Margaret Cotton, four of her husbands and countless children and stepchildren. Notorious even to this day, Mary Ann Cotton became one of Britain's first female serial killers and also one of the first women worldwide to be nicknamed after a black widow spider. But what had spurred this unremarkable woman to such despicable acts? Initially the most likely cause was money, the fear of not having enough to keep her from poverty, of being one of the hundreds of thousands who could barely survive in Victorian England. Later, however, one can only surmise that she had begun to enjoy the power she wielded over her victims. The Cotton home in Newcastle still stands to this day, and is said to be haunted not only by her ghost, but also by the ghosts of her numerous victims.

MARIE NOE

An Unlucky Parent

The Lord needed angels so we got a ton of them up there.
ARTHUR NOE, FROM AN INTERVIEW GIVEN TO STEPHEN FRIED,
PHILADELPHIA MAGAZINE, 1998

On 12 July 1963 an article appeared in *Life* Magazine, written by Mary H Cadwalader, which asked if Mr and Mrs Andrew Moore were the unluckiest parents in the whole of America. Mrs Moore had by that time lost each of her seven babies and was described as looking 'worn almost to gauntness... Her eyes are two enormous dark smudges in a face as gray as ashes. She seldom visits the children's graves. Courage, in her lexicon, counts more than tears. She stays close to home with her dog and her two cats.'[1] In fact, the names Andrew and Martha Moore were pseudonyms, the couple's real names being Arthur and Marie Noe, but by the end of the 1990s, far from being America's most pitied husband and wife, they were so despised that at her bail hearing in August 1999, the Assistant District Attorney said of Marie that she was 'as much a mass murderer as Ted Bundy'.

Marie Noe grew up in a troubled, disruptive environment. Her mother, a part-time cleaning woman, was often beaten up by Marie's bully of a father who was also an alcoholic. Police records show a constant string of court appearances, mostly brought about by his wife, who reported him for physical and mental abuse. Marie was separated from her parents and for a short period went to stay in an orphanage, where she celebrated her third birthday, before being reunited with her mother. Devastatingly, Marie came down with scarlet fever at the age of five and, as she herself says, she was used as a guinea pig, being made to take a variety of different drugs. As a result the drugs affected her mental abilities and when she went to school she was unable to keep up with everyone else.

By the age of twelve, Marie had packed up her studies so that she could help out at home instead. In particular she was to look after her younger siblings (one of whom, it is said, was actually the illegitimate daughter of Marie's older sister). Until she was married she gave every penny she earned from various menial jobs directly to her mother. To add to her misery, Marie's mother, following her husband's example, often used to beat her children with a whip. It was not, by anyone's standards, the ideal American family and unsurprisingly events took their toll on the children. One of Marie's siblings was sent to a psychiatric hospital for treatment and, according to court documents from that period, was diagnosed as suffering 'post-traumatic personality disorder'.

By the time Marie eloped with her husband-to-be, Arthur Noe, on 12 July

1949, she was desperate to escape the family home. Arthur was twenty-four years old while Marie was only eighteen, but it was love at first sight. They had met at a neighbourhood social club and had 'stepped out' together for several months before running away, but it still came as a shock to her new husband that his young bride could neither read nor write. 'I was practically illiterate,' said Marie. 'My problem was never mentioned when I was growing up, but when I got married and seen how other people could talk, could read, could understand things better than I could, I understood I had a disadvantage.'[2] Nevertheless, Arthur was patient with Marie and soon taught her the rudiments so that she could begin to improve herself. The couple jogged along nicely until, in May 1950, barely a year after they were married, their first child was born at Temple University Hospital, Philadelphia. He was christened Richard Allen Noe.

Richard was seven pounds eleven ounces on delivery and aside from suffering a slight case of jaundice (which is common in newborns) he was a perfectly healthy baby. Marie and Arthur were delighted with their son and soon took him home, but after only a few days Marie Noe brought him back to the hospital, saying that Richard had vomited and that she wasn't sure what was wrong. Richard was admitted for what the doctors believed was a touch of colic, but having fully recovered after a few days he was returned to his mother. Tragically, one month after Richard was born, Arthur Noe discovered his son lying lifelessly in his cot. Arthur immediately rushed the child over to a neighbour who drove father and son straight to the Episcopal Hospital, but it was too late. The cause of death was cited by the coroner as 'congestive heart failure due to subacute endocarditis', but it was not thought necessary to conduct an autopsy.

After Richard Allen Noe died, Marie Noe had a further three babies in swift succession, but each birth ended as tragically as the first.

In April 1951 Elizabeth Mary Noe was born at Northeastern Hospital. Like her brother, Elizabeth was a normal child with no health problems to speak of until October 1951, when her mother found the five-month-old lying in her cot vomiting up a mixture of blood and milk. Marie acted swiftly and called the emergency services, after which the child was rushed into Temple Hospital. She was declared dead on arrival. The cause of death was stated as bronchopneumonia but, according to the autopsy report, no internal examination was made of Elizabeth's body, and bronchopneumonia is almost impossible to detect without swabs being tested microscopically.

The third Noe child to die was Jacqueline, who was born on 23 April 1952. Like the others, no health problems arose until, three weeks after her release from hospital, Marie said she had found her vomiting and turning bright blue. Jacqueline was dead on arrival at the Episcopal Hospital and this time the cause was put down to an inhalation of vomit.

Nowadays, of course, if three babies from the same family died before reaching the age of one, the parents, but in particular the mother, would almost certainly be under suspicion of murder. But the 1950s was a more innocent age, and although Sudden Infant Death Syndrome (also known as SIDS) wasn't common vernacular, the coroners did believe it could be the cause of death. At that time (and to a certain extent to this day[3]) SIDS was thought to run in the family.

Arthur Noe Jnr was born three years after Jacqueline on 23 April 1955, but twelve days later he was rushed into the Episcopal Hospital after his mother said she had found him suffering from breathing problems. The doctors, however, could find nothing wrong and the child was sent home with its mother. The next day Arthur Noe Jnr was rushed into hospital once again, this time by the emergency services. With a dismal ring of familiarity, he was declared dead on arrival.

On 24 February 1958 Marie then gave birth to her fifth child, Constance. The baby was, like all Marie's previous children, healthy, except for a mild case of conjunctivitis. And yet, according to the *Philadelphia Magazine* article that was published in 1998, one of Constance's doctors later recalled that when Marie was told he would be helping out with the child's care, she turned round and said: 'What's the use? She's going to die just like all the others.' True to form, a couple of weeks later Marie rang her own doctor to say that Constance wasn't breathing too well and, due to Marie's tragic history, the doctor had Constance admitted to hospital, fearing she might have a rare blood disorder. As it turned out, nothing of the sort was wrong and three days later the baby was discharged with a clean bill of health.

Two days after that, Constance was dead. It could hardly have been worse for the Noes. How could such a terrible thing happen not just once, but five times? They themselves put it down to an act of God, but alarm bells had finally begun ringing among hospital staff, who instigated an investigation by the Philadelphia Office of the Medical Examiner in conjunction with the police.

Initially an autopsy was ordered on Constance's body, one which was carried out by Doctor Marie Valdes-Dapena (herself a mother of ten), who was a paediatrics pathologist on the staff of Philadelphia's St Christopher's Hospital for Children. At the time of Constance's death, Mr Noe had stated that, on finding the child lying lifelessly in her cot, he had attempted to resuscitate his daughter, only to find milk curds slipping out of both her mouth and nose. At the time this had been put forward as one of the most likely causes of death, i.e. the aspiration of vomit, but Valdes-Dapena thought otherwise. She stated that the aspiration was a result, not a cause, of death. She put Constance's body through a battery of tests, including a toxicology report, but nothing showed up and Valdes-Dapena signed the case off as 'undetermined, presumed natural'.

Meanwhile, the police interviewed both Mr and Mrs Noe, but like the coroner's officer before them, they turned up very little other than the fact that Mrs Noe obviously suffered from a very low IQ.

A much more sympathetic picture of Marie was only forthcoming when her mother talked to *Life* Magazine, saying that 'after that funeral, Martha [Marie] just sat here for a while not hardly saying a word. Seemed like she couldn't stand to go home. She was just all filled up.'

None the less, it wasn't long before Marie fell pregnant again, but on 24 August 1959 she went into premature labour and delivered a stillborn child, Letitia. This time no shadow of doubt was cast over either Marie or Arthur and the couple were sent home with everyone's heartfelt sympathy.

Little was heard of Marie Noe after the death of this sixth child. Then three years later she turned up, pregnant with her seventh child, born by caesarean section on 19 June 1962. Mary Lee, as the baby was called, was in good health, although the child was kept in hospital for just over one month, perhaps because Marie had suffered a vascular collapse during the operation and was anaemic, or perhaps because hospital staff wanted to monitor the baby's progress. None the less, at the end of the month both mother and child were discharged and although Marie did not take her baby back to the hospital suffering from any significant complaints, she did ring her own doctor frequently.

By this time the Noes had changed family physician and now saw a man by the name of Columbus Gangemi, who later reported to the Chief Medical Examiner that Marie Noe rang him up constantly demanding advice on how to cope with her child. Gangemi also added that Marie sounded edgy and that she was tired of her baby's constant crying. This state of affairs did not last too long, however. On 4 January 1963 Mary Lee was rushed into hospital suffering from breathing difficulties, and was pronounced dead on arrival.

Police asked Mr and Mrs Noe to accompany them down to the station, where they were to be questioned. At the same time an autopsy was ordered on Mary Lee's body, to be carried out by the Assistant Medical Examiner, Doctor Halbert Fillinger. The interviews revealed that, as previously concluded, Mrs Noe was not an intellectually capable woman but, as far as the child was concerned, the police could find nothing out of the ordinary. 'The body,' their report said, 'had no bruises and was well cared for… The baby wore a white shirt, diaper, plastic pants and white socks and was wrapped in a pink blanket and purple towel… The house was clean and well heated. The crib was clean and had a sheet on it…'

The autopsy drew a blank as well. Fillinger, together with Valdes-Dapena, ran every test they could on Mary Lee's corpse, but again neither of them came up with any conclusive results. Eventually they agreed to state the cause of death as 'undetermined', as opposed to the previous autopsy report on Constance Noe, which had said 'undetermined, presumed natural'.

Their most pressing concern, however, was Marie Noe, who was by then pregnant with her eighth child. Desperate to prevent another tragedy occurring, Fillinger offered the Noes free prenatal and antenatal care in return for being allowed to study their new child for genetic faults. The Noes (apparently on the advice of Columbus Gangemi) refused the offer. In the end it was all academic as the eighth child to be born, Theresa, died after only six-and-a-half hours of life. At this point the story of the Noes seems nothing less than a nightmare, a treadmill of births and deaths from which no one could alight. But then the *Life* Magazine article appeared which, far from accusing either of the Noes of foul play, held them up as figures to be pitied. In fact *Life* saved most of its vitriol for the coroner's office. 'In that period,' it said, 'the coroner's office left a good deal to be desired: it boasted not a single microscope, no laboratory to speak of and equipment which the present Health Department now describes as "butcher knives, carpenters' saws and household scissors."' After the article appeared, the whole of America was stunned by the Noes' tragedy. Added to this, infant mortality was soon a nationwide topic, because only a few weeks later the President, John F Kennedy, and the First Lady, Jackie Kennedy, lost their own infant son.

Patrick Bouvier Kennedy was born prematurely on 7 August 1963 (only three months before the President was assassinated in Texas) but died two days later having suffered respiratory problems. In the meantime the autopsy report on Theresa Noe came back with the cause of death put down as 'congenital hemorrhagic diathesis', a blood disorder that no one could have foreseen. That two of the Noe's children (Theresa and Letitia) had died either before they were born or hours afterwards only served to baffle investigators further. There was no clear-cut pattern to the Noe deaths, no clear trajectory that anyone could follow with any degree of certainty.

By 1964 Marie Noe was pregnant with her ninth child to whom she gave birth on 3 December at St Joseph's Hospital. With all the press attention and public scrutiny, no one was going to take any chances with this baby, christened Catherine Ellen. For the first three months of her life, she remained in hospital under strict supervision.

St Joseph's, as its name suggests, was a Catholic hospital and many of the nurses were also nuns, particularly in the paediatric department. One nun, a Sister Victorine, bonded well with baby Catherine and was to have constant access to her throughout her stay. As a result she also came into daily contact with the baby's parents, and her statement to those investigating the Noes makes for very interesting reading. Of them she said, 'Mr Noe always was much more affectionate toward the child than was Mrs Noe, [who] seemed to prefer to remain detached and aloof and dispassionate in her feelings... Mrs Noe would make a pretense [*sic*] of warming up to the baby, as if she felt it was required of her... [and] would utter inane little offerings that would have no bearing on the moment.'[4]

Either Marie's 'non-display' of emotion was a result of having lost eight previous children and therefore she felt too scared to form a strong bond with this, her ninth baby, or, as most people suspected, there wasn't a maternal bone in her body. As if to substantiate this, Sister Victorine also swore that she overheard Mrs Noe threatening to kill baby Catherine when the child wouldn't take to its bottle quickly enough. Ironically, it was during this period that Doctor Gangemi began treating Marie Noe with hypnosis, in the hope that it would instil her with enough patience to bring up Catherine successfully. In early 1965, the baby was then discharged from St Joseph's and for a good few months everything seemed to go well. The summer came and went with no mishaps, but as soon as autumn began Doctor Gangemi began receiving numerous phone calls from a panicked Marie. One in particular caused a great deal of concern, namely that the baby had got hold of a PVC dry-cleaning bag and had almost suffocated. Given that several of Marie's children had died of respiratory failure, Gangemi was naturally furious. Nor did he hide his anger from Mrs Noe, shouting at her to explain how an eight-month-old could get hold of such an item. Marie said she didn't know, but wasn't it fortunate that she'd been on the scene to save her child from suffocating? Gangemi couldn't recall what he said next, but no doubt several expletives were muttered under his breath.

Of course, if SIDS was a relatively under-researched syndrome in the mid-sixties, then Munchausen's Syndrome by Proxy (MSBP) would have sounded like a diagnosis from another planet. In retrospect, however, and with the above incident involving the dry-cleaning bag taken into consideration, it does come closest to explaining what might have been happening within the Noe household. MSBP usually sees a mother claiming that her child is sick or making her child sick in order to garner attention for herself. Famously, in England between 1991-93, Nurse Beverley Allitt (who later become known as the Angel of Death) murdered four children under her care and injured nine others while suffering from MSBP. Fortunately she was caught and is now serving thirteen life sentences in a top-security mental institution, but it took hospital staff over a year before they realized anything was seriously wrong.

But with Marie Noe, although everyone believed something was amiss no one, including the doctors, could put their finger on it and, as Marie Valdes-Dapena pointed out when interviewed by investigative journalist Stephen Fried: 'when an adult suffocates a baby by doing this [Valdes-Dapena placed her own hand over her mouth] the autopsy shows nothing, zero.'[5]

Everyone's hands were tied. Short of taking the child away from its parents, which would have been almost impossible without any evidence, no one could do anything except watch and wait.

Luckily Catherine survived her encounter with the PVC bag, but to be on the safe side the medical staff decided to keep her in hospital for a period of five weeks. During this time Catherine thrived, but only weeks after she had been discharged, she was rushed into hospital again having inexplicably collapsed and gone limp while Marie was holding her. Again the baby was admitted, this time for a period of three weeks. She even celebrated her first birthday in hospital, the

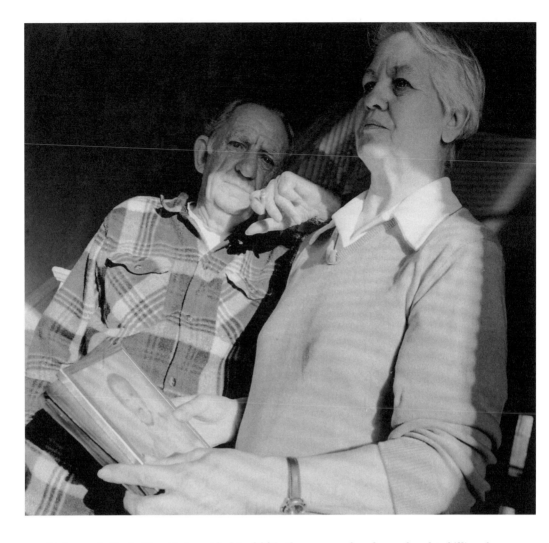

Arthur and Marie Noe, photographed in 2001, three years after she confessed to killing four out of eight of her babies who died. She maintained that she could not remember how the other four had died, but was charged with eight murders. (© DAVID FIELDS/CORBIS SYGMA)

only Noe child to reach the age of one. Catherine was discharged from hospital only to be returned less than two weeks later having suffered yet another turn. Perhaps inevitably, on each occasion Catherine was admitted she never displayed any abnormalities while under the hospital's supervision. Instead she was a normal, bubbly baby to whom all the doctors and nurses displayed enormous affection. Once again her stay at the hospital was a little over three weeks, but this time on her release the Noes purchased an oxygen-delivery system, which everyone thought might alleviate Marie's fears. In some respects they were correct, for ten days later Marie put the machine to good use when she said Catherine had experienced a slight seizure. But on 14 February Marie insisted that Cathy had suffered another attack. This time she rang Doctor Gangemi as well as using the oxygen. He could find nothing wrong with the child, but as a precaution prescribed an anti-seizure drug called Dilantin that could be administered in an emergency. Two weeks later, on 25 February 1966, Marie found Cathy lying on her stomach in her playpen turning blue. Cathy was rushed into another of Philadelphia's hospitals, but didn't survive the journey and was pronounced dead on arrival. A later autopsy concluded that the cause of death was, as it had been on prior occasions,'undetermined'.

This time the police, in the form of Investigator Remington Bristow and the Medical Examiner, Joe McGillen, were on the case within a matter of hours. Together they interviewed Mr and Mrs Noe and though Mrs Noe was somewhat nonplussed at all the fuss being made, her husband put up a worthy defence of his wife and insisted she was not capable of doing anything to harm her children.

However, it wasn't long after these interviews that another twist emerged when an unknown source informed police that the Noes had now begun talking of adopting a child. That such a thought could have crossed the Noes' minds must have horrified many, but it was a course open to them. In the meantime the investigation crawled on, with both Bristow and McGillen digging deeper and deeper into the Noes' private lives. Most of the material they found was nothing out of the ordinary, but every now and then disturbing information would appear.

Doctor Gangemi, who was interviewed several times during this period, provided police with some startling insights. For instance, he said that he looked on Marie as 'an unstable schizophrenic personality who quite possibly is psychotic'.[6] He also pointed out that Marie loved the attention that her babies' deaths had provided and that she felt something of a celebrity. The schizophrenic personality reinforced another extraordinary fact about Marie; for years she had experienced spells of temporary blindness. In the *Philadelphia Magazine* article she confessed that these episodes had started from the time of her first period when she was fourteen years old and they were accompanied by terrible migraines. Then, at the age of twenty, just after the death of her first son, Richard, Marie went blind again. This time she was hospitalized by a doctor, who in turn referred her to a psychiatrist. Both men agreed that her condition was probably 'conversion hysteria' due to having lost a dearly beloved son. The psychiatrist suggested that Marie be treated with a 'truth' drug, sodium amytal, to which she agreed. Under the drug's influence she admitted that she wanted another child but that her husband wasn't so enthusiastic. The psychiatrist and Marie also covered several other topics and would probably have gone on to conduct other 'sodium amytal' sessions, except that the next day Marie regained her sight and discharged herself from the hospital.

Meanwhile, the police, in addition to examining Marie's history of mental instability, were also looking into another possible reason why all of the Noe children had died: insurance. Save for Theresa and Letitia the other babies had all had policies taken out on them for between $100 for the first few children and

$1,000 a child thereafter. The Noes had only experienced difficulty obtaining insurance on one child, namely Catherine, presumably because the company had become suspicious after previous claims for Arthur Junior, Constance and Mary Lee. Despite this, Mr Noe managed to persuade a different insurance firm to cover Catherine for $1,500. Understandably he never mentioned all the previous children of his who had died, but there was also one further discrepancy. On the day that the insurance company salesman stated that he had seen Catherine alive and well in the house she was actually on a hospital ward. When Catherine died, the insurance firm refused to pay out, although later they settled with the Noes for $500.

And as for the idea of adopting a child, as anyone who has ever gone through this process is bound to be aware, it is a long, painfully slow procedure. The Noes were unimpressed. After Catherine died they wanted a child immediately, and when none appeared after five months they complained to the church adoption agency. At the same time, Halbert Fillinger, the Medical Examiner who had performed the autopsy on Catherine, found himself in the bizarre position of being cited as a reference by the Noes on their adoption application form. According to a later statement he said that one of the nuns had rung him up and asked him for his opinion of the couple. He replied that if they gave Marie Noe a child then it would probably end up dead, although if everyone was wrong and Marie was not guilty of killing her offspring then nobody was more deserving than she was.

Neither of these options came to fruition, however, for Marie, to the horror of everyone involved in the case, suddenly announced that she was pregnant again.

Baby number ten was born on 28 July 1967. Christened Arthur Joseph Noe, he was delivered by caesarean section, but during the operation Mrs Noe's womb was ruptured and the medical team had to perform a full hysterectomy. Before the birth, doctors, together with the Medical Examiner, had expressed their concerns over Mrs Noe's ability to care for a child to the Department of Health's 'Maternal and Infant Care Project'. Perhaps the child could be removed from Mrs Noe? Sadly, the reply came back that nothing could be done. As yet there were no laws by which anyone could intervene between a mother and child. Besides, although plenty of people had concerns over Arthur Noe's future, this was the 1960s. As has been mentioned already, child abuse, SIDS and Munchausen Syndrome were not common parlance. There was no proper authority for people to direct their concerns, so the baby would just have to take its own chances and, with this in mind, everyone involved in the case stood back and watched.

For the first two months of his life Arthur (whom the Noes referred to as 'Little Arty') remained in hospital under the supervision of several experienced doctors, including the Noes' own physician. During this time Gangemi noted with some severity that 'the child appears normal in every respect. NEVER has this child displayed any... respiratory embarrassment [as] described by the mother [in] her

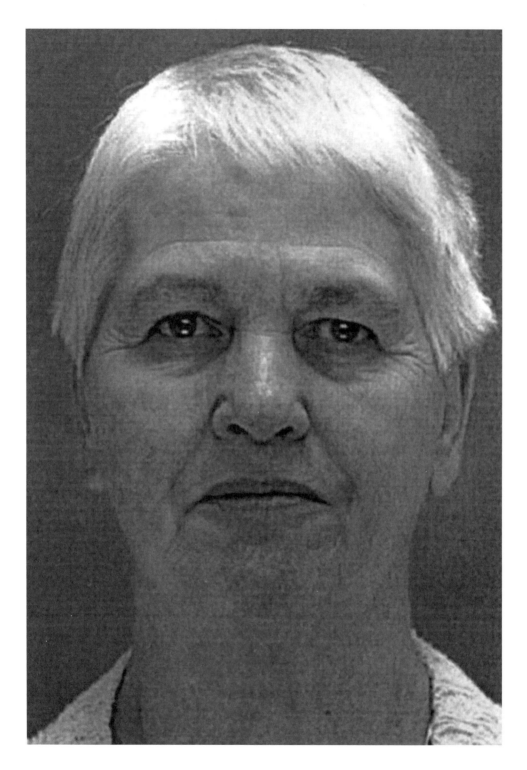

Marie Noe at the time of her arrest in August 1998. She pleaded guilty to all eight counts of second-degree murder, and received a sentence of twenty years' probation, with five years to be spent under psychiatric treatment. In her confession, she said that she had longed for the police to uncover her crimes against her own children. (© POPPERFOTO)

other now-deceased infants.'[7] Arthur Noe then left hospital on 29 September 1967 accompanied by his parents. Gangemi was to write in his discharge notes: 'In God We Trust!'

It took less than thirty days for the baby to return. Initially he was taken to St Christopher's Hospital, having suffered what Marie described as respiratory problems. She said Arthur had turned blue, after which she had given him mouth-to-mouth. Marie then rang Emergency Services who rushed the child to hospital. From St Christopher's Little Arty was transferred to St Joseph's to be under the care of Doctor Gangemi. He was to stay there nineteen days, during which time he was X-rayed and monitored, but nothing could be found wrong. The only oddity during this whole episode was that Marie Noe only visited her child once in nineteen days. Arthur Noe Senior didn't show up at all.

Little Arty was sent home at the end of the nineteen days, but returned five weeks later when, according to Marie, a cat had lain over his face and stopped him from breathing. At this point, the fact that the child was not removed from its mother's care is profoundly disturbing. Everyone must have agreed that something was seriously amiss, yet later that same day the baby was returned home. Twelve days later Little Arty was dead.

According to a statement that Marie later gave to police, she had gone into the baby's room to find him turning blue: 'I immediately lowered the side of the crib and started mouth-to-mouth resuscitation. This did not appear to be doing any good.' She called Emergency Services and tried mouth-to-mouth again, but nothing worked; her baby was pronounced dead on arrival at hospital.

An investigation swung into action almost immediately. Marie and Arthur were questioned, as were friends and neighbours, doctors and other hospital staff. The couple even underwent a polygraph test, which they both passed, although there is some doubt as to its authenticity, given that no one was aware of Marie's previous psychiatric history. The piece of evidence that helped the Noes more than any other came from the Medical Examiner's office. Joseph Spelman, who had conducted the autopsy on baby Arthur, concluded that there was nothing to indicate an unnatural death. However, Spelman did write two letters concerning the Noes: one to the Philadelphia agency which oversaw adoptions and one to a similar state office. Both letters were prompted by Marie Noe saying that she now again wanted to adopt a child or at the very least foster one. The letters (which were identical) didn't say anything outright, but they did imply that Spelman had grave doubts over the Noes and that he did not believe SIDS was the cause of their children's deaths. Nothing could be proved; there was no firm evidence with which to prosecute Marie and so, in 1969, the investigation was finally brought to a close. That might have been the end of the story, were it not for a book published in 1997 called *The Death of Innocents: A True Story of Murder, Medicine and High-Stakes Science*, written by Richard Firstman and Jamie Talan.

In it, the main case under discussion was that of Waneta Hoyt who, from 1964 to 1971, killed five out of her six children. At her trial Hoyt's lawyers defended her, saying that the children had died as a result of a relatively unknown syndrome called SIDS. Consequently she was found innocent of their murders, thus validating the cause of death and leading experts to believe that SIDS could and did run in families.

However, in 1994 Hoyt exploded this theory by confessing to having killed all five babies and in 1995 she was sent to prison for life.

For legal reasons, the Noes weren't mentioned by their real names in *The Death of Innocents*, but a few references were made to their case and in turn this led to Stephen Fried's *Philadelphia Magazine* article, both of which prompted police to reopen the case. Years after the death of her last child, Marie Noe was once again being questioned by police, only this time something extraordinary occurred; she confessed to smothering four out of eight of the children. Of the other four she insisted she had no memory, but police now had enough to arrest the most famous bereaved mother in America, which they did on 5 August 1998.

Some people believed that Marie's confession was dubious, especially given her learning difficulties, while others still thought that there could be a medical explanation as to why all eight children had died, ranging from an inherited blood disorder called mitochondrial DNA disease to peanut allergy. None the less, despite not remembering what happened to four of her children, Marie Noe pleaded guilty to all eight counts of second-degree murder. On 29 June 1999 she was given twenty years' probation with five years to be spent under psychiatric treatment.

The sentence caused outrage; how could someone who had murdered eight babies be given such a light penalty? But Deputy District Attorney Charles Gallagher defended his decision, saying: 'This was the most humane way we could have dealt with Mrs Noe. Rather than spend millions of dollars housing her in prison, we're spending the money on treatment and research. Maybe we'll learn why she did it. Maybe after a series of treatments we'll get to the bottom of it, which is important, very important.'

His words couldn't be truer. SIDS still afflicts thousands of families across the world and unfortunately, in a small number of cases, so does Munchausen Syndrome By Proxy and other equally dangerous psychiatric illnesses.

In her confession to police Marie Noe insisted that her husband knew nothing about what she was doing and that she had longed for the police to discover her crimes. 'I was hoping that they [police] would. I knew what I was doing was very wrong,' she confessed.

ROSE WEST

The House of Horror

**We will always be in love…The most wonderful thing in my
life is that I met you. How our love was special to us. So love,
keep your promises to me. You know what they are.**
LETTER FROM FRED WEST TO ROSEMARY WEST, NOVEMBER 1994

The year was 1969, the end of the 'Swinging Sixties', the beginning of the
harsher Seventies. Drug culture was at its zenith, birth control was widely
available and the Vietnam War was drawing to a close. In the middle of
that year, a young girl called Rosemary Pauline Letts was working at a bakery in
Cheltenham. A nondescript child of fifteen, every day she would take the bus to
and from her home in Bishop's Cleeve. It was on this journey that she first came
to the attention of Frederick West. Twelve years Rosemary's senior, West
immediately made a play for the young school-leaver, later coming into the
bakery and presenting her with a gift of a lace dress and a fur coat. Fred also
asked Rose to go for a drink, an offer she accepted. It was a momentous occasion,
the meeting of two people who would later go on to commit crimes so lurid that
the British tabloid newspapers would feed off the stories for months.

Born on 29 November 1953, Rosemary Letts was one of seven children. At the
time her parents were living in Northam, a small village in North Devon.
Although a gloomy, isolated place, it was also the type of community within which
it might have been ideal to bring up a young family. Sadly, however, Bill and Daisy
Letts were far from ideal parents. At the time of Rose's birth, Daisy Letts was
undergoing electro-convulsive therapy (ECT) for depression at a psychiatric
unit. The most probable cause of her illness was her husband who, it has been
suggested, was a schizophrenic. Bill Letts was a highly unstable character. He was
a bully, a violent man who had to have his own way, and Rose's early years were
marked by the beatings that Bill Letts meted out to his wife and children. As
Andrew Letts, Rose's brother, later recalled:

> **If he felt we were in bed too late, he would throw a bucket of cold
> water over us. He would order us to dig the garden, and that
> meant the whole garden. Then he would inspect it like an army
> officer, and if he was not satisfied, we would have to do it all over
> again. We were not allowed to speak and play like normal children.
> If we were noisy, he would go for us with a belt or a chunk of
> wood. He would beat you black and blue until Mum got in
> between us. Then she would get a good hiding.[1]**

In 1960 the family moved to Plymouth, but barely two years later they had decamped to Chipping Campden, near Stratford-upon-Avon. Not long after that they moved again, only to settle in Bishop's Cleeve. Rose was a teenager by this time, and although she never admitted to being sexually abused by her father, according to various testimonies Bill Letts had begun a sexual relationship with his daughter, one that would continue until his death. As if this wasn't horrific enough, it was during these early years that Rose also became an abuser herself. She had two younger brothers, Graham and Gordon, and at night she would often climb into their beds and masturbate them.

By 1969 Daisy Letts had taken enough beatings from her husband and, along with Rose and her younger children, she left Bill and went to live with her eldest daughter, Glenys, and Glenys's husband, Jim Tyler. Jim was a car mechanic, but he also owned a mobile transport café that was set up in a lay-by on the outskirts of Cheltenham. With Rose due to leave school, the Tylers gave her a job serving tea and snacks from their café. This was an ideal opportunity for Rose. Already sexually precocious, she was now in a situation where she met men all day long. Often Jim Tyler would drop in at the café to make sure everything was running smoothly, only to be confronted by a dishevelled Rose, alighting from a lorry. It was also at around this time that Rose claimed she was, on two separate occasions, raped by different men. The first rape occurred when she was sixteen. Rose had been picked up by a man after a party, and instead of driving her home, he'd taken her to a local golf course where he'd assaulted her, although Rose never reported the incident to the police.

The second rape happened in 1969, approximately five months after the first. Rose had left work for the day and was standing at her bus stop when a man began chatting her up. Rose wasn't interested, but the man wouldn't take any notice and she began to feel so frightened that instead of waiting at the bus stop she ran into a nearby park. The man followed her and raped her, but, as with the first rape, Rose never reported it to the police. A few months later Rose Letts met Fred West.

At the time, Fred was still married to a woman called Catherine Costello (better known as Rena) although they were separated. Rena, who worked as a prostitute, was living in Glasgow, while Fred had set up home near Cheltenham. The couple had two children, Anne Marie, aged five (who was Fred's child) and Charmaine, aged six (who was Rena's child by another man). Fred had taken the girls away from their mother and set himself up on a caravan site. During the day he worked as a driver for an abattoir. Throughout his life Fred was to have a series of low-paid, unskilled jobs. He was a lorry driver for a timber company, a milk-delivery man for Model Dairies, a fibreglass-presser at Permali's factory, a machine operator at Gloucester Wagon Works, an odd-job man and part-time builder. It was a shambolic existence: a life lived without structure. Neither the hours Fred worked nor the Lakehouse caravan park made for an ideal situation in which to bring up the children but Fred, being an opportunist, turned it to his advantage. He soon realized that the two little girls provided the perfect excuse to lure young women into his life by offering them work as untrained nannies. More often than not the girls then ended up sleeping with him. Also, to add to this backwoods scenario, it was during this time that Fred committed his first murder. Ann McFall was a friend of Rena Costello's, but when Fred and Rena went their separate ways, Ann decided to stay on with Fred in the caravan and soon began a relationship with him. It wasn't long before she fell pregnant, but when the foetus was eight months old something untoward occurred. Fred was to tell people he loved Ann McFall so it is not beyond reason that her death might have been an accident, the result of some sado-masochistic sex session. Whatever the case, Fred murdered the mother of his second child and later buried her body in a field near to his childhood home of Much Marcle.

This, then, was the set-up when Frederick West entered Rose Letts's life: a union that was to lead to her becoming one of the most prolific female serial killers in British legal history.

After Fred had taken Rose out for a drink, he invited her back to his caravan and Rose, wanting to impress him, immediately made a fuss of the children. This was a pattern that was to repeat itself over the following few weeks until Rose finally gave up her job at the bakery and went to work full-time at the caravan. No more than a child herself, she was now keeping Fred's home, looking after his children and no doubt sleeping with her new boss. But all hell broke loose when Rose's father, on discovering his daughter's new relationship, tried to put a stop to it by placing her into the hands of Social Services. She was sent to live in a home for troubled teenagers and was specifically told not to get in touch with her boyfriend. Rose, however, being a headstrong, wilful girl, ignored the rules and not only wrote him letters but arranged to meet him whenever she could. No one was going to stand in her way and, on leaving the home, aged sixteen, she immediately she fell pregnant with Fred's child. At this time her parents had reunited, but the family home was far from peaceful. When she told her parents about the pregnancy her father booked her into an abortion clinic. Determined not to allow him to spoil her chances with her boyfriend, Rose ran away with Fred and within days of leaving her parents she had set up home with him in a bedsit at 9 Clarence Road in Cheltenham. From there the couple moved to a flat at 25 Midland Road in Gloucester, and on 17 October 1970 Rose gave birth to the first of her children, a girl whom they named Heather.

Disaster was soon to strike, however, because on 4 December 1970 Fred was given a nine-month prison sentence for the theft of some tyres. Suddenly Rose was left to bring up three children by herself. Barely seventeen years old, living in less than salubrious conditions and with little or no money, it cannot have been easy. Rose began to beat Anne Marie and Charmaine. One day a young friend of Charmaine's popped in to visit her playmate, only to find her standing

Fred and Rose West moved to 25 Cromwell Street, Gloucester, not long after their marriage in January 1972. By then Fred West had already murdered Ann McFall, as well as his first wife, Rena, and her daughter by another man, Charmaine, burying their bodies in fields near his childhood home . (PA PHOTOS)

on a chair with her hands tied behind her back while Rose stood ready to hit her with a wooden spoon. In addition, according to Anne Marie's later testimonials, Rose often left the two girls tied to their beds for hours at a time without access to a toilet and with no food or water. Heather, thankfully, fared much better. She was still only a baby, and it has been noted that Rose was a good mother when her children were small and dependent upon her for their every need. It was only when they grew a little older and developed strong characters and wills of their own that she would turn on them and treat them like dirt.

On Fred's release from prison the couple united in their mistreatment of the children, but the beatings and the daily humiliations the two older girls suffered were nothing in comparison to what occurred next.

Charmaine had never been a favourite of Fred's. Fathered by another man, looking as different as she could from her stepfather and stepsister, she was always on the wrong side of Fred's temper. Then, in August 1971, Rena suddenly turned up wanting to take her children with her to Scotland. By her own account, Anne Marie was now told that Charmaine had gone back to Scotland with her mother. The same information was given to the school that Charmaine attended. Indeed, whenever anyone inquired after the child, that was the story they were given. The reality, however, was that both Charmaine and her mother Rena had been killed at some time near the end of August 1971. Their bodies were buried in the next field over from that in which Ann McFall had been interred and, although Rose was never charged in connection with their murders, a question mark still hovers over whether she was party to their killings.

In January 1972 Fred West married Rose Letts and shortly afterwards Rose gave birth to her second daughter, May. By November of that same year she was pregnant again with her third child. In total, Rose gave birth to four children by Fred (Heather, May, Stephen and Barry) as well as four children by different men (all of whom Fred accepted as his own, calling them his and Rose's 'love children'). And yet, though Fred's libido was obviously high, the truth of the matter was that when it came to sex, he preferred to be a spectator, especially where his wife was involved. Much given to pornographic magazines and to boasting to others of his sexual prowess, Fred also harboured an almost fetishistic attitude towards his work tools. Every surface of any home he lived in was always cluttered with spanners, screwdrivers, car jacks and pliers. He would constantly boast to friends how he could 'fix' women, make them more sexually active and provide them with home-made abortions. During his early relationship with Rose he had made it clear to her that he was interested in every detail of her sex life. After they were married this interest translated into Fred wanting to view Rose having sex with black men because they were genitally bigger than white men. In later interviews with the police Fred was to say that:

> **Rose didn't want the gentle part of it. She wanted some big
> nigger to throw her down and fucking bang on top of her, and**

**treat her like a dog... 'I don't want none of that soppy shit.'
she said. 'I want fucking, not fucking about with...' I'd come
home from work and she'd sit deliberately on the edge of the
settee with her legs wide open and say 'Look at that... I bet
you wish you had something that could fill that.'[2]**

In September 1972, the couple moved to 25 Cromwell Street, an address that was
later to become as synonymous with evil as 10 Rillington Place.

To begin with Fred rented the house from its owner, Frank Sygmunt, an
elderly Polish gentleman who later sold the premises to Fred at a very reasonable
price. Fred worked night and day dividing the house into bedsits which he and
Rose then rented out to a series of lodgers. Just as the caravan site had housed
misfits and drifters, so 25 Cromwell Street soon filled up with similar characters.
Fred, eager to encourage an 'anything goes' atmosphere, made it clear to all his
lodgers that he was liberal-minded enough to allow drugs on his premises. He
also encouraged his lodgers to talk about their sex lives, and there is firm
evidence that he drilled holes into most of the bedroom walls so that he and Rose
could spy on their tenants. In addition to this he removed all the locks not just
from the bedroom doors, but also from the bathroom doors. According to
various statements later given to the police, he and Rose would often burst in
while their lodgers were taking their baths.

It was also during these early days at 25 Cromwell Street that Rose slept with
several of the house's occupants, and presumably Fred watched the proceedings.
Sex was very much at the forefront of their lives, a vital component in their
emotional make-up, and nothing illustrates this more clearly than what
happened during the summer of 1972 when Fred began converting the cellar of
their house into separate rooms. Ostensibly one of these rooms was to be an area
for the children to use, but at some point it became the scene for the torture and
rape of Anne Marie West.

One day, while Anne Marie was playing upstairs, Fred ordered her down into
the cellar. She recalls that she was very uneasy about this; there was something in
the tone of his voice, something in the way her stepmother looked at her. None
the less, she didn't disobey her father. She went down into the cellar, only to
discover what looked like a large metal frame lying in the centre of the room.
What occurred next makes for very uncomfortable reading. Anne Marie was
stripped naked, tied to the frame, beaten and raped by her father while Rose
looked on. When Fred had finished, Rose assaulted the child with a vibrator.
Later Fred was to explain that it was a father's duty to introduce his daughter to
sex and to break her virginity. Anne Marie should be thankful that he was so
caring. 'I made you,' he would, according to her account, tell her. 'You are my
flesh and blood. I am entitled to touch you.'[3]

On several occasions after this, Anne Marie (or sometimes one of the other children) ended up in Accident & Emergency at a local hospital with various scratches, bruises and cuts, but the authorities failed to take action, always believing the stories Rose fed them. Then, in October 1972, Caroline Raine (later Caroline Roberts) moved in to 25 Cromwell Street, taking on the position of live-in nanny.

Fred and Rose had picked Caroline up one night while she was hitching a lift back home after an evening out with her boyfriend. The couple appeared friendly and during the journey Fred had mentioned that he and his wife required someone to take care of their children. A few days later Caroline moved in with the Wests. Only seventeen years old herself, she got on well with Anne Marie and Heather, but early on felt very uncomfortable in Rose's presence because Rose kept bursting in on her while she was taking her baths and touching her inappropriately. She also became highly suspicious of Fred due to a conversation they had when Fred told her that Anne Marie was no longer a virgin. According to Caroline, when Fred saw the look of horror on her face he changed his story, saying that she'd had an accident on her bicycle and that was how her hymen had broken.

Eventually Caroline left the Wests' employment, but on 6 December 1972, while again hitching back to her parents' house, Fred and Rose stopped to pick the teenager up. The chances of them being out on two occasions when Caroline was hitchhiking cannot be ignored; it seems the Wests often drove around at night looking for victims and, though slightly embarrassed that she had walked out on her employers, Caroline none the less got into their car. Immediately Rose changed seats and climbed into the back. As soon as Fred started driving, Rose began touching the teenager, trying to kiss her and stroke her legs. Caroline struggled but she was no match for her two assailants. Rose held her down and when Fred had a chance he turned around and punched Caroline so hard that he knocked her out. At that point Caroline was bound hand and foot and driven back to Cromwell Street, where Fred locked her in his bedroom.

Caroline was stripped naked and had sticky tape wrapped round her face (something which the police later discovered was a trademark of Fred's). She was then tied to the bed where Fred West beat her vaginally with the buckle end of a belt. Afterwards she can remember Rose West sexually assaulting her and Fred explaining that his wife had always had very strong lesbian urges when she was pregnant. Later that night Fred raped her and Caroline remembers that she fully expected to die, but by next morning the Wests appeared to have calmed down, to such an extent that they began asking Caroline if she would like to come back and resume her position as live-in nanny. It is testimony to the attitude of both Fred and Rose West towards their victim that such a suggestion could even be raised. Neither can Fred have seen Caroline as anything other than an insensate object, something to which he could do whatever he liked. Acting to save her life, Caroline went along with the Wests' suggestion and it was only a few days afterwards that she finally escaped Cromwell Street and went straight round to her mother's house. On seeing the state her daughter was in, Mrs Raine contacted the police.

The Caroline Raine case was heard on 12 January 1973. By rights, Fred West should have been charged with rape and Rose West with sexual assault, but when it came to the crunch both were charged only with the latter offence. The Wests' solicitor then managed to downplay the abduction and explained away the sexual assault as a consensual threesome that had gone slightly awry. It was a harmless bit of fun, he said, and sadly the court agreed. Fred and Rose were ordered to pay a £100 fine and, as far as the courts were concerned, that was the end of the matter. But if Fred and Rose West had learnt any lesson from being arrested then it was this: that they shouldn't allow any future participants in their sex games to go free. Next time they would have to be twice as thorough, twice as ruthless.

Lynda Gough was seventeen years old when she disappeared. She had started visiting 25 Cromwell Street some time in 1973 and it was during this period that she babysat for the Wests and had relationships with two of their numerous lodgers. When she went missing it was a mystery to everyone who knew her, but in particular to her parents, who began their search at the Wests' house. Lynda's mother went round to 25 Cromwell Street and asked Rose if she had seen her daughter, but Rose denied all knowledge that such a person existed. It wasn't until Mrs Gough noticed that Rose was wearing Lynda's slippers and that some of her daughter's clothes were hanging up on the washing line that Rose regained her memory. She said that she did recall someone answering to that description but that the girl had left to go to Weston-super-Mare. Lynda's parents then tried to track their daughter down in that town, but nothing came of their search and, although unsettled by the whole business, they never reported the incident to the police.

When Fred had killed Ann McFall, Rena Costello and her daughter Charmaine, he had disposed of their bodies in open countryside, but from the murder of Lynda Gough onwards, he changed locations and decided to bury all further victims in and around 25 Cromwell Street. With this in mind, Lynda Gough's body was dismembered (as were all of Fred and Rose's victims) and the body parts stuffed underneath the ground floor bathroom.

Fred continued to work on the house, demolishing the garage, building a new bathroom and laying concrete floors. The house was his pride and joy, a place he slaved over during the whole twenty-odd years that he and Rose lived there, most of the materials being odds and ends that he stole from various building sites. There wasn't an inch of the house that he hadn't adjusted, but there was one room that soon became Rose's alone: a room that was set aside for her flourishing prostitution business. It had its own doorbell so that when her clients called round they didn't disturb the rest of the household. Advertisements

Frederick West surrounded by children at a New Year gathering in January 1970; his girlfriend, the then Rose Letts, is at the back at far left. West killed himself in prison while awaiting trial on multiple counts of murder and sexual offences, thereby cheating justice. (© MATTHEW POLAK/CORBIS SYGMA)

appeared in the local newspapers. Of course Fred was in on the act, watching and listening to everything that went on. After each session he insisted Rose keep a record of how big her client's genitals were and how they scored out of ten. If he wasn't methodical about anything else, then Fred was insistent on keeping precise details of each and every one of Rose's sexual encounters.

In November 1973, only a few months after the birth of their third child, Stephen West, a fifteen-year-old local girl called Carol Cooper disappeared. She was last seen waiting for a bus that would have taken her to her grandmother's house. Carol had lived in care for quite some time and was in search of any kind of affection. When the Wests drove up in their car and offered her a lift, she no doubt saw nothing to be afraid of; here were two people willing to go out of their way to help a young girl.

One month later, in December 1973, the couple abducted another young woman. Lucy Partington was a twenty-one-year-old, third-year student of medieval history and English at Exeter University. She was also the niece of the novelist Kingsley Amis. Lucy had been visiting a disabled friend in Cheltenham and had been waiting at a bus stop when she disappeared. The most likely explanation is that Fred and Rose drove past and offered her a lift, or that they forced her into the car. Either way she ended up at 25 Cromwell Street. Almost twenty years later it has been speculated that she was kept alive in the cellar for up to a week, because seven days after her disappearance Fred West attended Casualty with a severe wound to his hand which in all likelihood was the result of his dismembering her body.

During all this time Anne Marie West was also suffering further abuse and

A police photograph of Rose West issued after she had been imprisoned for life on ten counts of murder, including the killing of one of her own daughters, in November 1995. She maintained her innocence to the last, and in October 2000 made a formal application to have her conviction reviewed by the Criminal Cases Review Commission (© PA PHOTOS)

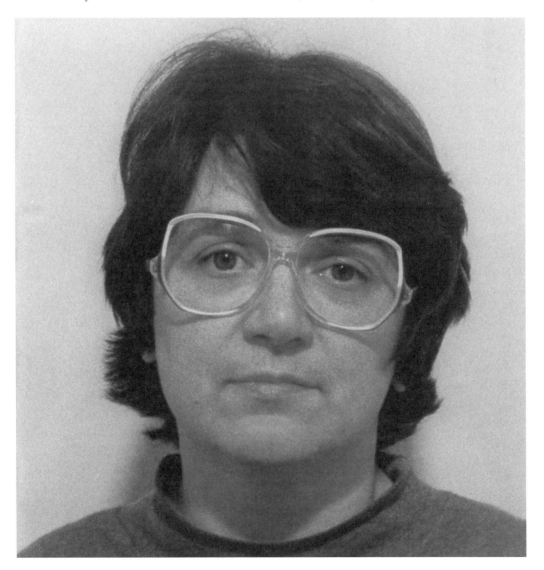

humiliation at the hands of her father and stepmother. On one occasion she was ordered to strip off and the younger children were then allowed to cover her body in finger paint. Afterwards Rose joined in, forcing Anne Marie down on all fours and writing the words 'BLACK HOLE' on her back with an arrow pointing towards her anus. Anne Marie was made to stay like that all day until Fred returned home. Everyone found it very amusing, but one can scarcely imagine how humiliating this episode must have been for the child herself.

In addition, Fred and Rose also introduced Anne Marie to prostitution, forcing her to have sex with several of Rose's 'black men', as well as being raped by Fred. It has also been suggested that she was abused on more than one occasion by Rose's father, Bill Letts, who was now a regular visitor to the house.

In April 1974 a fourth young woman disappeared off the streets of Cheltenham, this time a Swiss girl called Thérèse Siegenthaler. She was twenty-one years old, a student of sociology studying in London, hitchhiking to Wales at the time. Her body was found years later buried adjacent to that of Lucy Partington under the cellar floor at 25 Cromwell Street and, as with all the previous victims, her corpse had been dismembered and a certain number of small bones were missing.

Thereafter, in short succession, two further murders were committed. Shirley Hubbard, aged fifteen, disappeared in November 1974 and Juanita Mott, aged eighteen, disappeared in April 1975, after which there was a break in the killings. Instead Fred began hanging round a place called Jordan's Brook House, which was a home for delinquent teenage girls. He would befriend the girls and then invite them back to Cromwell Street to hang out with him and Rose. In particular he asked one young girl (in court she was only referred to as Miss A) to stay at Cromwell Street after she ran away from Jordan's Brook. According to her later testimony it was here that Rose involved her in an orgy and also where she was raped several times. Afterwards Miss A was allowed to wash herself and go back to Jordan's Brook, but she was so traumatized that she didn't report the incident to the police. It was only years later, after Fred and Rose had been arrested, that she finally came forward.

Early in 1977 Fred West set his sights on yet another young woman, Shirley Robinson. He had met Shirley in a café and later asked her if she'd like to be one of his lodgers. Shirley moved in to 25 Cromwell Street in late April 1977. At first the three of them – Fred, Rose and the new lodger – got on very well. Shirley helped out around the house and did some babysitting, but at some point the relationship turned sexual. Fred and Rose began a threesome with their young guest and it was only a matter of time before Shirley fell pregnant with Fred's child. Inevitably Rose grew jealous and Fred was then heard to say that Shirley would 'have to go'. Of course everyone thought he meant that Shirley would have to leave the house, but in retrospect it is easy to see that he had something else in mind.

A note from Fred West, dated 4 March 1994 while he was in prison awaiting trial, to Detective Chief Superintendent John Bennett, who headed the investigation into the murders and whose police teams uncovered the grisly evidence buried at 25 Cromwell Street, Gloucester. In the note, West admits to the killings for which his wife was subsequently found guilty. (© PA PHOTOS)

Shirley Robinson disappeared in May 1978. As with every other victim of the Wests, when her body was discovered it had been dismembered. But there were even more gruesome revelations when it was also discovered that the eight-month-old foetus had been cut out of its mother's womb and buried near by.

Rose West gave birth to her first mixed-race child (Tara West) in December 1978 and two months later she was pregnant again with Louise West. It was during this second pregnancy that Fred began working as an odd-job man at Jordan's Brook and, having already met and abused Miss A, he then struck up a relationship with a seventeen-year-old girl called Alison Chambers. Fred invited Alison to live at 25 Cromwell Street where a threesome was started once again, but by September 1979 Alison was dead and her body dismembered and disposed of in the back garden.

Heather West appears to be Fred and Rose's last victim, though she was by no means the last person that they abused. At fourteen years old she was a quiet, withdrawn child who had made few friends at school. Desperate to leave the family home, she applied for a job at a holiday camp, but was rejected. Inconsolable, Heather moped around the house for weeks until one day she mysteriously disappeared. Fred and Rose insisted that their daughter had gone to Wales and even pretended that she had phoned home to say that she was happy and well. But in reality Fred, and possibly Rose, had strangled their daughter, cut and twisted her head off, sliced the rest of her body into small pieces and later buried the remains in a hole in the back garden, not far from where they had concealed Alison Chambers.

After Heather's death, Fred began doing some odd jobs on one of his neighbour's houses, a woman called Kathryn Halliday. She soon revealed that she was bisexual and it wasn't long before Fred and Rose began a threesome with their new acquaintance. However, Kathryn found that Rose was increasingly violent: 'Rose West wanted me to do things to her which were very, very aggressive... She wanted orgasms all the time, like a machine.'[4] As a result, Kathryn decided to move out of the area. Thereafter, things seemed to calm down. Rose continued her work as a prostitute and Fred began making pornographic films, using his wife as a model. In fact, it wasn't until the summer of 1992 that anything untoward was suspected about the Wests' conduct. One day Fred abducted a young child and both raped and sodomized her while filming the incident. Afterwards the child, who was deeply traumatized, told a friend what had happened and the friend told the police.

Immediately the five surviving West children were placed in care. On being questioned Stephen West said he had not been abused (either emotionally or physically), but Anne Marie was more forthcoming (although later she retracted her statement). But the damage was done. Fred was incarcerated pending the court case for rape and Rose was left at home to fend for herself. It was during this separation that questions started being asked as to the whereabouts of Heather. It had long been a family joke that Heather was buried under the patio, though of course none of the children believed this, but when no trace of Heather could be found and further questions were raised concerning the whereabouts of Rena Costello and Charmaine, the police began a thorough search of 25 Cromwell Street.

The rest, as they say, is history. In all, twelve bodies were exhumed from number 25, while Ann McFall, her unborn child, Rena, and Charmaine Costello, were discovered near Much Marcle.

On being questioned, Fred tried to protect his wife, saying over and over again that she had no knowledge of the murders. In contrast, Rose remained silent. The only time she showed any real reaction is when she was informed of the murder of her daughter, Heather. Due to this, some people have speculated that she wasn't involved in her daughter's murder, although it is hard to countenance this, because if she knew and was involved in the other murders then it is more than likely that she was involved in this final, heinous act.

On 30 June 1994 both Fred and Rosemary West were formally charged and a date was set for their trial. Standing together in the dock Fred tried to touch Rose on the shoulder, but she shied away from him, evidently trying to dissociate herself from him completely. However, Fred still attempted to keep in touch with his wife, mainly through the letters he wrote to his children in which he would ask after their mother. Finally he wrote a short note to Rose on New Year's Day, 1995. 'All I have is my life,' he said. 'I will give it to you, my darling.' Fred West committed suicide a few hours later by hanging himself with a makeshift rope, which he tied to bars in his prison cell.

Rose West's trial opened on 3 October 1995 at Winchester Crown Court. Of the witnesses, none were more damning than Caroline Raine and Fred West's own daughter, Anne Marie, who portrayed Rose as a callous, sadistic woman who would stop at nothing to achieve sexual gratification. Rose, on the other hand, tried to convince the jury that she was a timid woman, a woman totally under the influence of her husband: a victim herself. But on taking the stand – a move her own counsel advised against – Rose became her own worst enemy as she laughed, grew angry, made a series of bad jokes and on more than one occasion criticized one or other of the dead girls.

After a six-week trial, Rose West was convicted of participating in ten murders and the judge recommended that she never be allowed out of prison. Today she is incarcerated in Durham Gaol, and in a move reminiscent of the Myra Hindley case, consecutive Home Secretaries have intimated that she will never be released.

On 7 October 1996, 25 Cromwell Street, which had been dubbed the 'House of Horror' by the tabloid press, was demolished. Every brick and piece of concrete was taken away and reduced to dust, and everything that was flammable was sent to RAF Innsworth where it was disposed of in an incinerator.

GRACE MARKS

A Teenage Temptress

I sat before my glass one day,
And conjured up a vision bare,
Unlike the aspects glad and gay,
That erst were found reflected there –
The vision of a woman, wild
With more than womanly despair.
MARY ELIZABETH COLERIDGE,
'THE OTHER SIDE OF THE MIRROR', 1908

In 1853 the author Susanna Moodie wrote a book entitled *Life in the Clearings versus the Bush,* in which she devoted a chapter to a prison visit where she made the acquaintance of Canada's most notorious murderess. Over a century later this prisoner also became the subject of a novel by Canada's foremost author, Margaret Atwood. The novel was entitled *Alias Grace* and the prisoner in question was a young woman by the name of Miss Marks. Only sixteen years old at the time of the murders, Grace Marks's story held the Victorian public in thrall, combining as it did a heady mix of sex and violence woven together with that most wicked of sins: a servant's insubordination.

> [Grace Marks] is a middle-sized woman, with a slight graceful figure. There is an air of hopeless melancholy in her face which is very painful to contemplate. Her complexion is fair, and must, before the touch of hopeless sorrow paled it, have been very brilliant. Her eyes are a bright blue, her hair auburn, and her face would be rather handsome were it not for the long curved chin, which gives, as it always does to most persons who have this facial defect, a cunning, cruel expression.[1]

So wrote Susanna Moodie after her first visit to Kingston Provincial Penitentiary. Moodie had gone there, accompanied by her husband, in order to research prison conditions for a sequel to her first book, *Roughing it in the Bush,* which had been a rather dismal account of pioneering life in Upper Canada.[2] *Life in the Clearings versus the Bush* was intended as a study of the more civilized western side of Canada, and with this in mind, Moodie made it her duty to visit several official establishments.

Kingston Provincial Penitentiary had opened in June 1835 under the reign of King William IV, so it was a relatively new building when Grace Marks first appeared within its walls. Although it housed some of Canada's most evil male convicts, Marks swiftly became its most famous inmate. Referred to by Moodie as that 'celebrated murderess', the author went on to describe the crimes for which Marks had been tried and subsequently convicted.

The story began at Richmond Hill, Upper Canada, when, at the beginning of July 1843, a gentleman by the name of Thomas Kinnear[3] hired a young Irish emigrant, Grace Marks, as a 'servant of all work'. Marks was the daughter of a stonemason and, according to a testimony which later appeared in the Toronto-based *Star Transcript & General Advertiser*, in 1843 Grace Marks had, 'four sisters and four brothers, one sister and one brother older than I am.' Coming from such a large family it was of great importance that she should leave home and earn a living of her own as soon as she could manage. Grace therefore began work as a servant at the age of thirteen, which meant that by the time she was employed by Thomas Kinnear (for a paltry $3 a month) she had already had several years experience of being in service. No doubt she was certain she knew it all. Perhaps she thought that being an old hand at the job she wouldn't be obliged to do all the menial tasks alone. But Grace hadn't counted on Thomas Kinnear's other servant, a woman by the name of Nancy Montgomery.[4]

Before Grace's arrival, Nancy had done all the hard graft herself, but as soon as Grace appeared on the scene, all that stopped. Nancy Montgomery, who was having an illicit affair with her employer, wanted nothing more than to fashion herself as mistress of the house. In short, Grace had to wait upon Nancy hand and foot, and she was also required to do all the undesirable jobs, which in those days was no small order. Maids of all work were expected to sweep, dust, polish, scrub, fetch and carry from dawn until dusk, and so from the outset of her employment within Thomas Kinnear's house there was no love lost between Grace and Nancy Montgomery.

Sadly, little is known about Thomas Kinnear except that he originated from a family who lived near Fife in Scotland and that, according to Robert Stamp in his book *Early Days in Richmond Hill*, he was a 'gentleman farmer' who lived a very comfortable life thirty miles outside of Toronto. This information is also backed up by a 1997 interview given by Margaret Atwood to David Wiley, in which she speculated that Kinnear was probably 'a gentleman in easy circumstances...a remittance man.[5] Younger son, doubtless sent to the Colonies because of his soft and loose ways by the older who has inherited the property and who wishes to cut a respectable figure.'

However, if little is known about Thomas Kinnear then even less is known about the fourth player in the drama: James McDermott. Hired as Kinnear's manservant, with duties that included maintaining the livery, he had started out life in Ireland, where as a wild, reckless teenager he had served for a short time as a soldier in the army. But not being the kind of boy who enjoyed taking orders, this career didn't last long and McDermott deserted his post, deciding instead to emigrate to Canada. According to his confession (which McDermott later gave to a Mr George

Walton while he was in jail), on arrival in his newly adopted country he enlisted into the 1st Provincial Regiment of the Province of Lower Canada and then moved regiments once more, enrolling in the Glengarry Light Infantry Company. However, after he had been discharged from this latter post he travelled to Toronto where he secured a job on Kinnear's farm. Of course McDermott's new employer knew very little about his new servant's background, only that he was Irish: something he was to have in common with Kinnear's next employee, Grace Marks. It all boded so well. But within three weeks of Grace Marks joining the household, two of its members were dead and McDermott, who was said to have been only twenty years old at the time of the murders, was swinging from the end of a rope.

Interestingly, in light of the fact that he was not the most reliable of men, it is through James McDermott's eyes that Susanna Moodie chose to tell the whole sorry tale, for although she didn't interview him personally, McDermott gave his lawyer – a man by the name of Kenneth McKenzie – a full and frank account of how the murders occurred. This version of events was afterwards related by McKenzie to Moodie, although it is by no means accurate as Moodie often added or invented material to suit her own purposes. (Indeed very few facts in this case are corroborated by more than one source, making it almost impossible to state with absolute certainty what is truth and what is mere speculation.) None the less, Moodie's account begins with McDermott saying that, 'Grace was very jealous of the difference made between her and the housekeeper, whom she hated, and to whom she was often very insolent and saucy.'[6] The animosity between the two women was so bitter that McDermott insists Grace talked of little else. 'Every little complaint Nancy made to Grace was repeated to me with cruel exaggerations till my dander was up, and I began to regard the unfortunate woman as our common enemy.'[7] On top of this McDermott further accused Grace of trying to poison Nancy and Kinnear by lacing their porridge with a noxious substance. (However this accusation was made on 20 November 1853, i.e. several weeks after McDermott had been sentenced to death, so one can only conclude he was lashing out at Grace in the unlikely hope that he might still save his own skin.)

The tension in the house was palpable, and while Nancy was carrying on with Thomas Kinnear, Grace began flirting with James McDermott. At least, this is how Moodie portrays the scene, all the while painting Grace as a femme fatale. This is a common enough stereotype during the 1840s and 1850s, although one can't help but feel that this description had more to do with Moodie's wish to make her story more scintillating. After all, what could be better or more salacious than a sixteen-year-old girl enticing a young man into committing two horrendous, despicable crimes. Of course, Grace herself had a different version of events to relate, for according to her confession (given to the same Mr George Walton to whom McDermott had spoken) McDermott had already formulated a plan to kill both Montgomery and Kinnear even before Grace showed up at the house. His motivation appears to have been Montgomery's threat to have him sacked: '...the housekeeper several times scolding McDermott for not doing his work properly, she gave him a fortnight's warning, that when his month was up he was to leave… About a week after this, McDermott told me [Grace Marks] if I would keep it a secret he would tell me what he was going to do with Kinnear and Nancy.'[8]

Undoubtedly, the truth of the matter lies somewhere between the two versions, but whatever the case, on 28 July 1843, Thomas Kinnear announced that he was riding in to Toronto to do some business with his bank, and that he would be away overnight. After his departure Nancy went out to visit some neighbourhood acquaintances, while Marks and McDermott remained alone at the farm. 'This was an opportunity too good to be lost,' Moodie has McDermott say, 'and, instead of minding our work, we got recapitulating our fancied wrongs over some of the captain's whisky.' The author then launches into a bitter tirade against Grace Marks, implying that she was a she-devil who, without the slightest prick of conscience, enticed McDermott down a path of evil. Of course, if nothing else, this again illustrates the extremely ambiguous attitude held towards women during the Victorian era. Women were godly creatures, so weak and feeble, both physically and mentally, that they could never be involved in crimes of such an evil nature. But if every cloud has a silver lining, the opposite can also be observed; running counter to this rose-tinted view, it was commonly believed that under certain circumstances women could be twice as evil as men, wicked temptresses with unnatural powers. That Moodie chose the latter option was most likely for dramatic purposes because, as previously mentioned above, a sixteen-year-old siren makes for better copy than a naïve, sulky, adolescent girl duped into doing something she didn't quite understand. So, according to Moodie, Grace Marks wormed her way into McDermott's affections and, bit by bit, persuaded him that Nancy was nothing if not evil.

> **'Dear me,' said I [McDermott], half in jest, 'if you hate her so much as all that, say but the word, and I will soon rid you of her for ever.'**
>
> **I had not the least idea that she would take me at my word. Her eyes flashed with a horrible light. 'You dare not do it!' she replied, with a scornful toss of her head.**
>
> **'Dare not do what?'**
>
> **'Kill that woman for me!' she whispered.**
>
> **'You don't know what I dare, or what I dar'nt do!' said I, drawing a little back from her. 'If you will promise to run off with me afterwards, I will see what I can do with her.'**
>
> **'I'll do anything you like, but you must first kill her.'**
>
> **'You are not in earnest, Grace?'**
>
> **'I mean what I say!'[9]**

The two servants subsequently set about planning the murder. Grace describes to McDermott how, although Nancy Montgomery was supposed to sleep in a bed with her, on some nights she would be absent, implying that Nancy shared Thomas Kinnear's bed. According to Margaret Atwood's research, Nancy had given birth to an illegitimate child before being employed by Kinnear. At the time of her autopsy she was discovered to be pregnant a second time. All this, according to Moodie, compounded an already bleak situation and, with sexual tensions running high, Marks and McDermott settled on a plan to bludgeon Nancy Montgomery to death while she slept. This course of action is also backed up by a brief account of the murders, which appears in a text entitled *The Lives of the Judges of Upper Canada and Ontario*, which explained 'Mr Blake was the Crown Prosecutor in the case of the Queen v McDermott and Grace Marks, in 1843, for the murder of Thomas Kinnear... These two, McDermott and Marks, became jealous of the position Nancy Montgomery had, and determined to get her out of the way.'[10]

Finally Nancy returned home and the three servants spent a pleasant evening together. According to Grace Marks in her confession, a man by the name of James Walsh came over from his cottage, which stood on the same farm as Kinnear's house, and played the flute while the two women danced round the kitchen. Then at 10 o'clock or thereabouts, everyone retired to bed.

With Kinnear in Toronto, Nancy opted to sleep with Grace, and accordingly the two women retired upstairs leaving McDermott behind in the kitchen with nothing to do but wait until his victim was asleep. This he did, all the while nursing an axe in his hand but, in Moodie's view, he was torn between carrying out the crime or abandoning it. His main motivation for the former appeared to be that if he didn't act then Grace Marks would tease him mercilessly. However, according to Marks's *Star Transcript & General Advertiser* testimony, she claimed 'I entreated him not to do so that night, as he might hit me instead of her. He said, "Damn her; I'll kill her then, first thing in the morning."'

The night came and went without further incident, but on the following day the three servants rose, and depending upon which version of events is believed, Grace either taunted McDermott into murdering Montgomery or the two of them colluded in the crime. Either way, at some point on 29 July 1843, Nancy was killed. 'I found her at the sink in the kitchen, washing her face in a tin basin. I had the fatal axe in my hand, and without pausing for an instant to change my mind – for had I stopped to think, she would have been living to this day – I struck her a heavy blow on the back of the head with my axe. She fell to the ground at my feet without uttering a word.'[11]

Nancy's body was then dragged down into the wine cellar where, according to Moodie, she recovered enough to try and stand on her feet, and attempt to escape. McDermott then tied a handkerchief around her neck and, giving Grace one end, they both pulled it so tight that Nancy's eyes 'started from her head', after which she fell to the floor, dead. (In Grace Marks's testimony, McDermott alone strangled Nancy.) Gruesomely McDermott is then said to have cut his victim's body into four pieces, although no mention of this dissection was made during his trial, in which witnesses described Nancy's body as having been discovered under a washtub.

The crime over and done with, the two perpetrators once again set about their daily duties. Interestingly, it was at this point that, according to Marks's version of events, she agreed to help kill their employer, saying to McDermott that she couldn't help him to kill a woman, but that she would assist him to murder Kinnear. That decided, the two servants dutifully began tidying the kitchen, clearing up the utensils that Nancy had dropped on being struck from behind, not to mention the blood which was smeared all over their hands and clothes. A little later their labours were interrupted by the arrival of a dishevelled-looking pedlar from whom McDermott purchased two shirts, before he went on his way.

At around midday, Thomas Kinnear arrived back home and, seeing that Nancy was not present either in the house or in any of the surrounding farmyard buildings, asked after her whereabouts. Not wishing to raise suspicion, McDermott informed his master that she had gone to visit friends the day before and had not yet returned. Kinnear seemed a little disgruntled but soon afterwards settled down, retiring to the parlour to read. However, by lunchtime, he was worried about Nancy's absence. She knew that he was due to return from Toronto, so the fact that she was not at home waiting for him caused him considerable concern. To put his mind at rest he decided to go out and ask after Nancy in the neighbourhood. This alone was enough to panic McDermott who, having been ordered to saddle up Kinnear's horse, retired to the harness room. There he loaded an old duck gun, which he hid behind the door, after which he went inside the house in order (so he said) to try and persuade Kinnear not to go out asking after Montgomery.

McDermott told Kinnear that his saddle had been vandalized, presumably during the night. He said that it had been cut into pieces and that it was unfit to use. But Kinnear was highly suspicious, and instead accused his servant of having cut the saddle up himself. Kinnear then went outside to inspect the offending object, but on entering the harness room (in Grace Marks' testimony, which is by far the more reliable, the murder occurred in the kitchen), McDermott grabbed the duck gun and shot his master through the heart. 'I heard the report of a gun,' said Marks later. 'I ran into the kitchen and saw Mr Kinnear lying dead on the floor and McDermott standing over him; the double-barrelled gun was on the floor. When I saw this, I attempted to run out; he said "Damn you, come back and open the trap door."'[12] But Grace says that she refused to do what McDermott requested, and as a consequence, of which he fired at her. Luckily the bullet missed Grace, and lodged itself in the jamb of the back kitchen door. McDermott then apologized to her, saying that he hadn't thought there was a second bullet in the gun; that he'd only intended to scare her. After that they made their peace with each other, then disposed of Kinnear's body by throwing him into the wine cellar alongside Nancy Montgomery. 'Very little blood flowed from the wound,' McDermott noted. 'He bled internally. He had on a very fine shirt and, after rifling his person and possessing myself of his pocketbook, I took off his shirt and put on the one I had bought of the pedlar.'[13]

Grace also changed clothes, slipping out of her own dress into a new one belonging to Nancy. Thereafter, there was very little left to do apart from steal as many valuables from the house as they could possibly carry away with them, then make their escape. This is perhaps the most dramatic part of the story: the two fugitives fleeing not only the state, but also the country.

> **After this double murder, they both fled to Toronto, and the following morning took the boat for Lewiston, in the State of New York. Mr F.C. Capreol of Toronto, hearing of the murder and escape, chartered a boat in the afternoon of the same day, secured the services of the Chief Constable of Toronto, and the two proceeded on the chartered boat to Lewiston during the night, and before the next morning had the fugitives under arrest.[14]**

At this juncture, Grace Marks provided another interesting insight into her relationship with McDermott, saying that, far from sleeping in the same bed as him, they took separate rooms on the boat. This might have been to keep up appearances, neither party wishing to draw attention to themselves, but more likely it was due to the fact that, however salacious the press wanted the murders to appear, in reality Grace was not having an intimate relationship with McDermott, indeed she had never had an intimate relationship with him.

The following morning the two were arrested and brought back to Toronto, where they were imprisoned awaiting trial, an event that eventually took place before a huge public audience in the Justiciary Courts on 3 November 1843.

In the interim, Grace was kept in prison from where a report was filed that appeared in Toronto's *Chronicle and Gazette* on 12 August 1843. 'The girl, instead of exhibiting any traces of broken rest and a guilty conscience, appears quite calm, with her eye full and clear as though she slept sound and undisturbed.' Of course this view was nothing less than idle speculation; the observation had more to do with how the public perceived Grace than anything the journalist had witnessed. None the less the description would have reinforced what the public had already been led to believe, until the trial proper began and everyone could see the accused with their own eyes.

After several months in jail, both prisoners were brought before the courts, although James McDermott's trial was held before that of his partner in crime. Strangely, however, only the murder of Thomas Kinnear was heard, as both the prosecution and defence lawyers decided there was no point repeating everything twice. The punishment would be the same, i.e. the death penalty, so Nancy Montgomery's killing was put to one side.

A jury of twelve men was sworn in and, despite a small setback when those gathered in the courtroom thought that the floor was going to give way due to there being so many spectators packed into such a small space, the trial began at midday. It was a short affair, lasting less than twelve hours, during which time a variety of witnesses for the prosecution were brought forward. These included James Newton (one of Kinnear's neighbours) who found his friend's body dumped in the cellar, and another neighbour by the name of Francis Boyd, who said that they had 'discovered the body of Mr Kinnear in a dark part of the cellar, lying on the back, with the left hand over the forehead, the feet about nine inches apart, the eyes partly open; had no shoes on; had on a light coat; there was no appearance of having struggled.'[15] Other witnesses included David Bridgeford, a Coroner for the Home District, who stated that he was present when the body of Nancy Montgomery was found under a tub. Bridgeford also testified that, on examination, Nancy was found to be pregnant.

James Walsh, who had spent the evening playing the flute with the three servants, also testified, as well as a woman by the name of Hannah Upton, who said that McDermott had visited her house asking to borrow gunpowder the day before Kinnear was shot. But perhaps the most damning evidence of all came from George Kingsmill, who had arrested both McDermott and Marks after they had made their escape, and who found several of Kinnear's belongings, including a bag of his clothes and a gold snuff box, in both prisoners' possession.

It was an open and shut case, at least McDermott's defence counsel (led by Kenneth McKenzie) obviously thought so, because apart from cross-examining the prosecution's witnesses, he conducted an unusually half-hearted campaign; he brought forward no witnesses to testify to his client's innocence, and the only evidence he submitted to the jury for consideration was the lack of an eyewitness 'of the actual commission of murder' by his client.

At one o'clock on Saturday 4 November the jury retired to decide James McDermott's fate, and less than ten minutes later they returned, declaring the prisoner guilty.

Now it was Grace Marks's turn in the dock. Would she fare any better? Would she escape the rope? The following day Marks was duly brought to the courthouse and, as with James McDermott, a series of witnesses took the stand to give evidence against her. However, whereas most people had disparaged McDermott's character and testified to his being untrustworthy, of Grace they nearly always alluded to her exemplary behaviour and good manners. Her defence counsel (once again led by Kenneth McKenzie) also put up a much better fight for their client, stating that she had been forced into doing what she did by James McDermott, who told her that if she didn't help, he would kill her. To back up this evidence, the defence counsel pointed to the bullet in the back kitchen door, saying that it was irrefutable evidence that she had been threatened. In addition to all this, standing in the dock, only sixteen years of age, Grace no doubt cut a very innocent figure. Surely such a pretty young girl couldn't have been involved in so gruesome an act? Surely she must have been coerced into the plot?

But the strategy didn't work (at least, not initially); when the jury retired to consider their verdict, they returned only a few minutes later to say that she was guilty as charged. At this point Grace, who had remained composed throughout the proceedings, is said to have fainted. However, when the judge summed up the case, although he said that he held out no hope of a pardon, he would forward 'to the proper authorities the recommendation of mercy by the jury'.[16] Fortunately for Grace, luck (no doubt combined with her tender age and youthful looks) was on her side; only a few days later, her death penalty was commuted to a life sentence.

James McDermott received no such mercy; while Grace entered the Provincial Penitentiary in Kingston on 19 November 1843, two days later McDermott was hanged in front of a huge assembly of people. Nor, according to Kenneth McKenzie, did he go to the gallows with any degree of humility. On being told that, unlike Grace, his sentence would not be commuted, McDermott 'dashed himself on the floor of his cell, and shrieked and

THE TRIALS

OF

JAMES McDERMOTT,

AND

GRACE MARKS,

AT TORONTO, UPPER CANADA, NOVEMBER 3RD AND 4TH, 1843 ;

FOR THE

MURDER

OF

THOMAS KINNEAR, ESQUIRE,

AND HIS HOUSEKEEPER

NANCY MONTGOMERY,

AT RICHMOND HILL, TOWNSHIP OF VAUGHAN, HOME DISTRICT, UPPER CANADA,
ON SATURDAY, 29TH JULY, 1843 :

WITH THEIR CONFESSIONS SINCE THEIR TRIALS,

AND THEIR PORTRAITS.

REPORTED EXPRESSLY BY MR. GEORGE WALTON.

TORONTO:
STAR AND TRANSCRIPT OFFICE, 160, KING-STREET, TORONTO.

1843.

The title page of a pamphlet published in Toronto in 1843, after the conviction of Grace Marks and James McDermott, and the execution of the latter, for the murders of their employer and his housekeeper. Grace was eventually released in 1872, but what happened to her thereafter remains a mystery. Her case was a sensation in its day, and interest in it was reawakened in 1996 with the publication of Margaret Atwood's prize-winning novel, Alias Grace.
(© Canadian Institute for Historical Microreproductions, Ottawa)

raved like a maniac, declaring that he could not, and would not die; that the law had no right to murder a man's soul as well as his body.'[17]

In contrast, Grace declared that she would have preferred to have died alongside McDermott rather than suffer the torments of her conscience. Instead she was left to rot in prison, for although Kingston Penitentiary was a relatively new establishment, its regime was by no means modern. Children (both male and female) could be incarcerated there from the age of seven, and punishments for misbehaviour included being whipped, starved or sent to solitary confinement. Dickensian is an apt description of the conditions, especially when one reads Susanna Moodie's explanation of one particular punishment: 'There is a sort of machine resembling a stone coffin, in which mutinous convicts are confined for a time.'

It was a harsh regime, designed to maximize an inmate's discomfort. It is therefore unsurprising that shortly after Susanna Moodie encountered Grace Marks at Kingston, the prisoner was sent to a lunatic asylum in Toronto. It wasn't unusual for inmates to be transferred in this way; either they were legitimately ill or, as is more likely, they were feigning lunacy in order that they might escape the Penitentiary's unpleasent conditions for a short while.

Moodie, having determined to visit the asylum as well, once again came across that 'celebrated murderess'. Her experience was far from pleasant. Even taking into account Moodie's preference for 'purple prose', no doubt a kernel of truth can be found in the following description:

> Among these raving maniacs I recognized the singular face of Grace Marks – no longer sad and despairing, but lighted up with the fire of insanity, and glowing with a hideous and fiend-like merriment. On perceiving that strangers were observing her, she fled shrieking away like a phantom into one of the side rooms. It appears that even in the wildest bursts of her terrible malady, she is continually haunted by a memory of the past. Unhappy girl! When will the long horror of her punishment and remorse be over? When will she sit at the feet of Jesus, clothed with the unsullied garments of his righteousness, the stain of blood washed from her hand, and her soul redeemed, and pardoned, and in her right mind? It is fearful to look at her, and contemplate her fate in connexion with her crime. What a striking illustration does it afford of that awful text, 'Vengeance is mine, I will repay, saith the Lord!'[18]

However, within a few weeks of this encounter, and despite a pregnancy scare, Grace Marks had recovered enough to be removed once again into the care of the Kingston Penitentiary.

Over the following twenty-eight years, Marks appears infrequently in the less-than-complete prison records, although it can be discerned that she acquitted herself well, and several accounts mention the fact that she spent time working in the Governor's house. Although no one elaborates on who the Governor was, generally he is believed to be the head of the Penitentiary. It wasn't unusual in those times (especially in North America) for prisoners to be put to work outside the prison, and women in particular would often be hired out as day labour in the homes of the rich.

Margaret Atwood in her novel *Alias Grace* picks up on this theme, and begins her story with Grace pacing the Governor's yard: 'I am a model prisoner and give no trouble. That's what the Governor's wife says, I have overheard her saying it. I'm skilled at overhearing. If I am good enough and quiet enough, perhaps after all they will let me go.'[19]

Over the years Grace Marks became a minor celebrity, and several prison visitors made it their duty to petition the Crown for a pardon on her behalf. Much the same occurred in the case of Myra Hindley in Britain, whose friend Lord Longford campaigned for many years for a conclusion to her sentence and ultimately for her release. However, whereas Hindley died in hospital under armed guard in 2002, Grace Marks was more successful in her bid for freedom, which she finally won in 1872.

Little is known of Marks's life after she was released. She travelled to New York State alongside a prison warden and his daughter, where she was provided with temporary accommodation. After this, all trace of Marks vanishes, and although some writers have claimed that she married, there is no firm evidence to suggest that this was ever the case. Most likely Marks changed her name and disappeared in order to live quietly somewhere far off the beaten track.

An enigma during her own lifetime, Grace Marks remained so until the time of her death, the date of which is also unknown. No wonder then that she has provided such a marvellous canvas upon which writers have been able to inscribe their own stories and project their own prejudices.

Coincidentally, the graves of her two victims, Thomas Kinnear and Nancy Montgomery, which are located in Richmond Hill Presbyterian cemetery, have almost vanished without trace as well. Unmarked at the time of their burial, even the picket fencing which was set around each site was later removed, thus making it impossible to locate either grave.

AILEEN CAROL WUORNOS

Damsel of Death

My conclusion from the interview is, today we are executing someone who is mad. Here is someone who has totally lost her mind.

NICK BROOMFIELD, WHO TRIED TO CONDUCT
AN INTERVIEW WITH WUORNOS IN 1993

There are no redeeming features in the case of Aileen Carol Wuornos. From beginning to end this is an unrelentingly bleak, desolate tale, a story of teenage pregnancy, child abuse, extreme poverty, rape, vagrancy and prostitution. If a person's background could ever be used as mitigating circumstances for the crimes they committed, then surely this would be it.

Aileen Carol Wuornos was born on 29 February 1956 to Diane Pitman. Pitman was only seventeen when she gave birth to Aileen, but she had been married to Leo Pitman, Aileen's father, since she was fifteen, and had already produced a son, Keith. Leo Pitman was a diagnosed paranoid schizophrenic and would later be convicted of paedophilia for sodomizing ten-year-old boys. He later committed suicide in 1969 while in prison.

Aileen never knew her father, instead spending the first few months of her life alone with her mother and brother. Diane Pitman found it increasingly difficult coping with two young children and eventually she abandoned them at her parents' house and then disappeared to go and lead her own life.

Pitman's parents (who later legally adopted the two children, giving them their surname 'Wuornos') were far from suitable carers. Lauri and Britta Wuornos, originally from Finland, lived in Rochester, Michigan. Lauri, the grandfather, was a violent man who drank heavily and frequently beat his wife. With two children in the house he took to beating them as well. His wife, Britta, was little better. She never protected the children from her violent husband and she would often drink as much as he did. With the limited amount of money the couple had being spent on alcohol, the children often went without food. This didn't help either youngster when it came to going to school. Concentration was difficult, if not impossible, and it has been suggested that it was during this time that Aileen began offering sexual favours to the older boys in her school, in return for sandwiches and biscuits.

After a difficult early childhood, Aileen's life took another bad turn when, at the age of thirteen, she accused a male friend of her grandparents of raping her. The crime was never investigated, but shortly afterwards Aileen fell pregnant, first claiming the child was the result of the rape, then saying that it was her grandfather's fault and, later still, that the child was the consquence of a relationship she had had with her brother, Keith. Whatever the truth of the matter, Aileen was swiftly packed off to a home for unmarried mothers, where the staff reported that she was a difficult child; highly uncooperative, with a very aggressive attitude towards any form of authority. She was also, or so the staff said, unable to strike up any friendships with the other girls. Finally Aileen gave birth to a baby boy who was later put up for adoption. The year 1971 was not, as it turned out, an auspicious one for the Wuornos family. In July, Britta died from what most people believed was liver failure due to her heavy drinking, although there were several others, Diane included, who were convinced that Lauri might have murdered his wife.

Diane Pitman (Aileen and Keith's natural mother) now reappeared, offering her two estranged children a home with her in Texas, but the siblings refused. Both went into care, but Aileen soon dropped out of school, abandoned her new home, and took to hitchhiking around the country, making money through prostitution. Keith also turned his back on his mother and began a life of petty crime, no doubt to feed an ever-increasing drug habit. In 1976, Lauri Wuornos committed suicide by locking himself in his garage and starting the engine of his car to inhale the fumes. Only a few months later, on 17 July, Keith Wuornos died, having been diagnosed with throat cancer. Surprisingly he left Aileen $10,000 from a life-insurance policy, and had she been better prepared for life as an adult, she might have sought out some kind of stability by buying a mobile home, or putting down a deposit on an apartment. Sadly this never happened. Instead, Aileen wasted all the money on drink, drugs and a new car, which she wrecked only a short time after she'd purchased it.

Aileen now headed for the warmer climes of Florida, and it seemed that she might have fallen on her feet when she met up with a sixty-nine-year-old man called Lewis Fell. Despite the gap in their ages, the two were married and Fell, being a moderately wealthy man, might have made Aileen happy. But the marriage soon fell apart. Fell alleges that Aileen kept at him for more and more money and, when he finally refused, that she hit him with his own walking stick. She was also arrested for beating a bartender over the head with a pool cue. Fell was so frightened of his wife that he obtained a restraining order on her to prevent her from going near him again. The marriage was annulled and with no other choice Aileen went back to living on the road.

Aileen Carol Wuornos now drifted into a life of drink, drugs, prostitution and petty crime. She began forging cheques and finally tried her hand at armed robbery, for which she was arrested and subsequently jailed. On her release she was quickly arrested again for yet another attempt at forging a cheque. She was

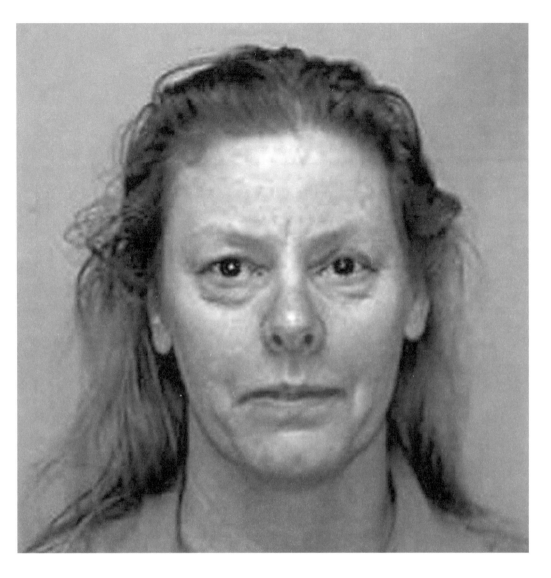

Aileen Carol Wuornos, an undated photograph taken at some time after her arrest in 1991. She was convicted of the murders of six men, for which she received six death sentences, and came to be widely, though erroneously, regarded as America's first female serial killer. (© PA Photos/EPA)

also up in front of the courts for stealing a car and a gun. Throughout her life of crime, the police recall she was a very detached young woman, showing not the slightest bit of remorse, let alone fear. The primary emotion Aileen displayed was one of sheer, unadulterated rage.

In the summer of 1986 Aileen met a woman called Tyria Moore in a Daytona gay bar. There was an instant attraction between the two women, which developed into a relationship, and they began renting an apartment together. Tyria, who worked as a motel maid, then left her job because Aileen didn't like her having contact with other women. Instead the couple lived off Aileen's earnings as a prostitute. She frequented truck stops, highway cafés, bars, motels, arcades, pool clubs and back alleys: anywhere that she thought she could meet and pick up clients. But a successful career as a prostitute often depends on how good the woman looks, and Aileen's long abuse of drink and drugs had sadly taken their toll on her physical appearance. She put on weight, her skin grew increasingly grey, her hair turned lank and soon she was unable to attract enough male customers to earn a living. Without any money coming in, she and Tyria couldn't even afford to stay in cheap motels. Instead they drifted from place to place, often sleeping outside or if they were lucky, in a shed or farm outbuilding. The strain on the relationship must have been enormous and the need for money equally so. Tyria, who was later to turn state's evidence, said it was around this time that Aileen began talking to her more openly about the abuse she'd received as a child and the yearning she had for revenge.

Richard Mallory's body was discovered in Volusia County on 13 December 1989 in a wooded area north-west of Daytona Beach. He had been shot three times in the chest with a .22 calibre pistol. The owner of a small electronics company, with a reputation for heavy drinking, he had made several enemies at work by sacking his employees on a regular basis. Fifty-one-year-old Richard Mallory was also in the habit of visiting porn theatres and topless bars. However, although an unsavoury and unpopular character, the police could uncover no clues as to who had killed him.

In fact, Richard Mallory's last hours had been spent in the company of Aileen Carol Wuornos. He had picked her up in his Cadillac and, after drinking large amounts of vodka, and driving for a couple of hours, they had decided to have sex in Daytona Beach woods. Aileen had other plans, however, and had shot her client and afterwards stolen his money, his credit cards, his watch, a radar detector and camera. Finally Aileen covered up his body with an old scrap of carpet that she found lying around in the woods. She then left the scene using Mallory's car as a get-away vehicle, only to abandon it later somewhere deep in the countryside.

Only a few months afterwards, Aileen murdered again, this time killing a forty-three-year-old construction worker called David Spears, who had picked her up in his truck while she was hitchhiking. Aileen shot Spears six times with the same gun she had used on Richard Mallory, after which she dumped his body (which was naked except for a red baseball cap) in woodland near Tampa.

In the space of only a few months Aileen then murdered a further five men.

Charles Carskaddon picked up Aileen Wuornos on 6 June 1990 while he was driving to Tampa to meet his fiancée. A part-time rodeo worker from Boonville, Missouri, he was feeling lucky that day as he'd just landed a new job. At some point in the journey Carskaddon stopped the car, presumably to have sex with his prostitute passenger, but instead she shot him nine times in his lower chest and abdomen, and afterwards stole not only his money and some jewellery, but also his gun: a .45 automatic.

On 7 June 1990 Peter Siems, a sixty-five-year-old missionary, disappeared. His body has never been discovered, though police believe its most likely resting place is at the bottom of one of Florida's numerous swamps. Siems had been driving his car (the backseat of which was stacked with bibles) to New Jersey, where he was going to visit relatives. At some point, however, he stopped to pick up a hitchhiker. According to Wuornos's later testimony, she climbed into the car and a short way into the journey she shot him dead.

Less than a month later, on 4 July 1990, Wuornos and Tyria Moore were involved in a car crash when the vehicle they were driving, Peter Siems's Pontiac Sunbird, veered off the road. The accident was witnessed by a couple of people who later gave the police a description of the two women they had seen running away from the scene of the crash. It was crucial evidence, but by the time police had identified the car as having belonged to Peter Siems, Wuornos and Moore had vanished from the area.

Meanwhile, Aileen had set her sights on yet another victim. Eugene Troy Burress was murdered on 30 July 1990. The fifty-year-old meat-delivery driver from Ocala had left the factory where he worked to make his normal rounds in his van, only to pick up Aileen somewhere along the road to Daytona. Aileen shot him once in the back and once in the chest, and his decomposing body was later discovered by picnickers, buried in a shallow grave within the environs of Ocala National Forest on State Road 19 in Marion County.

The date of the next murder is slightly more vague, but on either 10 or 11 September 1990 Charles 'Dick' Humphreys, a former police chief, offered Wuornos a ride in his car, after which he was shot seven times in the head and torso. True to form, Wuornos then stole his car, although she abandoned it less than a week later.

Aileen Wuornos's seventh and final victim was Walter Jeno Antonio, a sixty-two-year-old truck driver who had picked her up and then driven her somewhere quiet so that they could have sex. His body was found near a remote logging path in Dixie County, with three bullet wounds to the back and one to the head, but by this time police were on the case, having released sketches of the two women seen running from the crash involving Peter Siems's vehicle.

Fortunately, the police had a good response to the pictures and several people rang in to identify Tyria Moore and Aileen Carol Wuornos as the suspects. Aileen was also recognized under several different surnames because, during her years as a truck-stop prostitute, she had used various aliases. The fact that the pair were publicly wanted by the police must have put another, even more enormous strain on their relationship. Tellingly, it was now that Tyria chose to leave her lover, travelling to Pennsylvania in order, she said, to visit relatives.

Aileen had, meanwhile, begun selling off some of the items she had stolen during her killing spree. She went mainly to pawnshops, where she received cash in return for Richard Mallory's radar detector and camera. The same week she also pawned a ring belonging to Walter Antonio, and some tools that had been owned by David Spears. However, in Florida, anyone using pawnshop outlets is required by law to leave a thumbprint on the receipt and the police, desperate for any lead in the recent spate of roadside killings, had already begun trawling the area for just such material. It was not long before they turned up a docket in Daytona for a camera and radar detector which, when they were traced using serial numbers, turned out to belong to Richard Mallory. The thumbprint on the receipt was that of one Cammie Marsh Greene, one of Aileen's numerous pseudonyms. The same print also showed up on an outstanding weapons warrant for a Lori Grody (again another of Aileen's fake names).

Aileen was eventually arrested by Larry Horzepa of the Marion County Sheriff's Office, after a lengthy undercover police operation. At the time of her arrest she was living rough, sleeping on the front porch of a biker bar called the Last Resort in Orange Springs, near Florida's east coast. Over the years, the Last Resort had become like a home to Aileen. Both she and Tyria had frequented the place during their early courtship, shooting pool, using the jukebox, joking and drinking with the men. Aileen in particular had enjoyed the biker culture that surrounded the establishment. It was therefore fitting that she was arrested there, though on being detained she was informed it was due to an outstanding weapons violation, not for the murder of seven men. At this point the police didn't have enough evidence to charge her with the murders because they had neither discovered a murder weapon nor found Tyria Moore.

The second problem was soon resolved when Tyria Moore was located living in Pennsylvania. She was staying with her sister and, on being cautioned and sworn in to tell the truth, she gave a statement to the effect that yes, she had known about the murder of Richard Mallory, because after killing him, Aileen had driven home in his Cadillac and told Moore precisely what she had done. Moore then said that Aileen had shown no regret over her actions, subsequent to which Moore had asked her lover not to say anything else. 'I told her,' Moore said, 'I didn't want to hear about it… And then any time she would come home after that and say certain things, telling me about where she got something. I'd say I don't want to hear it.'[1] According to Moore, she herself was never involved in the murders; they were entirely Aileen's doing.

The police then flew Moore down to Florida where she was going to 'assist' them further by pretending to talk to Aileen in confidence.

On 14 January 1991 Tyria Moore spoke to Aileen Wuornos in prison via the phone. The call was being closely monitored by police and, eager to reassure her lover, Aileen told Tyria that she had only been arrested for a weapons offence. It must have come as a shock therefore when Tyria, prompted by detectives, told

Aileen that she had in fact been detained on suspicion of killing seven men. In a subsequent phone call, Aileen then told Tyria that she would not let her lover go to jail, that she alone would confess to the murders, and on 16 January 1991 this is precisely what Aileen Carol Wuornos did.

In the beginning Aileen insisted that all seven murders had been in self-defence. 'If I didn't kill all those guys,' she said during one interview, 'I would have been raped a total of twenty times maybe. Or killed. You never know. But I got them first.'[2]

In the case of the first murder, that of Richard Mallory, this might have been true, for as the reporter, Michele Gillens, later discovered, Mallory had served ten years for a violent rape in another state. But this evidence never surfaced at Wuornos's trial and, several years after her conviction, she confessed that her earlier plea of self-defence was a lie. In the meantime, Wuornos's team of lawyers managed to persuade her to plead guilty to the six subsequent murders in exchange for escaping the death penalty and receiving six consecutive life sentences instead. This plan was put into operation and, had it not been for one state attorney pressing for the death penalty, she might still be alive today.

On 14 January 1992 Aileen Wuornos went on trial in Florida for the murder of Richard Mallory. The evidence against her was damning. Dr Arthur Botting, the Chief Medical Examiner who had performed the autopsy on Mallory, explained that the victim had probably taken between fifteen to twenty painful minutes to die. But the most damning evidence of all came from Aileen Wuornos's former

On the day of Aileen Wuornos's execution, 9 October 2002, anti-death-penalty campaigners gathered outside the prison in which she was to die. After one stay of execution in September that year, Florida's Governor Jeb Bush, the President's brother, confirmed her sentence.
(© JOE SKIPPER/REUTERS)

lover, Tyria Moore, who again said that on returning home after killing Mallory, Aileen hadn't seemed in the slightest bit upset, nor was she drunk or high on drugs. Tyria also added that Aileen hadn't mentioned Mallory trying to assault her. The prosecution then went on to present the jury with evidence of the other killings. In the state of Florida there is a law known as the Williams Rule,[3] which states that evidence relating to other crimes of a similar nature to the one being tried can be admitted as evidence if these crimes show a pattern that has been established. Without a doubt Wuornos's case of self-defence would have been ten times more likely to succeed had the other murders[4] not been brought into evidence. Instead the prosecution accused Wuornos of being a money-seeking murderess: 'She killed out of greed. No longer satisfied with the ten, twenty, thirty dollars, she wanted it all. It wasn't enough to control his body, she wanted the ultimate – his car, his property, his life.'[5] The prosecution rested its case.

Less than two weeks into the trial, it was the defence's turn to try and prove that Aileen was, if not innocent, than at least provoked into the attack. Tricia Jenkins, one of Aileen's lawyers, tried to dissuade Aileen from taking the stand, but nothing would stop Wuornos from having her day in court. Contrary to her original testimony, where she stated that she had shot Richard Mallory in order to rob him, Aileen now insisted in very colourful terms that he had raped, sodomized and tortured her. 'I said I would not [have sex with him],' she said when she took the stand:

> **'Yes, you are, bitch,' he replied. 'You're going to do everything I tell you. If you don't, I'm going to kill you and have sex with you after you're dead, just like the other sluts. It doesn't matter, your body will still be warm.' He tied my wrists to the steering wheel, and screwed me in the ass. Afterwards, he got a Visine bottle filled with rubbing alcohol out of the trunk. He said the Visine bottle was one of my surprises. He emptied it into my rectum. It really hurt bad because he tore me up a lot. He got dressed, got a radio, sat on the hood for what seemed like an hour. I was really pissed. I was yelling at him, and struggling to get my hands free. Eventually he untied me, put a stereo wire around my neck and tried to rape me again. We struggled. I reached for my gun. I shot him. I scrambled to cover the shooting because I didn't think the police would believe I killed him in self-defence.[6]**

On cross-examination by John Tanner, however, Wuornos's evidence was torn to shreds and she grew increasingly angry. Tanner accused Wuornos of lying, saying that everything she had stated in court was contrary to her original taped confession. At this point her defence team advised Aileen not to answer any more of Tanner's questions, and during the rest of the cross-examination she did indeed heed their advice, invoking her Fifth Amendment right against self-incrimination a grand total of twenty-five times.

It had been a huge mistake for Wuornos to take the stand and the defence could only reiterate its original argument that Wuornos was a mentally ill woman with a borderline personality disorder.

On 27 January 1992 Judge Uriel Blount sent the jury out to consider their verdict. Two hours later they returned to announce that they found Aileen Carol Wuornos guilty of first-degree murder. In response Aileen shouted, 'I hope you get raped, scumbags of America!'

The following days were then taken up with the penalty phase of the trial and expert witnesses for the defence were called to give evidence of Aileen's mental condition. They testified that she did indeed suffer from a borderline personality disorder and that her violent childhood had only exacerbated this. The following excerpt is from Aileen's later appeal, which documents her original trial and sentence:

> **One expert, Dr Krop, testified that Wuornos lacked impulse control and had impaired cognition. Dr Toomer said that Wuornos believed she was in imminent danger at the time of the murder, and that the remorse she exhibited revealed she did not suffer antisocial personality disorder. The State's expert psychologist, Dr Bernard, agreed that Wuornos had borderline personality disorder, but also found that she suffered antisocial personality disorder. Dr Bernard also agreed that she had an impaired capacity and mental disturbance at the time of the crime, but believed the impairment was not substantial and the disturbance was not extreme. Dr Bernard agreed there was evidence of non-statutory mitigating evidence including Wuornos's mental difficulties, alcoholism, disturbance, and genetic or environmental deficits.**

Tricia Jenkins also described Aileen as 'a damaged, primitive child', but nothing would deter the jury from announcing a unanimous decision in favour of the death penalty, and on 31 January Judge Blount sentenced her to the electric chair.

Aileen Wuornos was put on Death Row in Breward County. Shortly afterwards, on 31 March, she then pleaded guilty to the murders of Dick Humphreys, Eugene Troy Burress and David Spears, for which she was again given three death sentences. In June she pleaded guilty to the murder of Charles Carskaddon and in July to that of Walter Gino Antonio. Once again Aileen was handed death sentences for each murder. And this might have been where the story of Aileen Carol Wuornos ended, were it not for the American TV chat show alongside various feminist groups intent on making Aileen into a major *cause célèbre*. Several women's groups insisted that Aileen had not only acted in self-defence but that she hadn't received a fair trial; that she was inadequately represented by her own counsel; that the introduction of the 'Williams rule' had prejudiced her case; and, as if all that wasn't enough, that the entire criminal system was prejudiced against both lesbians and prostitutes.

But the most curious supporter of Aileen came in the shape of a middle-aged, born-again Christian called Arlene Pralle, who had seen Aileen's photograph in a local newspaper and had written to her while she was in gaol. The letter began, 'My name is Arlene Pralle. I'm a born-again. You're going to think I'm crazy, but Jesus told me to write you.' Pralle included her telephone number in the letter and, far from finding her crazy, Wuornos rang Pralle up and the two soon became firm friends. Pralle went on to become one of the most ardent defenders of Wuornos and soon she was giving interviews on TV chat shows and to newspapers and magazines. In an interview with *Vanity Fair*, Pralle described her friendship with Aileen as 'a soul binding. We're like Jonathan and David in the Bible. It's as though part of me is trapped in gaol with her. We always know what the other is feeling and thinking.' And to anyone else who would listen she would tell of Aileen's horrific childhood, the abuse she received at the hands of her maternal grandfather, her early teenage pregnancy as a result of rape and the subsequent abuse she suffered while working as a prostitute. On 22 November 1991 Arlene Pralle and her husband legally adopted Aileen as their daughter, saying that God had told them to do so.

Not long afterwards Pralle then began to handle all the film and TV offers[7] which had begun to pour in. Although Wuornos, as a convicted criminal, could not make any money from these movies, several deals were struck. In particular the talk shows *Montel Williams* and *Geraldo* both paid in the region of $7,000 – $10,000 to interview Wuornos while she was on Death Row. There was also a TV film called *Overkill*, which was an almost completely sanitized version of the Wuornos story. It starred an actress called Jean Smart who was much prettier than the woman she was portraying, especially when you consider Aileen's drink- and drug-ravaged face. In fact the film gave the lie to the whole sorry tale, making Aileen out to be an attractive *femme fatale*, when in actual fact she was a rather dowdy, tough-looking woman who worked as a prostitute and who hung around bars.

In fact, the most truthful account of the Aileen Wuornos story was that made by a British documentary filmmaker, Nick Broomfield. His work was entitled *Aileen Wuornos: The Selling of a Serial Killer*. In it, Arlene Pralle, alongside a lawyer called Steve Glazer, were filmed requesting money (in the region of $10,000) from Broomfield as payment for an interview with Aileen. Aileen had given Pralle and Glazer exclusive rights to her story, saying that they could sell it after her execution. It was virtually a licence to print money and, as Broomfield

The hearse carrying the body of Aileen Carol Wuornos after her execution. She was only the second woman to be executed in Florida since before the US Civil War, which began in 1861; the state reintroduced the death penalty in 1976. (© JOE SKIPPER/REUTERS)

experienced, one that they exploited to the full. But it wasn't just these two who were taking advantage of the situation. Nearly everyone who came into contact with Aileen was trying to sell something. This included Tyria Moore and, most incredible of all, the police. According to Broomfield's documentary, the police had been planning to sell Hollywood exclusive rights to their investigation one month *before* Aileen was arrested. If true, this was an appalling display of greed and betrayal, at the centre of which sat Aileen Carol Wuornos with six death sentences hanging over her head. Her lawyers did their best to get these overturned, repeatedly stating that she was mentally unstable at the time her crimes were committed, but Aileen was less than impressed by their efforts, stating in an interview with an ABC reporter in February 2001, 'I was sentenced to death. I need to die for the killing of those people.'

The Governor of Florida, Jeb Bush, agreed, although he did issue a stay of execution in September 2002, asking for further mental examinations of the prisoner. After three psychiatrists had interviewed Aileen and had all stated that she was fully cogniscent of her crimes and knew precisely why she had been sentenced to death, Jeb Bush lifted the warrant.

At 9.47a.m. on 9 October 2002, Aileen Carol Wuornos was put to death by lethal injection (by this time the use of the electric chair had been abolished in the State of Florida). Aileen was allowed to make a final statement on which there was no time limit, but in the event it probably took her no longer than thirty-five seconds to give the following garbled message: 'I'd just like to say I'm sailing with the rock, and I'll be back like Independence Day, with Jesus June 6. Like the movie, big mother ship and all, I'll be back.'[8] After this she was led to the execution chamber, where she was strapped on to a table after which three needles were pushed into her veins containing a deadly concoction of muscle relaxants and heart-stopping chemicals. She was the tenth woman to be executed in the USA and the second woman in Florida to be executed since the death penalty was resumed in that state in 1976.

Troy Burress's sister, Leta Prater, who witnessed the execution said, 'I want to know she is absolutely gone. I would have liked to see her get the electric chair. My brother didn't go to sleep. He was shot more than once… I was absolutely devastated [by his death]. I still am. He was more than a brother. He was my best friend. I miss him so much.'[9]

Aileen Carol Wuornos is often cited as America's first female serial killer. That she was female and that she killed several people has never been in dispute. However, there have been women who killed serially before the Wuornos murders occurred. Instead, what makes her case unusual is first the method she used in that she shot her victims, and second the fact that they were all men who, up until the time of their deaths, were unknown to her. Women who kill tend to use either poison or, if in a domestic environment, the first thing that comes to hand, which is normally a knife. The gun is a weapon most often employed by men. Women also usually murder people they know, members of their immediate family, friends, lovers and so on. For a woman to go out and murder a complete stranger is very rare indeed.

Having said all that, Aileen Carol Wuornos was not the first woman to use a gun to murder a stranger and sadly, given the world in which we live, she will not be the last.

MYRA HINDLEY

The Face of Evil

There is a small group of once popular Christian names that have fallen out of use because of their association with one hated individual. In Germany, Adolfs under 50 are thin on the ground. And you can count on the fingers of one hand the Myras born in this country [Great Britain] since 1966.'
PETER STANDFORD, FROM THE *GUARDIAN*, 15 NOVEMBER 2002

It had all the elements of the opening to a horror film for, on a dark winter's night, in freezing rain, an unsettling scene was being played out at the Cambridge Crematorium. Under police escort a coffin was being carried through a stone gateway beneath a Latin inscription, *Mors Janua Vitae* – Death is the Gateway to Life. Inside, to a small gathering of people that included one representative of the Prison Service, Albinoni's Adagio was being played. The coffin was laid at the front of the room on a small catafalque and the service began.

This was the cremation of one Myra Hindley, who had died, aged sixty, from pneumonia after suffering a heart attack. Initially the service had been planned to take place close to the hospital in which she had died, but the staff at West Suffolk Crematorium refused, saying they would be deeply unhappy carrying out such a request. No one was surprised. Myra Hindley was the most reviled person in the country. Due to a particular photograph taken of her at the time of her arrest in 1966, she had also become an icon of evil, her name synonymous not just with murder, but with everything that was held to be perverted and wrong.

Myra Hindley was born on 23 July 1942 in Manchester. Her parents, Hettie and Bob, were a working-class couple, with Bob employed as an aircraft fitter and Hettie as a machinist in a textile factory. Due to the war, Bob was absent for the first three years of Myra's childhood, but on his return he hardly endeared himself to the family. He was a bully, a man who thought nothing of hitting his wife and children and spending most of his earnings down at the pub. When Hettie's second child, Maureen, was born in 1946, Myra was sent to live with her maternal grandmother. It was only meant to be a short stay, just until Hettie had got on her feet again, but in the event Myra remained with her grandmother until her late teens.

At school Myra was always considered a bright, mature girl, but she was often absent from class, her grandmother (who was only in her early to mid-fifties) preferring to keep Myra at home for company. Her absences meant that Myra didn't get the best schooling. Instead of gaining entrance to the local grammar school, she had to settle for a secondary modern, Ryder Brow. None the less,

Myra made the best of a bad situation and quickly showed an aptitude for creative writing and poetry, as well as enjoying athletics and swimming. She was also in demand as a popular babysitter and many people remember her being very competent in this role, demonstrating a genuine affection for children.

At the age of fifteen Myra made friends with a boy called Michael Higgins. It was an unusual pairing as Michael was a shy, fragile child, two years younger than Myra. Yet the two were the best of friends. Myra protected Michael, and she was inconsolable when he drowned one summer in a local reservoir. She blamed herself, Michael having asked her to join him for the swim. For weeks afterwards she cried and, according to her mother, suffered from severe depression. She collected money for a wreath that she wanted to lay on Michael's coffin, and it was not long after his death that she left school without any qualifications.

Her first job was at Lawrence Scott and Electrometers, where she was a junior clerk. It was uninspiring work, repetitive and monotonous. But, this aside, Myra enjoyed herself, dating boys, going to dances, smoking and drinking. She also experimented with make-up and started dying her hair to make herself look older. Perhaps this was why, at just seventeen years old, she became engaged to Ronnie Sinclair. It was the adult thing to do – to settle down, get married and have a family – but the engagement didn't last very long. Myra grew bored of what she began to think of as a mundane way of life. She was fed up with the unexceptional, unambitious people who surrounded her; she wanted something better. During this period Myra changed jobs four times and considered enlisting in the armed forces, or going abroad to work as a nanny. But as luck would have it, in January 1961 she met a man who was to inspire her more than any other individual ever had or ever would. The man's name was Ian Brady, and together he and Hindley would form one of the twentieth century's most notorious criminal partnerships.

Of all the employees at Millwards (an old-fashioned chemical firm in Manchester), Ian Brady had to be the strangest. He was an aloof young man, someone who kept himself to himself, someone who seldom smiled. He enjoyed reading, though his tastes were questionable because he was obsessed with Nazism. His library included Hitler's *Mein Kampf*, as well as various existentialist texts and books on sex and torture, the Marquis de Sade being one of his favourite authors.

Brady had been born in 1938 in the Gorbals, one of the roughest slum areas of Glasgow. His mother, Margaret (later known as Peggy) Stewart, was unmarried at the time and never told the young Brady the name of his father, except to say that he was a journalist who had died while she was pregnant. When Ian was three months old, his mother, unable to cope with a baby as well as having to go out to work as a waitress, advertised for someone to adopt her child. Mary and John Sloane were the couple that answered her plea. They already had four children, but Ian Brady soon joined their throng.

As a young boy Ian was constantly in trouble. He was a tearaway, a tough Glasgow teenager involved in countless burglaries. At the age of sixteen he was put on probation and ordered to return to live with his mother Maggie, who by this time had remarried and moved to Manchester. But the biggest shock to Brady at this time was not that he had been put on probation, but that Mary Sloane was not his real mother. Maggie had visited Ian as he was growing up but had always been introduced as a friend of the family. Now he was told of his real parentage and for the first time in his life he had to face the fact that he'd been adopted.

In Manchester Brady found it hard to fit in. He had a strong Glaswegian accent which meant that the local boys teased him. He hardly knew his mother and wasn't overly fond of his stepfather. By seventeen he was in a Borstal institution for young offenders on a two-year stretch for aiding and abetting a burglary. On his release Ian withdrew even further into himself. He found work as a labourer and for a time enjoyed the job, but in 1959, having polished up his bookkeeping skills, he began work as a stock clerk at Millwards Ltd. A year after he began his job, Ian Brady was introduced to his new secretary, a young woman named Myra Hindley. In a letter which she later sent to journalist and documentary filmmaker Duncan Staff, Hindley describes her infatuation as follows: 'I'd always been a romantic dreamer falling in love with film stars – I was crazy about James Dean and Elvis – and had read and heard the phrase "falling head over heels in love", but never thought it would happen to me. But as soon as Ian Brady looked at me and smiled shyly, that's exactly what happened.'

From 1963 onwards, several children began to go missing in the Manchester area. The police, who mounted massive searches, even using dogs and frogmen, and who printed hundreds of posters and interviewed thousands of people, thought that the disappearances were linked, probably the work of one or two men.

The first child to disappear was a sixteen-year-old girl called Pauline Reade. She had been on her way to a dance at the Railway Workers' Social Club and was supposed to meet up with some girlfriends. According to their later testimonies, however, as soon as their parents learnt alcohol was to be served, they refused to let their children attend. Joan Reade (Pauline's mother) didn't know about the alcohol and so Pauline, dressed in her best frock, set out alone.

By midnight Mrs Reade was beside herself with worry. Pauline had still not returned home and so she and her husband went out to search for their daughter. By morning, however, they were still none the wiser as to her whereabouts and in desperation they informed the police, who in turn conducted a thorough search of the area. It seemed as if Pauline had dropped off the edge of the earth.

Having become work colleagues at Millwards, Brady and Hindley had taken their relationship on to a more intimate footing. Myra needed someone to give her life meaning and Brady fitted the bill. In comparison to her ordinary, every-day friends, Brady cut a glamorous figure, always dressing in black, keeping his hair neatly slicked back. Although largely self-taught, he also seemed a well-read young man. Hindley began studying the same books as him and listened attentively while he spouted out his 'philosophies'. Before long Ian Brady had moved in to Myra's grandmother's house and the couple were ever afterwards inseparable, although it was during these early days that Myra probably first grew aware of her lover's darker side.

Brady introduced Myra to pornography and at some point she also claimed he drugged her as an experiment to see how long she would remain sedated. The incident frightened Myra enough to want to escape, so she applied to the NAAFI (the organization that provides canteens and others services to the British armed forces) for a clerking job in Germany. Myra travelled to London for an interview and when she returned home told her family she had got the job. However, they hated the idea of her going abroad so much that she eventually cancelled her plans and continued seeing Ian.

Given that her boyfriend was obsessed by the books that he read, with their existentialist theories about love and life, perhaps it is not surprising that the young couple soon after began talking about abducting and killing a young girl. Later, in letters she sent to the *Guardian*, Myra justified her actions by implying that she had had no choice in the matter:

> I knew [that] by the time he began talking about the perfect murder that I was going to help him, that I had very little choice. Again, even if I went to the police there was no proof, only my word against his. And then he would know what I'd done if the police had told him I'd made these allegations against him, and although I knew he wasn't stupid enough to do anything to draw attention to himself, I also knew that he would bide his time while he thought of what to do and how to do it without raising suspicion.
>
> I would have to leave my job, which wasn't a problem; I could go away and lose myself somewhere, but how could I possibly tell my family all that had happened and been said by him without terrifying them?
>
> They couldn't move; a family just can't uproot itself and move somewhere and find places to live, jobs etc.; and still live in fear, looking over their shoulders all the time. I knew I was trapped and would have to do what he wanted of me.[1]

As a means of justifying her actions, this letter is at best shaky, but what it does reveal is that Myra was allowing herself to be turned into a woman who would do whatever her lover requested. After all, it was exciting, even thrilling, not like

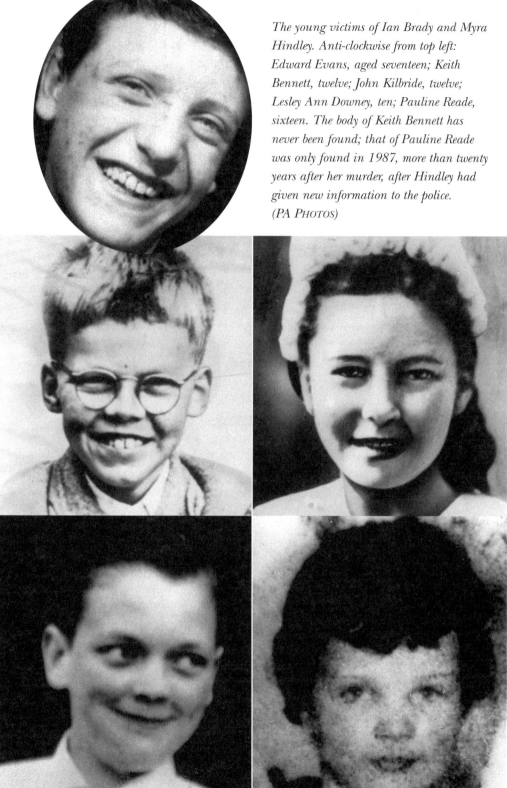

The young victims of Ian Brady and Myra Hindley. Anti-clockwise from top left: Edward Evans, aged seventeen; Keith Bennett, twelve; John Kilbride, twelve; Lesley Ann Downey, ten; Pauline Reade, sixteen. The body of Keith Bennett has never been found; that of Pauline Reade was only found in 1987, more than twenty years after her murder, after Hindley had given new information to the police. (PA PHOTOS)

going to the pictures or the bingo, pastimes her workmates enjoyed. Brady's requests made Myra feel superior; they excited her. Pauline Reade didn't stand a chance.

On the night Pauline disappeared Myra stopped her car and asked the young girl if she could help look for a glove. Pauline lived only two doors down from Myra's seventeen-year-old brother-in-law, David Smith (who was married to Myra's sister Maureen) so she already knew the young girl if not well, then at least well enough to say 'hello' to. Myra explained that she had dropped the glove earlier in the day up on the moor. As a reward, she said that she would give Pauline some gramophone records; their search wouldn't take long.

Pauline jumped into the car and Myra drove to Saddleworth Moor with Brady following behind on a motorbike. Saddleworth is a bleak place typified by its millstone-grit scenery. Having driven Pauline up there it is impossible to say precisely what happened next, but by the end of her ordeal Pauline Reade had been raped by Ian Brady and had then had her throat slit. Her body was buried in a shallow grave, after which Hindley and Brady made their respective ways home.

The second child to disappear was twelve-year-old John Kilbride, who lived in Ashton-under-Lyne, near Manchester. The date was 11 November 1963, just four months after Pauline Reade had vanished.

John had been at the cinema in the afternoon along with a friend of his called John Ryan. After the film finished the two young boys went down to the local market to see if they could earn some extra pocket money helping the stallholders pack up. It was the type of work they loved doing, helping out and getting paid a few pennies for their trouble. John Ryan last saw his friend standing by a stall that sold carpets.

When John Kilbride didn't come home for his dinner, Sheila and Patrick Kilbride began to grow worried. Eventually they rang the police but, despite a massive search, it seemed as if he too had simply stepped off the edge of the earth.

This time both Hindley and Brady had picked up their victim, though no doubt John only got into the car because he saw a woman was present. He was driven out to the moor where he was raped and then strangled with a thin piece of string. His body, like Pauline Reade's, was then buried in a shallow grave.

Years later, in one of her letters to the *Guardian*, Hindley again tried to explain how she'd felt at the time:

With the killing of John Kilbride, a child, I felt I'd crossed the Rubicon.

He [Brady] said good, admitting to having crossed the Rubicon was tantamount to admitting what he'd tried to drum into my head: that what was done was done, and couldn't be undone, there was no going back and even after the first murder we were irrevocably bound together and more so after the second one.

> **Just then he looked up at the TV – there was either a football match on or late sports news. He said: 'Look at that massive crowd. Who would miss one person, two, three, etc from all the millions of people in this country?' I didn't say their parents and family – he never gave them a thought and I knew I'd really have to steel myself to do the same.[2]**

Once again, in retrospect and with no foreseeable end to her imprisonment in sight, Hindley was trying to show how regrettable she thought her actions had been, but at the same time she was also subtly attempting to shift the blame on to Brady's shoulders alone.

Keith Bennett was Brady and Hindley's third victim. Also twelve years old, he was abducted while he was on his way to his grandmother's house. Like John Kilbride he was raped, strangled and buried out on the moor (but unlike the other victims, his body has never been recovered).

The fourth killing occurred six months later, on 26 December 1964. Out of all Brady and Hindley's heinous crimes, this one in particular (for reasons that will soon become clear) has remained the most repellent.

Lesley Ann Downey was ten years old. She lived in Ancoats, another district of Manchester, and had been at a local fun fair with two of her brothers and some friends when she became separated from the group and was later abducted. Hindley and Brady took her back to their house (Myra's grandmother was away visiting relatives) and told the child to take off her clothes, all except her shoes and socks. She was then made to pose for pornographic photographs, which Ian later hoped to sell on the black market. The photographs showed her with her hands tied and at one point her mouth was gagged with a black scarf.

There was a tape recorder in the room, which Ian switched on. The first thing to be heard when the seventeen-minute tape was later played back in court was a child's scream, after which Lesley Ann can be heard crying, 'Don't… Please God, help me.' The next voice on the tape is Brady's, ordering her to be quiet and to do as she is told. Lesley Ann then says that she has to get home; her mother will be expecting her, after which Myra's voice is heard saying, 'Don't dally.' A little bit later, after Lesley Ann has begged Myra to help her, Myra tells her to shut up or she'll hit her.

After her trial Myra was to say that she was out of the room when Brady killed Lesley Ann, but on the tape Ian threatened to cut Lesley's throat and Myra was definitely heard in the background, so she must have known the child was about to be murdered. The following day Lesley Ann's body was bundled into their car, taken to Saddleworth Moor and buried.

The last of Ian Brady and Myra Hindley's victims, but the first to point the police in their direction, was a young man called Edward Evans. On the night of 6 October 1965, Ian Brady met Edward Evans, who was only seventeen, in the

Acting on their suspicions but on very little hard evidence, police searched Saddleworth Moor,
a wild and remote area of the Pennines on the borders of Lancashire, Derbyshire and
Yorkshire, in October 1965, following Brady's arrest for the murder of Edward Evans.
Eventually the police teams found two bodies – those of Lesley Ann Downey and John Kilbride
– and Brady and Hindley therefore went on trial for these three murders in April 1966.
(© PA PHOTOS)

Central Station buffet where he had gone to pick up some beer. Brady invited
Evans back to his house for a drink and Evans accepted the offer, getting into a
car that Myra was driving. Back at their house Myra, on the pretext of making
some arrangement with her mother, went round to the home of David Smith.
Smith was utterly in thrall to his sister-in-law's boyfriend and, like Myra before
him, had become totally immersed in the type of books Brady read, the way that
he talked and the things that he talked about. He would often spend whole
evenings drinking and chatting with Brady, and it's not unreasonable to assume
that Brady had begun to view Smith as a possible second accomplice who could
help Myra lure victims to their death.

At approximately 11.40p.m. Myra asked Smith to accompany her back to her
own house, something he was quite happy to do. On reaching the house, Myra
then asked Smith if he would like to come in for a drink. He agreed and they
entered the premises where Brady showed Smith into the kitchen. There were a

few miniature bottles of spirits on the sideboard and Brady told Smith to help himself, after which he left the kitchen and returned to the living room, leaving the door slightly ajar. David Smith had no idea that there was someone else in the living room, but moments later he heard a terrifying scream, followed by Myra shouting out for Smith to help. According to his later testimony, Smith thought someone had broken into the house and was attacking Brady so he rushed into the living room, only to find Brady smashing an axe down on the head of what looked like a shop dummy. The next moment the 'dummy' was lying on the floor with Brady hitting it repeatedly with the blunt end of the axe while all the time shouting obscenities. To his horror, Smith then realized it wasn't a dummy at all, for he could see blood seeping all over a rug.

Edward Evans died from fourteen axe blows to the skull. Later, when David Smith gave evidence, he said that Myra might have been in the kitchen throughout most of the attack. It was all so frenzied and it had blurred in his memory. However, whether she was in the kitchen or in the living room, Myra would have been fully aware of what was happening.

Brady, Hindley and Smith, who had been told that he had to help as he was now implicated in the murder, began to clean up the mess. They scrubbed the walls, rugs and lino with detergent and at one point Smith recalls Brady saying 'that was the messiest yet'. Finally, Evans's body was wrapped in polythene and bundled round with sheets and blankets then dumped in a cupboard under the stairs.

David Smith went home at approximately 3.00a.m. He felt sickened and numb from the experience, and when he reached home blurted out what had happened to Myra's sister, Maureen. The following morning the couple went to a call box and phoned the police, telling them that they believed the body would still be in the house.

Ian Brady was arrested on 7 October 1965. Police discovered the body of Edward Evans exactly where Smith had told them it would be, in the locked cupboard under the stairs. What the police didn't realize at that point was the significance of the arrest in connection with the missing children, but it was to be only a matter of time before that came to light.

Over the next five days, while Brady was being interviewed about the Evans murder, Myra insisted on staying at the police station, awaiting his release. The police eventually requested that Myra's mother should come and fetch her daughter home. Only then did Myra understand that Brady was not going to come back. It was a shock from which it took her days to recover. Meanwhile, Brady had asked her to try to destroy various papers of his, but the house was sealed off and still being examined by the forensics team, so Myra couldn't get near it. Crucially, she couldn't get near Brady's car either and it wasn't too long before the police discovered a wallet which, on further inspection, contained several bits of paper with instructions for the disposal of a body. At the same time the police, searching Hindley's grandmother's house, discovered a notebook,

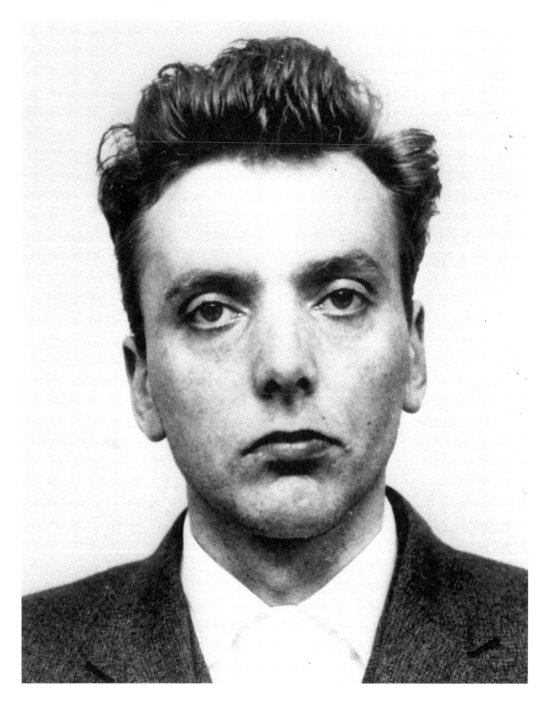

also belonging to Brady, which contained, alongside various scribbles, a list of names. One line read as follows: 'John Sloan, Jim Idiot, Frank Wilson, John Kilbride, Alec Guinness, Jack Polish…'

Superintendent Talbot, who was leading the inquiry, put this book together with some photograph albums that contained shots of Brady and Hindley posing

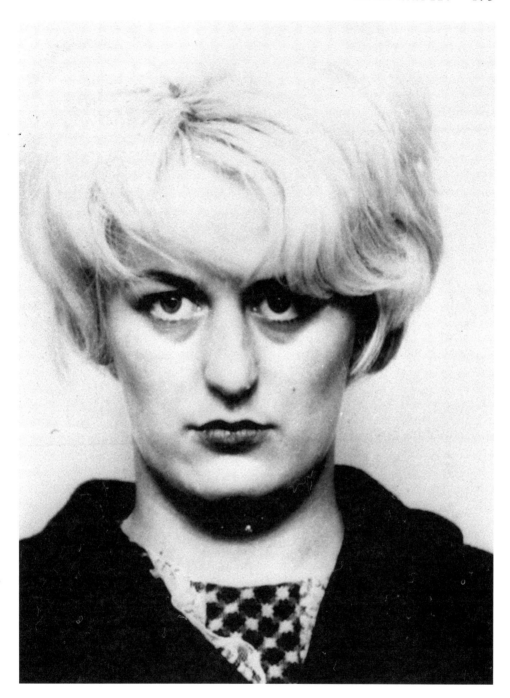

Ian Brady and Myra Hindley at the time of their arrest in October 1965. It was not until 1987 that Hindley told police of the murders of Pauline Reade and Keith Bennett. In the meantime, this photograph had become an icon of evil, and remains so to this day. Both Brady and Hindley were fortunate to escape the death penalty, for capital punishment was abolished in Britain only four weeks before their arrest. (© PA PHOTOS)

out on Saddleworth Moor. David Smith had told the Superintendent that the couple frequently picnicked up there. He also said that Brady had told him that he'd used the place to bury victims. On being questioned, Brady denied this, saying simply 'it was all part of a fiction to impress him'. None the less, the police now began a search of the moor, a thankless task given the size of the place, and one that was destined to fail. The crucial piece of evidence, which would link both Brady and Hindley to the disappearance of the children, was only found during a second search of Hindley's grandmother's house, when officers discovered a left-luggage ticket: No. 74843. This ticket led the police to Manchester Central station and in turn to two suitcases. Among the contents they discovered the pornographic photographs of Lesley Ann Downey, as well as the tape of her being tortured.

Almost simultaneously, up on the moors, a policeman had stumbled across something that resembled a bone sticking out of the ground. Initially it was thought to be the body of John Kilbride, but in fact these were Lesley Ann's remains.

On 21 October 1965, at Hyde Police Court, Ian Brady and Myra Hindley were charged with the murders of Edward Evans and Lesley Ann Downey. All through their interviews they denied both charges and tried to implicate David Smith in the murders, saying that it had been he who had lured Lesley Ann back to the house for Brady to photograph and that Lesley Ann had later left the house with Smith, unharmed.

Fortunately for Smith, the police weren't convinced. The evidence pointed towards Brady and Hindley and attention now centred on finding John Kilbride's body. The police were convinced that it was somewhere up on the moors and after a painstaking study of Brady's photographs, their hard work paid off. John Kilbride's final resting place was found and his murder added to Brady and Hindley's growing list of crimes.[3]

Their trial opened on 19 April 1966 at Chester Assize Court. Curiously, both the prosecution and the defence objected strongly to women being present on the jury (the case was thought to be too distressing) so it was decided instead to swear in twelve men. Equally strange, considering that Hindley had played a lesser role in the murders, was that she and Brady were going to be tried together. This can have done her no favours as she would be standing beside Brady as almost every depraved act he had ever committed was discussed openly in court. The case was headlined in the newspapers as the 'Trial of the Century', for this was the first time in British legal history that a woman was believed to have been involved in sex murders involving children. So great was the public outcry over the nature of these crimes that a bullet-proof glass screen had to be erected around the area where the defendants were to sit.

When the trial began, Brady and Hindley denied any involvement in the deaths of Edward Evans, Lesley Ann Downey and John Kilbride, but the evidence (in particular the Lesley Ann Downey tape, all seventeen minutes of which were played in court) was strong enough to refute their numerous lies.

On 6 May 1966, after the jury had retired for two hours and fourteen minutes, Ian Brady was found guilty of what Mr Justice Fenton described as 'three calculated, cool, cold-blooded murders' and consequently was given three life sentences. Hindley was convicted of the murder of Edward Evans and Lesley Ann Downey, but only of 'being an accessory after the fact' to the killing of John Kilbride, for which she received two life sentences plus seven years.

The *Guardian* reported their reactions as follows: 'Brady, who seemed unmoved, walked down the dock steps flanked by two prison officers. Hindley left the dock fully composed.'[4]

They escaped the death sentence only by the narrowest of margins, because The Murder Act 1965, which abolished the death penalty, had been passed just four weeks before the couple were arrested.

In prison Myra Hindley continued her infatuation with Brady, corresponding with him by letter almost every week. The rift between them only began when they learnt of each other's very different perspectives concerning their life sentences. Brady, after his incarceration, almost immediately acknowledged that he would never be released and in 1978 made a very rare public statement saying that he did not intend to apply for parole: 'I accepted the weight of the crimes both Myra and I were convicted of justifies permanent imprisonment, regardless of expressed personal remorse and verifiable change.'[5]

In stark contrast, however, Hindley fought her destiny tooth and nail and by 1970 had stopped all communications with her partner in crime, instead turning to a variety of sources to back up her cause, including lawyers, newspapers and certain influential friends she gathered along the way. The most prominent of this last group was Lord Longford, a former Labour cabinet minister, who began to visit Hindley in jail in 1969. She also formed a friendship with David Astor, a former editor of the *Observer* who funded part of Hindley's legal campaign, fighting for her release. And fight she did, almost until the last.

Hindley's first application for parole was heard in 1985, twenty years after her imprisonment, by the then Home Secretary, Leon Brittan. It was rejected and Brittan added that Hindley's case should not be heard for another five years (although in his opinion she should serve at least fifteen years more). Then, in 1986, Hindley was struck a further blow when the European Court of Human Rights classed her case 'inadmissible'. Perhaps this is what prompted Hindley in 1987 to admit that, as police had suspected all along, she was not only involved in the three crimes she had been convicted of, but also in the murders of Pauline Reade and Keith Bennett. With Hindley's help the police then instigated a new search of the moors and, on 1 July 1987, Pauline Reade's body was finally located.

But despite further attempts, release was still not forthcoming. Successive Home Secretary's passed her case on from one to the other like a poisoned chalice. To Hindley and her supporters it appeared (with some justification) that her crimes had, with the passing of time, grown worse. After all, having expressed remorse over the murders and having served over thirty years in prison (her trial judge had suggested a tariff of twenty-five years), she now met all the criteria for parole, but she hadn't reckoned on one crucial factor: public opinion.

The simple fact was that no one could forgive Myra Hindley for being that most unnatural of creatures: a woman involved in the murder of children. That Brady had committed the crimes was one unpalatable truth, but that a woman could have aided and abetted him made Hindley the target for most, if not all, of the public's outrage and disgust.

Ironically, in addition to this the more her supporters stressed that Hindley's rehabilitation was genuine, that she was a reformed character and a committed Catholic, the more the public believed instead that she was a cynical, manipulative monster who would say and do anything to gain her freedom. Keeping Hindley in jail became, as the journalist Peter Standford stated in 2002, 'an article of faith'. At the time of her death her case, alongside the whole dilemma of whether politicians should have the right to override a trial judge's decisions, were once again on their way to the European Court of Human Rights.

Hindley did not enjoy good health during her last years, suffering from angina, osteoporosis, a brain aneurysm and several suspected strokes. However, it is widely believed that she had instructed doctors that should she lapse into a coma, she was not to be resuscitated. Aged sixty, she must have realized that death was going to be her only form of release.

Perhaps the last word should go to the mother of Keith Bennett, Mrs Winnie Johnson, who said, 'I was hoping that [Hindley] would say something before she died but it looks as if she hasn't, so I have got to live with it again, yet again. She's as bad as [Brady]. In fact she's worse than him, she's the evilest one of the two of them. Brady's never wanted to come out of prison but she's tried from day one to get out. She will go straight to hell where she deserves to go. Don't ask me if I have got any sympathy for her because I haven't.'[6]

Let us hope that with Myra Hindley's death Mrs Johnson, and the parents of the other victims, have gained some iota of peace. God knows they deserve it.

KARLA HOMOLKA

Lovebirds

Never let anyone know our relationship is anything but perfect;
Don't talk back to Paul;
Always smile when you're with Paul;
Be a perfect girlfriend for Paul;
If Paul asks for a drink, bring him one quickly and happily;
Remember you're stupid;
Remember you're ugly;
Remember you're fat;
I don't know why I tell you these things because you never change.
FROM A NOTE FOUND IN ONE OF KARLA HOMOLKA'S EXERCISE BOOKS

Depending on whose story you believe, Karla Homolka is either guilty of being a leading player in three of Canada's most barbaric crimes, or she is simply a battered housewife whose every action was at the behest of her abusive, thought-controlling husband.

On 14 June 1991, Leslie Mahaffy left her parents' home in Burlington, Ontario, to attend the wake of a schoolfriend, Chris Evans, who had died along with three other teenagers in a car crash. A spirited young fifteen-year-old, Leslie Mahaffy knew she had a curfew of 10.00p.m., but in the past she had never bothered to keep it. Nor was this night any exception, for she only returned home at 2.00a.m., when she was to discover that her mother, Debbie Mahaffy, had locked the front door in order to teach her daughter a lesson. Undeterred, Leslie went to call a schoolmate to ask if she could stay over with her, but the schoolmate's mother answered and told Leslie to go home and face the consequences of her behaviour. Sadly, this is precisely what the teenager set out to do, but instead of knocking on the door and gaining entry to her house, Leslie Mahaffy mysteriously disappeared.

A little less than a year later, on 16 April 1992, another fifteen-year-old girl went missing. Her name was Kristen Dawn French and she had been walking home from Holy Cross High School when she passed by the adjoining parking lots of two churches in which sat a Nissan car driven by an attractive young woman. The woman asked Kristen French directions to the Pen Centre, but seconds later the unsuspecting teenager was held at knifepoint by a man who had crept up behind her and then bundled her into the back of the car. Kristen French was never seen alive again.

In fact, both young girls had been abducted and taken back to the home of Paul Bernardo and Karla Homolka.

From the outside, 57 Bayview Drive was a strikingly beautiful pink Cape Cod-style house built on the shores of Lake Ontario in Port Dalhousie, but on the inside the beauty ended. The house was a mirror image of the Bernardo's own marriage: on the surface a picture-perfect dream of a relationship, but underneath a dark, visceral nightmare.

Karla Homolka first met Paul Bernardo in 1987 when she was seventeen years old. She was on a work trip to Toronto and, seemingly, it was love at first sight. When she returned to her parents' house in St Catharines she could talk of little else. She described Paul to her friends as being incredibly handsome, not to mention the fact that he was studying to become an accountant. Soon Paul, who lived in Scarborough, was coming down to spend every weekend with his girlfriend at her parents' house. He endeared himself to the family (which included Karla's two sisters Lori and Tammy, besides Karla's parents) so quickly that Mrs Homolka started referring to Paul as her 'weekend son'. No one could fault Paul on anything; his appearance, his proposed career, his manners, everything seemed beyond reproach. When, in 1990, Karla announced that Paul had asked her to marry him, everyone was overjoyed.

The wedding was set for June 1991, but before it occurred tragedy struck the Homolka household when, on Christmas Eve 1990, their youngest daughter Tammy (who was sixteen years old) suddenly died from what the coroner later described as 'accidental' causes. It was a terrible blow to all concerned, but unknown to Mr and Mrs Homolka the reality of the 'accident' was more terrible than they could ever have imagined. Their beloved son-in-law-to-be, alongside their eldest daughter, had in fact instigated the whole sorry affair.

If you are to believe Karla Homolka (and there are plenty of people who don't), ever since the early days of her relationship with Paul Bernardo she was subject to his bullying. This took the form of putting Karla down about her appearance, her work, her family and her friends. The first time he hit her, Karla said, was in 1988. Immediately afterwards Paul had started crying and telling her how sorry he was, which in turn made Karla feel that she was the one who was at fault. But the real bullying only began in the autumn of 1990 when he hit, punched and kicked her in several vicious attacks. Karla said during her testimony in 1995: 'He used to tell me the reason I looked the way I did was because of him. He told me I was nothing without him and he would call me names, like slut, bitch, cunt, things like that. He made me feel I was totally dependent on him.'[1] Of course, to an outsider, the obvious question is why did Karla not leave him immediately after the first attack? Why did she persevere in such an abusive relationship? Karla's whole story is peppered with similarly uncomfortable questions; there are so many points at which she could have called a halt to everything, said 'no', rung the police, told her parents or a friend. Instead she remained silent, hid the abuse from everyone and carried on as if nothing was wrong.

In the summer of 1990 Paul first mentioned that he wanted to have sex with other women, and in particular with young girls. To his way of thinking, it was fine for a man to have more than one sexual relationship at a time, but not fine for a woman to act the same way. Ironically, it was at around this time that he was also requested by police to give a DNA sample in regards to an ongoing investigation into a series of violent rapes that had occurred in his hometown of Scarborough. The rapes had begun in 1987 with an attack on a young woman who, in addition to the sexual assault (which involved anal sex), was also punched in the face and partly strangled with electrical cord. Another victim, this time a fifteen-year-old girl, was also anally raped and forced to perform oral sex on her attacker. The attacks had continued on a regular basis until well into 1990, by which time a photo-fit picture of the suspect had appeared, accompanied by the headline 'Have You Seen This Man?' The article, written by Rob Lamberti for the *Toronto Sun*, went on: 'The Scarborough Rapist now has a face. And he looks like the boy next door. For the first time since the rapist's rampage of fear began in Scarborough in May 1987, a victim has been able to help police create a composite drawing of the man.'

Those who knew Paul thought the photo-fit amazing because it looked exactly like their friend. It was so close that one of his best buddies eventually phoned the police, putting Paul's name forward as a possible suspect. Of course Paul was among thousands of men being tested, but even though his friend had pointed the police in his direction, even though he gave a DNA sample, at the time no further action was taken against him.

In late 1990 Paul upped the ante and began talking of wanting to have sex with Karla's little sister, Tammy. 'I didn't want him to do it at all,' Karla said later in court. 'I was totally against the idea.' None the less, Paul persuaded his fiancée that this is what he wanted to do and that she was to assist him by procuring drugs from her workplace (Karla worked at the Martindale Animal Clinic) with which to lace Tammy's drinks. Desperate to keep her boyfriend happy and believing that he would only spend a couple of minutes with her sister, Karla complied.

On Christmas Eve, after her parents had gone to bed, Tammy, Paul and Karla sat up watching TV. As the night wore on, Tammy's drinks were laced with Halcion (a sleeping pill). Eventually she fell asleep. To make sure she wouldn't wake during her ordeal, Karla soaked a cloth in Halothane (an anaesthetic) and put it over her sister's face. Tammy was then stripped and, while Paul ran a video recorder, he began having vaginal intercourse with his young victim. Next Paul demanded that Karla strip off and play with Tammy's breasts as well as perform digital and oral sex on her sister. A sample from the video recording runs as follows:

Paul: Will you blow me?
Karla: Yes.
Paul: Suck on her breasts. Now. Suck!
Karla: Hurry up, please.
Paul: [He says something inaudible followed by] You're not doing it.
Karla: I am so.
[And a little later]

Homolka and Bernardo hamming it up in a swimming pool, a photograph that gives no indication of the viciousness, depravity and sexual sadism that infused their relationship. Homolka is due for release in July 2005, but is said to be fearful at the prospect – an Internet 'death pool' encourages visitors to its website to place bets on the date on which she will be killed after her release. (© TORONTO SUN)

Paul: Do it. Lick her cunt. Lick it up. Lick it clean. Lick it clean.
Karla: I am.
Paul: Put your fingers inside.
Karla: No, I can't.[2]

Throughout these horrific proceedings the camera keeps running. Although she does as her fiancé demands, it can be noted that Karla is neither enthusiastic nor willing. She wouldn't smile for the camera even though Paul specifically demanded that she do so; according to Karla, she was later beaten severely for ignoring this command. When she was shown smiling in later videotapes during the rapes of Leslie Mahaffy and Kristen French, Karla Homolka testified that she was only acting happy so that she didn't 'ruin' another of Paul's video films, thereby giving him an excuse to beat her.

With the rape of Tammy Homolka over, Paul and Karla began clearing up, but then Tammy began vomiting violently. Karla tried to clear her sister's airway by turning her upside down and Paul attempted mouth-to-mouth resuscitation, but neither was successful. Eventually Karla called 911 and while the couple waited for the ambulance to arrive, they hurriedly dressed Tammy and hid the video recorder, along with the tape.

Tammy Homolka was pronounced dead at St Catharines General Hospital later that night and both Karla and Paul seemed grief-stricken. They were taken to police headquarters where they each gave a statement to the effect that Tammy, over the course of the evening, had drunk a lot of alcohol, fallen asleep and then woken and started to vomit, at which point she had choked. The interviewing officer then asked why Tammy had curious red marks around her mouth and nostrils. The marks were so severe that they reminded the officer of the type of stains seen on the faces of people emerging from burning buildings. Karla at first said she had no idea why Tammy's face was in the condition it was, but a short time afterwards she offered up the thought that perhaps the marks were 'carpet burns' from when she and Paul had moved her sister in an attempt to revive her. Of course the marks were, as Karla knew all along, the result of her placing the cloth drenched in Halothane over her sister's mouth. But Karla didn't want to tell police anything about what had really happened, later testifying that this was because she didn't want her parents to hate her. She went on to say that afterwards, every time she refused to do what Paul wanted, Paul would threaten to show the videotape to her parents. 'I felt like I had to do whatever Paul said because he had this major, horrible thing to hang over my head. I didn't feel like I had a choice.' Later this was precisely the defence Karla used when a tape was found showing her dressed up in Tammy's favourite clothes pretending to be her dead sister while having sex with Paul. On the tape Karla is heard to say that Paul used to masturbate himself next to Tammy while she slept. Karla also puts on a high-pitched voice in intimation of her sister and says, 'I'm your little pervert. I love you so much. You make me so horny, coming inside me. Tell me you love me…' to which Paul replied that indeed he loved Tammy.

But if all this wasn't sickening enough, worse was to follow when, two weeks before their wedding, Paul kidnapped Leslie Mahaffy.

According to Karla's testimony in court, she awoke on the night of 14 June 1991 to hear Paul tell her that there was a girl in the house whom he had kidnapped and wanted to rape. Paul then disappeared and spent the remainder of the night and most of the following day locked in the guest bedroom with his victim. Later, when Karla was downstairs, he moved the girl to the master bedroom and directed Karla to go take a look. Karla found Leslie Mahaffy sitting on the floor with a blindfold round her eyes. What occurred next was a combination of mental cruelty and sexual abuse. Paul and Karla videotaped everything, including Karla sexually abusing the teenager and Paul having both vaginal and anal intercourse with her while her wrists and ankles were tied. Finally, after discussing whether or not Leslie Mahaffy should be killed, Karla found some Halcion sleeping pills and made Leslie swallow them. With the camera now switched off, Leslie was strangled. Karla insisted it was Paul who committed this final heinous act; Paul testified that it was Karla. Leslie Mahaffy's body was then dumped in the cellar where, on the following day, it was dismembered (again Karla accused Paul and Paul accused Karla) and the body parts set in concrete and thrown into Lake Gibson.

Less than two weeks later Karla Homolka married Paul Bernardo in a ceremony which friends described as being like a fairy tale. After the couple signed the register the hymn 'O Perfect Love' was sung and during the wedding feast a toast was made to the Homolka's youngest daughter, Tammy. At Karla's trial she insisted that she didn't want to marry Paul, but that she had no choice because he had the Tammy videotape in his possession, in addition to which he also had video evidence of her involvement in Leslie Mahaffy's death. Karla also insisted that, after Leslie died, Paul's physical and mental abuse of her escalated beyond all comprehension. Two friends who dressed Karla on her wedding day say they can remember dark bruises all over the bride's ribcage. None the less, the wedding went ahead and, as if everything wasn't bizarre enough, at some point during the day a radio broadcast announced that a middle-aged couple, along with some fishermen, had discovered human body parts encased in cement in Lake Gibson. The hunt was now on, not just for the Scarborough rapist but also for a child-killer. As yet, the police had no idea that they were one and the same man.

Karla and Paul Bernardo spent their honeymoon in Hawaii, during which time Paul's abuse of Karla continued. According to her, he hit her not only with his fists and feet, but also with an arsenal of other objects including a belt. On their return home the violence continued. It was part and parcel of everyday life, Karla said, and when Paul decided that a friend of hers called Jane (who was still a virgin) would be his next victim, Karla meekly went along with the plan.

Jane was invited over to Bayview Drive where Karla laced her drinks with Halcion. Shortly afterwards Jane fell unconscious, during which time Paul stripped her and had both vaginal and anal sex with her. Videotape also shows that Karla had oral sex with Jane, although at her trial Karla maintained that she could remember nothing about it.

Miraculously Jane survived the attack and woke some time later feeling drowsy and sore, but remembering nothing of her ordeal. Kristen French was not so lucky, however.

On Thursday 16 April 1992 both Paul and Karla abducted Kristen French from a parking lot in St Catharines and took her back to 57 Bayview Drive, where she was locked in the guest bedroom. Asked by the prosecution at Paul Bernardo's trial whether she, Karla, knew what was then going to happen to Kristen, Karla nodded.

'I knew she had to be killed,' Karla said, 'because I knew that she was going to see both of our faces in the car. And also because of what had happened to Leslie Mahaffy; she had been killed because Paul thought she could identify him.'[3]

Immediately after they got Kristen back to the house, Paul went upstairs to be alone with his victim. Several hours passed, after which Paul called Karla into the master bedroom where Kristen was kneeling on the floor. What happened next was in many respects a replay of the ordeal Leslie Mahaffy had endured, only with a few bizarre twists. For instance, on the second day of the kidnap, Paul left the house to buy pizza and videos, leaving Karla alone to stand guard over Kristen. Again the question was raised in court, why hadn't Karla tried to escape and set Kristen free? She had ample opportunity and could have saved the young girl's life, but Karla's excuse was much like all her other excuses. Firstly she said she was scared because, despite not wanting to be involved in what had happened, she undoubtedly was. Secondly she said that she was frightened that while they were trying to escape Paul would come back, go mad and kill them.

With the opportunity to escape past, Kristen's torture continued. Several more videos were made and on more than one occasion Paul is heard to say that he'll kill Kristen because she isn't performing her duties well enough. Paul's sadistic nature is in full evidence; he beats Kristen, he uses different household objects with which to penetrate her and he threatens to urinate over her and do other vile acts. At one point Kristen was made to crouch on her hands and knees with her back arched while Paul penetrated her from behind, threatening all the time to punch her back if she didn't keep it arched. He also demanded that Kristen perform cunnilingus on Karla and that Karla reciprocate in kind.

Horrifically, Kristen's ordeal lasted a total of four days. On Easter Sunday she was strangled. Paul and Karla dumped her body in the cellar and later drove over to Karla's parents for Easter dinner. On their return, Paul and Karla placed Kristen's body in the jacuzzi where Karla was left to scrub it from top to bottom to remove any forensic evidence, douching her so that no seminal fluid would be found anywhere on her body. Later, the pair of them dumped the corpse in scrubland near Burlington.

A few weeks afterwards, on 12 May 1992, two police officers called round to 57

Bayview Drive to ask Paul Bernardo where he had been on the day Kristen French disappeared. Karla was at work during this time, but she testified that when she returned home Paul was beside himself with mirth. 'He said that he got through the interview like he was cool as a cucumber and it went off really well and he felt very proud of himself.' Paul felt that the interview had gone so well that only a few days were to pass before he suggested they kidnap and rape yet another young girl. When Karla objected, Paul beat her so severely that she eventually called her father, who came and picked her up. But Karla's bid for independence lasted only twenty-four hours; by the following evening she and Paul had made up and the couple were reunited.

It wasn't until 5 January 1993 that Karla eventually left her husband for good. According to Karla, in between her first attempt to leave him and her second, she was subjected to numerous beatings and humiliations which included a sex session with a prostitute in Atlantic City, being chased round the house with a stun-gun and being made to sleep in the root cellar where they had kept Kristen's body. After she ran away for the second time, Karla was immediately checked into a hospital where she remained for three days undergoing treatment for severe pain and bruising, together with a battery of tests to make sure she hadn't broken any bones. On her release her parents decided the best place for her to go – so that Paul couldn't reach her – was to stay with an aunt and uncle, Calvin and Patty Seger. At no point, however, did Karla reveal to her parents what she and Paul had done in relation to either Leslie Mahaffy or Kristen French. Instead, it was the police who were finally to force Karla's hand.

Ever since Paul Bernardo had come to the police's attention in relation to the Scarborough rape investigation, officers had kept his name on file. Extraordinarily, in view of the seriousness of the crimes, the DNA samples that had been taken from Paul and numerous other men back in 1990 had never actually been tested. This was not, as some people have suggested, due to incompetence, but simply because the forensics system was overburdened with work at the same time as being painfully understaffed: a lethal combination in the light of the 'schoolgirl killings'. It wasn't until January 1993 that the results came back from the laboratories with the name Paul Kenneth Bernardo at the top of the pile. Paul was immediately put under surveillance – at which point police also went to visit his estranged wife, Karla.

On 9 February 1993 three officers from the Metro Toronto sex assault unit interviewed Karla at her aunt and uncle's house. They asked her a whole series of questions, including whether Paul enjoyed anal sex and, near the end of the interview, they informed her that Paul was on the verge of being arrested for a series of sexual assaults. After the police left, Patty Seger questioned her niece as to the nature of the crimes Paul had committed. At one point she asked Karla whether Paul had ever killed anyone. Karla said yes. Her aunt then asked if one of his victims had been Leslie Mahaffy. Again Karla answered in the affirmative.

The next day Karla found herself a lawyer, a man by the name of George Walker, and made an appointment to see him, during which time she confessed to her part in what had become known as the 'schoolgirl killings'. Meanwhile, police were still keeping Paul Bernardo under surveillance. They eventually decided to ring Karla's lawyer and tell him they were on the verge of arresting her husband not only on the rape charges but also in connection with the Mahaffy/French murders. Only then did George Walker indicate that Karla might be willing to strike a plea bargain with the police and give evidence against her husband in return for a reduced sentence. Consequently, on 17 February 1993, Paul Bernardo was arrested on suspicion of being both the Scarborough rapist and the schoolgirl murderer. A week later, a deal was stuck for Karla with the Crown Prosecution Service by her two lawyers: she would receive twelve years in prison for the two murders, but in return her trial would be very brief and with good behaviour she would be eligible for parole in a little over three years.

On 6 July 1993 Karla pled guilty to the manslaughter of both Leslie Mahaffy and Kristen French. To the shock of journalists, Karla's lawyer then stated that the court would also hear evidence 'surrounding her criminal liability in the death of her younger sister, Tammy Homolka'. In the interim period between the time Karla was charged and the beginning of her trial, she had written her parents a letter:

> **Dear Mom, Dad and Lori,**
>
> **This is the hardest letter I've ever had to write and you'll probably all hate me once you've read it. I've kept this inside myself for so long and I just can't lie to you any more. Both Paul and I are responsible for Tammy's death. Paul was 'in love' with her and wanted to have sex with her. He wanted me to help him. He wanted me to get sleeping pills from work to drug her with. He threatened me and physically and emotionally abused me when I refused. No words I can say can make you understand what he put me through. So stupidly I agreed to do as he said. But something – maybe the combination of drugs and the food she ate that night – caused her to vomit. I tried so hard to save her. I am so sorry. But no words I can say can bring her back… I would gladly give my life for hers. I don't expect you to ever forgive me, for I will never forgive myself.**
>
> **Karla XOXO**

Having already struck a plea bargain with the prosecution, Karla's trial was a brief affair. Victim-impact statements were read out for both the Mahaffy and French families, after which Karla's lawyers ran through a list of factors in defence of their client, including her relative youth, her spotless record up until the time of the murders, her abuse at the hands of her husband, together with psychiatric reports. In particular, the latter stated: 'She knew what was happening but she felt totally helpless and unable to act in her own defence or in anyone else's defence. She was in my opinion paralysed with fear and in that state she became obedient and self-serving.'

Judge Francis Kovac summed up the trial by stating that, although Karla's involvement in all three murders was 'monstrous and depraved', she was not the main player, that role being reserved for her husband. Without Karla's full co-operation with the police, Paul Bernardo might never have come to trial. To the horror of the public, Kovac then sentenced Karla to the already agreed terms that had been struck between the defence and the prosecution. The stage was now set for one of the highest-profile murder trials ever to be heard in a Canadian court of law: that of Paul Kenneth Bernardo.[4]

The prosecution's leading witness was of course Karla. True to her word, she took the stand and began describing how, a little less than a decade earlier, she had met and fallen under the spell of her future husband. She went on to describe in meticulous detail her abuse at his hands and later she took the jury through a step-by-step account of the rape and murders of Tammy, Leslie and Kristen. But it wasn't until Paul Bernardo's defence team were allowed their chance to question Karla that the fireworks really began.

On Independence Day, 4 July 1995, John Rosen began questioning Karla by slamming two photos of her sister Tammy down in front of her. The first photograph showed Tammy alive, the second was a picture of her corpse. 'I would have thought,' Rosen spat, 'that from December 24 1990, to January 1993, those pictures, that nightmare, would have bothered your conscience every living moment of your existence.' Karla replied that it did, at which point Rosen scoffed and showed her two photographs of Leslie Mahaffy. Rosen then went through the same procedure, telling Karla that surely her conscience would have been so disturbed by the second murder that it would have prompted her to do something. Rosen then showed her two photographs of Kristen French and again went through the same process, after which he pressed Karla to reveal why, once she had finally escaped from Paul, she didn't go straight to the police.

Karla's reply was, just as it had always been, that she was terrified of Paul Bernardo and of what he might do. But Rosen was having none of it. Instead he responded by saying that Karla hadn't confessed to the police until after she 'was guaranteed a deal you could live with… from January 1993 you held your silence until you were looked after.' Unsurprisingly, Karla disagreed, but Rosen's accusations were precisely what the public had been thinking ever since Karla first cut her deal with the Crown. Every time she repeated that she had had no choice but to go along with everything Paul Bernardo said, Rosen just scoffed. He brought up the fact that, over the course of her relationship with Paul, Karla had sent him over five hundred cards, letters and notes, all expressing her undying love for him. Some, of course, were more explicit than others, like the one on Paul's twenty-fifth birthday which offered him a choice of a 'quickie, plain fucking, fancy fucking, movies, picture taking'. Others were simple love letters: 'I love you, I love you, I love you with all my heart. You're the best, you big, bad businessman, you.' However, the implication was clear; if Paul were abusing her so much then why was she still writing the notes to him and why, when there were

A protester demonstrates outside the St Catharines courthouse as Karla Homolka is driven away to the federal prison in Kingston, Ontario, to start her twelve-years sentence for her part in the three murders. Canadian public opinion was outraged by the relative leniency of her punishment, especially given her part in the rape and consequent death of her sixteen-year-old sister. (© Toronto Sun)

so many opportunities, particularly when Paul began telling her he wanted to sleep with her little sister, didn't Karla confide in anyone? Karla's response was that she 'wished to God' she had, but Rosen was still not satisfied and continued to spar with her for days at a time. Naturally his endgame was to show that Karla was the sexually dominant partner, not Paul, that it was Karla who enjoyed kinky sex, and finally that is was Karla who had killed Leslie Mahaffy and Kristen French.

And to some extent Rosen succeeded, for no matter how abused Karla had been, most people could not understand why she had complied with Paul over the terrible abuse and murder of three young girls, let alone that one of them was her sister. As Rosen put it, 'You're living with someone you hate, and who is talking about abducting a girl right off the street, and yet you don't rush into the police station and say, "I'm living with a maniac and you've got to stop him before somebody else gets hurt." [5] But Rosen was not so successful when it came to proving that it was Karla who eventually murdered Leslie and Kristen. The fact was that Karla remained steadfast throughout the rest of her testimony and gave Rosen no room for manoeuvre. Finally she left the stand and returned to her cell at the Prison for Women, leaving Paul Bernardo to face the music alone.

Although he had been advised by his legal team not to take the stand himself, Paul Bernardo ignored their concerns and, on 15 August 1995, went into the witness box. According to Paul, it was Karla who had first thought of drugging Tammy and teaching her 'what sex was about', it was Karla who insisted on getting married and it was Karla who said that Leslie Mahaffy had to die. Paul, on the other hand, testified that he had wanted to release Leslie, particularly in light of the fact that she had been blindfolded throughout her ordeal and therefore couldn't identify her attackers. He gave much the same evidence when it came to the murder of Kristen French; that it was Karla who had strangled the girl while he was out of the room. After that, he said, his marriage had deteriorated rapidly. He was still angry about what had happened to Tammy and he admitted that he had hit Karla on several occasions. His testimony wasn't a long, drawn-out affair, lasting only a total of three hours. However, it laid bare the crucial question which the jury had to answer, namely which one of the couple was guilty of the schoolgirl killings? In the event, and without the opportunity to condemn Karla, the jury returned with a verdict of guilty and Paul Bernardo was sentenced to a life term without any possibility of being granted parole for a minimum of twenty-five years. Without a doubt the sentence was justified, but outside the courtroom and surrounded by reporters, John Rosen stressed that in condemning Paul Bernardo, the jury had in no way vindicated Karla or the deal that she had struck with the Crown.

'This verdict,' he said, 'represents the jury's opinion of the guilt or the innocence of Mr Bernardo based on the evidence that they heard and nothing more. I think that if the jury could speak then some, if not all of them, would tell you that they have personal opinions about the deal made with Karla Homolka that differs from the Crown's opinion. I'm sure this jury would have preferred to have both of them sitting in the box together so that they could judge both of them...'

Karla Homolka has now been in prison for a total of nine years and, according to a ruling on 17 January 2003 by the National Parole Board, she must stay there until her sentence is completed in July 2005. But it isn't only the parole board or the public who want Karla to remain behind bars; in another bizarre twist to the story, Karla herself is uncertain whether she wants to be released. For the most part this is due to the fact that her life has been indirectly threatened by the posting of an Internet 'death pool' where the general public can bet on the most likely day of the year on which she will be killed. One such site (for there are several) is called the 'Karla Homolka Death Pool: When the Game is Over, We All Win!' At the time of publication most bets have been placed for dates between 2005 and 2006.

NOTES

Introduction

[1] Although, as Oliver James points out in his excellent book *Juvenile Violence in a Winner-Loser Culture: Socio-economic and Familial Origins of the Rise of Violence Against the Person* (Free Association Books, 1995): 'Murder of children is the only violent offence that women are more likely to commit than men.'

LIZZIE BORDEN: The Fall River Murders

[1] For a triumphant fictional description of this scene one can do no better than read Angela Carter's short story 'The Fall River Axe Murders' which appeared in her collection *Black Venus* (Chatto & Windus, 1985). The opening lines are as follows: 'Hot, hot, hot . . . very early in the morning, before the factory whistle, but, even at this hour, everything shimmers and quivers under the attack of white, furious sun already high in the still air.'

[2] From transcripts of the closing arguments for the defence of Lizzie Borden.

[3] The first paragraph of this article reads: 'FALL RIVER, Mass, Aug. 4 – Andrew J. Borden and his wife, two of the oldest, wealthiest, and most highly respected persons in the city, were brutally murdered with an axe at 11 o'clock this morning in their home on Second Street, within a few minutes' walk of City Hall. The Borden family consisted of the father, mother, two daughters and a servant. The older daughter has been in Fair Haven for some days. The rest of the family has been ill for three or four days, and Dr Bowen, the attending physician, thought they had been poisoned.'

[4] To read the entire transcript of this testimony see the Fall River Police Department files at http://www.frpd.org.

[5] A term taken from Patmore's verse sequence in praise of married love, *The Angel in the House* (1854–63), which extols the virtues of grace, gentleness and simplicity, virtues that every Victorian lady was not only supposed to admire, but also to possess.

AUDREY MARIE HILLEY: Secrets and Lies

[1] From *Poisoned Blood* by Philip E. Ginsburg, Michael O'Mara Books, 1993.

[2] Ibid.

[3] The obituary ran as follows: 'Robbi L. Homan, 37, of Marlow, died Wednesday in Dallas, Texas, after a long illness. She was born in Buffalo, NY, March 25, 1945, daughter of Hugh and Cindi Grayson, and had lived in Marlow for two years. Mrs Homan was formerly employed by Central Screw Co. in Keene and was a member of Sacred Heart Church in Tyler, Texas. Survivors include her husband, John Homan of Marlow, and two sisters, Teri Martin of Dallas and Jean Ann Trevor of White Plains N.Y. Mrs Homan had requested that her body be donated to the Medical Research Institute in Texas and that no funeral be held. Contributions may be made in her memory to a favourite charity.'

VALERIA MESSALINA: A Roman Lolita

[1] From *The Twelve Caesars* by Suetonius (Gaius Suetonius Tranquillus, AD *c*.70–*c*.140), translated by Robert Graves, 1957; Penguin Classics edition (ed. Michael Grant), 2003.

[2] From *I, Claudius* by Robert Graves, Arthur Baker, 1934; combined edition with *Claudius the God*, Penguin, 1986.

[3] From *The Annals*, Book XI by Tacitus (Cornelius Tacitus, AD 55–after 115), translated by Alfred John Church and William Jackson Brodribb; this text is available at http://classics.mit.edu/Tacitus/annals.html.

[4] Ibid.

[5] Quoted from 'Death and the Romans', a lecture by David Noy of the University of Wales, Lampeter, at http://www.lamp.ac.uk/~noy/death3.htm, 1999.

[6] From Suetonius, trans. Graves, op. cit.

AGRIPPINA THE YOUNGER: Empress of Poison

[1] From *The Twelve Caesars* by Michael Grant, Weidenfeld & Nicolson, 2002

[2] From *The Twelve Caesars* by Suetonius (Gaius Suetonius Tranquillus, AD *c*.70–*c*.140), translated by Robert Graves, 1957; Penguin Classics edition (ed. Michael Grant), 2003.

[3] Ibid.

[4] From *The Annals*, Book XII by Tacitus (Cornelius Tacitus, AD 55–after 115), translated by Alfred John Church and William Jackson Brodribb; this text is available at http://classics.mit.edu/Tacitus/annals.html.

[5] From *Claudius the God*, by Robert Graves, Arthur Baker, 1934; combined edition with *I, Claudius*, Penguin, 1986.

[6] From Suetonius, trans. Graves, op. cit.

[7] Ibid.

[8] Ibid.

TZ'U-HSI: The Dragon Empress

[1] From *Two Years in the Forbidden City* by Princess Te-ling (Der Ling), Mofatt, Yard & Co., 1911; Dodd, Mead & Co., 1929. Te-ling was First Lady-in-Waiting to the Empress Dowager, and the text of her book is available on several websites, notably that of the University of Virginia Library at http://etext.lib.virginia.edu/toc/modeng/public/DerYear.html.

[2] Ibid.

[3] From *The Dragon Empress: The Life and Times of Tz'u-hsi 1835-1908*, by Marina Warner, Weidenfeld & Nicolson, 1972.

[4] Later, Tsai-ch'un's name was changed to T'ung-chih, which in translation meant 'Return to Order'.

[5] From Warner, op. cit.

[6] Ibid.

[7] Kuang-hsu was also known as Tsain-t'ien.

[8] From *China Under the Empress Dowager, Being the History of the Life and Times of Tzu Hsi; compiled from State Papers and the Private Diary of the Comptroller of Her Household*, by J. O. P. Bland and E. Backhouse, Lippincott, 1912; reprinted Taipei, 1962.

[9] From Princess Te-ling, op. cit.

[10] Pamphlets were distributed wherever the Boxers appeared to the effect that the 'conduct of Christians and barbarians is irritating our Gods and Geniuses, hence the many scourges we are now suffering… The missionaries extract the eyes, marrow and heart of the dead in order to make medicaments… As for the children received in orphanages, they are killed and their intestines used to change lead into silver.'

CATHERINE THE GREAT: Empress of All the Russias

[1] From Catherine II's *Memoirs*, which cover the first thirty years of her life but end before her accession, although they also contain 'Thoughts' and letters. They were discovered on her death in 1796 but not published until 1859, and then in a French edition.

[2] From *A Source Book for Russian History*, Vol. 2, translated by G. Vernadsky, Yale University Press, 1972.

[3] From *Catherine the Great* by Henri Troyat, Aidan Ellis, 1993.

[4] Apoplexy is generally the loss of all bodily sensations and motion as a result of a sudden haemorrhage or thrombosis in the brain.

[5] From *Documents of Catherine the Great*, translated by W.F. Reddaway, Cambridge University Press, 1931.

[6] From Catherine's Decree on Serfs, 1767.

[7] From *Prince of Princes: The Life of Potemkin* by Simon Sebag Montefiore, Weidenfeld & Nicolson, 2000.

[8] Ibid.

[9] Many historians believe that Catherine married Potemkin in a secret ceremony at the Church of St Sampsonovsky in St Petersburg some time in June 1774. However, no official records survive to prove this story true. The only real evidence, apart from contemporary accounts of how well Catherine treated Potemkin, was the way in which she addressed him 'Dear husband' in her numerous letters and signed herself as his 'devoted wife'.

QUEEN RANAVALONA I: Bloody Mary of Madagascar

[1] Anon.

[2] From *Flashman's Lady* by George MacDonald Fraser, Barrie & Jenkins, 1977.

[3] From *A History of the Island of Madagascar* by Samuel Copland, R. Clay for Burton & Smith, 1822.

[4] From *Friends in Madagascar* by James H. Fisher, Society of Friends, 1940.

[5] From Fraser, op. cit.

[6] From *The Book of Martyrs*, by Chenu Bruno 'and others', SCM Press, 1990.

[7] Anon.

[8] From the *New Englander and Yale Review*, August 1859.

[9] From *Madagascar: Mon Île-Au-Bout-du-Monde* by Jacques Hannebique, Laval (France), Siloë, 1987.

ELENA CEAUSESCU: Mother of the Fatherland

[1] From *Kiss the Hand You Cannot Bite* by Edward Behr, Villard Books, 1991.

[2] By 1989 approximately twenty-eight of Ceausescu's close relations held top positions within the Communist Party or the Romanian Army.

[3] From Behr, op. cit.

[4] From *Transcript of the Closed Trial of Nicolae and Elena Ceausescu*, 25 December 1989. The text is available on several

websites, including http://www.timisoara.com/timisoara/rev/trialscript.html.

[5] Ibid.

[6] Ibid.

[7] Ibid.

[8] United Press International, 25 January 1990.

[9] From *Transcript of the Closed Trial of Nicolae and Elena Ceausescu*, op. cit.

MARY ANN COTTON: The Black Widow

[1] Lucrezia Borgia (1480–1519), the sister of Cesare Borgia, was an Italian noblewoman and patron of the arts and education at the time of the Renaissance. During her lifetime she gained a reputation, quite unfairly, for wantonness, vice and crime, the latter including several murders by poisoning.

[2] From 'Mary Ann Cotton – Britain's Mass Murderess' by Bernard O'Donnell, an essay in *Should Women Hang*, W. H. Allen, 1956.

[3] Green wallpaper of a similar type is also supposed to have been the reason why Emperor Napoleon I of France grew increasingly ill from 1815 to the time of his death in 1821 while exiled at Longwood House on St Helena. In the mid-1950s Dr Sten Forshufvud, a Swedish biologist and toxicologist, conducted an analysis of Napoleon's hair. Several samples were tested and indeed the results revealed very high levels of arsenic. At first it was thought that this proved, as Napoleon himself thought, that he was being deliberately poisoned, but later it became evident that small amounts of arsenic were present in the green wallpaper throughout Longwood House. In addition, Longwood was also found to be a very damp residence, a fact that would lend itself to the arsenic becoming even more potent, for in wet conditions mould changes the green compound into a highly poisonous gas – arsenic trymethyl.

MARIE NOE: An Unlucky Parent

[1] From an article entitled 'One After Another' by Mary H. Cadwalader, in *Life* Magazine, 12 July 1963.

[2] From an article entitled 'Cradle to Grave' by Stephen Fried, in the *Philadelphia Magazine (and Metrocorp Publications)*, April 1988.

[3] Take, for example, the case of the British solicitor Sally Clark, who lost two of her children to what she insisted was SIDS or some other unknown illness, but who was none the less convicted of their murders in November 1999. Three years later Clark had her conviction quashed.

[4] From Fried, op. cit.

[5] Ibid.

[6] Ibid.

[7] Ibid.

ROSE WEST: The House of Horror

[1] From *Happy Like Murderers: The True Story of Fred and Rosemary West* by Gordon Burn, Faber & Faber, 1998.

[2] Ibid.

[3] Ibid.

[4] Ibid.

GRACE MARKS: A Teenage Temptress

[1] From *Life in the Clearings versus the Bush*, by Susanna Moodie, Richard Bentley, 1853.

[2] Upper Canada is now known as Ontario.

[3] In Moodie's account Thomas Kinnear is referred to as Thomas Kinnaird.

[4] In Moodie's account she is referred to as Hannah Montgomery, and in *The Lives of the Judges of Upper Canada and Ontario* (see below, n.10) she is referred to as Mary Montgomery.

[5] A 'remittance man' is someone who is dependent upon remittances (of money) sent from home, usually by his family.

[6] From Moodie, op. cit.

[7] Ibid.

[8] From *Voluntary Confession of Grace Marks to Mr George Walton*, 17 November 1843.

[9] From Moodie, op. cit.

[10] From *The Lives of the Judges of Upper Canada and Ontario: from 1791 to the present time*, Rowsell & Hutchinson, 1888.

[11] From Moodie, op. cit.

[12] From *Voluntary Confession of Grace Marks*, op. cit.

[13] From Moodie, op. cit.

[14] From *The Lives of the Judges of Upper Canada and Ontario*, op. cit.

[15] From *The Trials of James McDermott and Grace Marks, at Toronto, Upper Canada, November 3rd and 4th,* 1843.

[16] Ibid.

[17] From Moodie, op. cit.

[18] Ibid.

[19] From *Alias Grace* by Margaret Atwood, Bloomsbury, 1996.

AILEEN CAROL WUORNOS: Damsel of Death

[1] www.crimelibrary.com/series4/wuornos/8.htm.

[2] From *Women Who Kill* by Carol Ann Davis, Allison & Busby, 2002.

[3] The 'Williams Rule' is most often implemented in cases of child abuse where the accused has frequently accumulated many victims over the space of his/her lifetime.

[4] Aileen was never charged with Peter Siems's death, as his body was never discovered.

[5] From Davis, op. cit.

[6] From an article entitled 'Sexual Violence Against Women and a Woman's Right to Self-Defense' by Phyllis Chesler, Ph.D., *Criminal Practice Law Report*, Vol. 1, No. 9, October 1993.

[7] In fact Aileen's story was retold in three movies, two books, a comic book and, strangest of all, set to music for an opera by Carla Lucero, who said, 'I really felt for this woman. She never gave up on the concept of love, and she's been betrayed all the way down the line.'

[8] United Press International.

[9] From an article by Ron Word in the *Sarasota Herald Tribune*.

MYRA HINDLEY: The Face of Evil

[1] From an article entitled 'Myra Hindley In Her Own Words' in the *Guardian*, 29 February 2000.

[2] Ibid.

[3] The body of Pauline Reade was not discovered until 1987, and that of Keith Bennett has never been found.

[4] From an article entitled 'Life Sentences for Brady and Hindley' by Geoffrey Whitely, in the *Guardian*, 7 May 1966

[5] www.crimelibrary.com.

[6] Extract from the *Scotsman*, 16 November 2002.

KARLA HOMOLKA: Lovebirds

[1] From *Deadly Innocence* by Scott Burnside and Alan Cairns, Warner Books, 1995.

[2] Ibid.

[3] Ibid.

[4] In fact there was a two-year delay between Karla's trial and that of Paul, the latter beginning on 18 May 1995.

[5] From Burnside and Cairns, op. cit.